SNC-LAVALIN
THE FIRST 100 YEARS

Bibliothèque et Archives nationales du Québec
and Library and Archives Canada cataloguing in publication

Main entry under title:

SNC-Lavalin : the first 100 years

Issued also in French under title: SNC-Lavalin :
les 100 premières années.
Includes index.

ISBN 978-2-922417-86-9

1. SNC-Lavalin - History. 2. Engineering firms - Quebec (Province) -
History - 20th century. I. Rieder, Noel. II. SNC-Lavalin.

TA217.S62S6213 2011   338.7'620009714   C2011-940594-6

SNC-Lavalin : the first 100 years

Legal deposits
Bibliothèque nationale du Québec
National Library of Canada

Project supervision: Noel Rieder, SNC-Lavalin
Editorial co-ordination: IQ Press
Graphic design and page layout: Derome design
Printing: Friesens, Canada

ISBN: 978-2-922417-86-9

          1 2 3 13 12 11

Photo and Newspaper Clipping Credits

All photographs are from the SNC-Lavalin fonds except:

Bibliothèque et Archives nationales du Québec • Page 4: Establishment of L.J.A.
Surveyer, photographer unknown, 1891; Édouard-Zotique Massicotte collection,
Montreal. **BC Hydro** • Page 10: Inside the Stave Falls powerhouse, British
Columbia, circa 1920. Page 14: Stave Falls Railway. **Bernard Bohn** • Page 178: Taro
Alepian, Pierre Robitaille, and Roger Nicol. Page 179: Normand Morin, Tony
Rustin, and Michael Novak. *Canadian Business* • Page 211: Jacques Lamarre on
the cover of *Canadian Business*, April 28, 2003. **Canadian Centre for Architecture** •
Page 4: Arthur Surveyer and Louis-Joseph Surveyer. Page 8: Montreal Harbour,
circa 1915. Page 24: Arthur Surveyer. **Timmins Museum: National Exhibition
Centre** • Page 21: Noah Timmins. **Copibec** • Page 177: *Commerce* magazine,
July 7, 1996. **École Polytechnique de Montréal** • Page 5: École Polytechnique de
Montréal graduating class; and the École Polytechnique de Montréal building
behind the Académie du Plateau, 1902. Page 9: Augustin Frigon. Page 11: First
issue of the *Revue Trimestrielle Canadienne,* May 1915. Page 15: Advertisement
for Arthur Surveyer & Cie. *Engineering News-Record* / **The McGraw Hill
Companies, Inc.** • Page 116: Cover of the *Engineering News-Record,*
August 5, 1982. **Canada Science and Technology Museum** • Page 7: Port Arthur,
Ontario, circa 1910. Page 21: 1010 Sainte-Catherine Street West, Montreal.
National Post Inc. • Page 168: Guy Saint-Pierre on the cover of *The Financial
Post Magazine,* November 1994. *NCE International* • Page 81: Clipping: *NCE
International,* August 1979. **Quebec Order of Engineers** • Page 13: Logo of the
Corporation of Professional Engineers of Quebec. **Paul Labelle photographe
Inc.** • Page 132: Guy Saint-Pierre. Page 139: Assembly. Page 153: Merger
announcement; Guy Saint-Pierre addressing employees; and Armand Couture
speaking with the press. Page 158: Services Department. Page 164: Jacques
Lamarre. Page 164: Raymond Favreau. Page 169: SNC-Lavalin Management
Committee. Page 178: Gala dinner at the International Symposium.
Page 179: Markis. Page 191: Hitching a ride on the 407. Page 198: Jacques Lamarre.
Page 204: Pierre Duhaime, Marylynne Campbell. Page 206: Pierre Anctil.
Page 218: Jacques Lamarre presenting Award of Excellence. Page 219: Gillian
MacCormack. Page 226: Riadh Ben Aïssa. Page 236: Jacques Lamarre and Pierre
Duhaime. Page 237: Pierre Duhaime. Page 240: André Dufour **Rio Tinto Alcan** •
Page 20: Port Alfred, Quebec. Page 28: Dominion Square Building. Page 36: Red
mud treatment plant at Arvida, Quebec; and the castings quality control room
at Etobicoke Works, Ontario. **Société d'histoire et de généalogie des Hautes-
Laurentides** • Page 39: Construction of the Mont-Laurier Hospital: P115 Fonds
CHCR Antoine-Labelle. **Studio Aventure** • Page 215: Jim Burke, 2008. **Estate of
Serge Lemoyne / SODRAC (2011)** • Page 95: *Bleu,* by Serge Lemoyne, 1983-1984.
Université de Montréal • Page 23: Audience: Division de la gestion de documents
et des archives, Université de Montréal. Secrétariat général fonds (D0035).
GD0035100006.5. *Documentaire sur l'Université de Montréal,* Éditions Le Quartier
Latin, 1943. **Yves Beaulieu** • Page 179: Robert Tribe. **Yves Lacombe photographe** •
Page 242: Pierre Duhaime. **Washington State Historical Society** • Page 16: Grays
Harbor, Washington.

Newspaper Clippings

Reproduced with the permission of *The Globe and Mail:* pages 26, 31, 131, 137, 138,
143, 147, 154, 156, 159, 185, 193, 208, 219.
Reproduced with the permission of *La Presse:* pages 30, 48, 92, 131, 137, 145, 151.
Reproduced with the permission of *Sun Media Corporation:* page 147.
From *The New York Times,* May 3 © 1994 *The New York Times.* All rights reserved.
Used by permission and protected by the Copyright Laws of the United States:
page 163.
Reproduced with the permission of *Le Devoir:* pages 93, 102, 112, 129, 138, 152,
154, 163.

SNC-LAVALIN
THE FIRST 100 YEARS

TABLE OF CONTENTS

PREFACE

As I write this, SNC-Lavalin is entering its second century of existence. To have not only survived but also prospered and grown through 100 years of economic and social change is certainly something to celebrate. SNC-Lavalin now joins an exclusive club of organizations that have stood the test of time.

The greatest reason for SNC-Lavalin's longevity is its employees. We have had, and have, a remarkable pool of talented and dedicated employees. As an engineering firm, SNC-Lavalin owns few hard assets; our real strength resides in the creativity and determination of our people. Without their sacrifices, talent, and loyalty, SNC-Lavalin would have faded into economic history long ago.

Another reason for SNC-Lavalin's enduring success is its strong local roots. Today, SNC-Lavalin is a true multinational corporation in every sense of the word, but it grew to prominence first in Quebec, and then in Canada. I think this is something that we can take pride in even as we become increasingly global in our operations and outlook.

At a moment in time such as this, it is impossible not to speculate about what the next 100 years hold for SNC-Lavalin. The world will continue to evolve in ways that no one can foresee, but there is one thing of which I am certain: engineers will remain at the heart of that change. It is engineers who will design and build the projects that allow us to meet the great challenges of tomorrow, whether they are climatic, social, or resource-based. So I can say with confidence that SNC-Lavalin will continue to play a vital role, especially as we focus on growth in international markets.

With that, I offer this book to our employees, our clients who have always put their trust in us, and our friends. I hope you will appreciate, as I did, the chance to learn more about this great company and its remarkable people.

Pierre Duhaime,
President and Chief Executive Officer
SNC-Lavalin Group

FOREWORD

As a director of SNC-Lavalin for close to 20 years, I was actively and passionately involved in its development into one of the world's leading engineering and construction companies. This book tells the story of the firm and speaks for itself. Instead, let me make a few observations about what I feel led to the firm's success over the first 100 years.

An engineering company is built by people and leadership. Here, SNC-Lavalin has been fortunate. Montreal is a multicultural city that has for many years attracted highly qualified and ambitious people from all corners of the world. Montreal is also blessed with first-class engineering schools and one of the earliest French-language business schools. During World War II, the company was able to hire European refugees who were immensely talented and spoke a variety of languages. This set the example for the postwar period, when the company added top talent from other areas of the world.

The result was a highly multicultural workforce that made SNC-Lavalin a formidable international competitor in an increasingly globalized world. The company's plentiful internal talent also gave it the flexibility to pick the right leaders for the times, people who were highly respected by the entire workforce and who lived and advanced a disciplined culture.

Flexibility has ever characterized the best international companies, and having multicultural leadership, a relatively recent development, is the logical way to meet the demands of different markets. SNC-Lavalin has had this culture since early in its history. Great leaders build great companies, and this company's history is proof of an understanding of this principle.

Once again, the emphasis on discipline and top-quality work is not new to the company, and neither is the importance it places on professionalism. The emphasis on quality work to ensure client satisfaction has served it especially well. The company has always had an open horizon and gone where its clients' needs were, no matter how remote and forbidding the location—the Arctic, the African Sahara, the Andes, or the jungles of South America.

The firm also combines a strong financial business sense with a thorough respect for calculated risk, so essential to delivering projects on time and within budget. Add to this its respect for communities, environment, health, and safety, and you have the SNC-Lavalin I know.

I left the SNC-Lavalin board in 1996, after reaching the retirement age of 70 for directors. To this day, I retain all my shares in the company, and the clients of our money management firm, Jarislowsky Fraser Limited, together have the largest single position in SNC-Lavalin's shares.

Congratulations for 100 years of success, SNC-Lavalin, and to the thousands of men and women who have made you what you are today.

Stephen A. Jarislowsky, C.C., G.O.Q

PART

1 HOPEFUL
BEGINNINGS

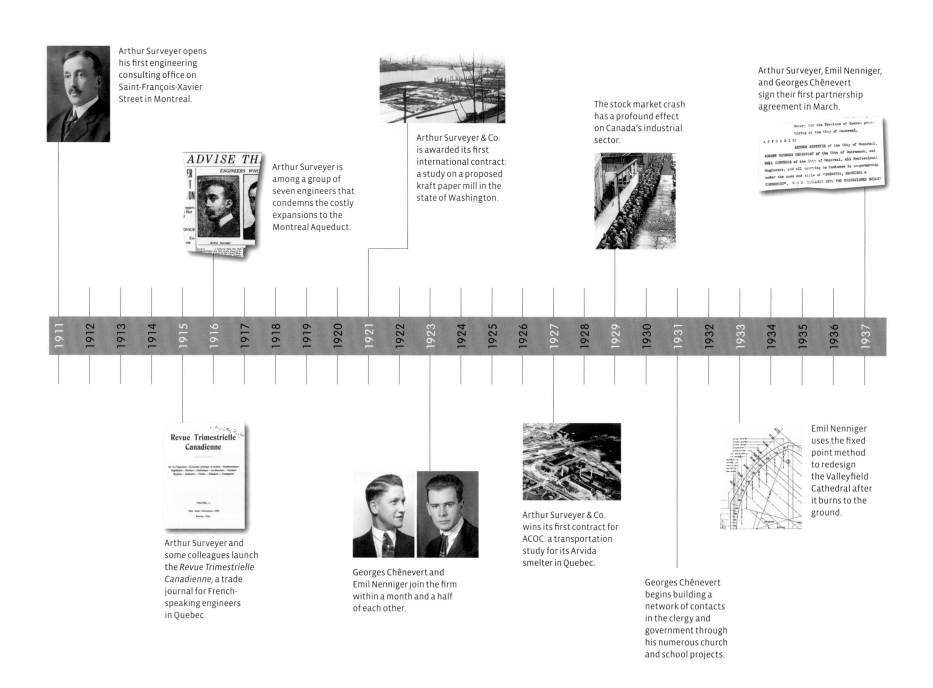

Arthur Surveyer opens his first engineering consulting office on Saint-François-Xavier Street in Montreal.

Arthur Surveyer is among a group of seven engineers that condemns the costly expansions to the Montreal Aqueduct.

Arthur Surveyer & Co. is awarded its first international contract: a study on a proposed kraft paper mill in the state of Washington.

The stock market crash has a profound effect on Canada's industrial sector.

Arthur Surveyer, Emil Nenniger, and Georges Chênevert sign their first partnership agreement in March.

Arthur Surveyer and some colleagues launch the *Revue Trimestrielle Canadienne,* a trade journal for French-speaking engineers in Quebec.

Georges Chênevert and Emil Nenniger join the firm within a month and a half of each other.

Arthur Surveyer & Co. wins its first contract for ACOC: a transportation study for its Arvida smelter in Quebec.

Georges Chênevert begins building a network of contacts in the clergy and government through his numerous church and school projects.

Emil Nenniger uses the fixed point method to redesign the Valleyfield Cathedral after it burns to the ground.

1911 1912 1913 1914 1915 1916 1917 1918 1919 1920 1921 1922 1923 1924 1925 1926 1927 1928 1929 1930 1931 1932 1933 1934 1935 1936 1937

PREVIOUS PAGE

A schematic of the Valleyfield Cathedral drafted using the fixed point method.

CHAPTER 1
ARTHUR SURVEYER, CONSULTING ENGINEER

In the spring of 1911, a 32-year-old engineer named Arthur Surveyer decides the moment has come to leave the Canadian Department of Public Works and open his own consulting firm in Montreal. He makes decisions only after great thought and internal debate, but he has no reservations. The start of the 20th century is a time when everything seems possible and engineers are taking their place as shapers of society. Surveyer will soon find his first partner in Augustin Frigon and win a first significant contract to design and supervise the construction of a hydropower station near Grand-Mère, Quebec.

The Grand-Mère powerhouse and dam in Quebec.

Blanche, and took the bold step of striking out on his own. He knows he could have made a comfortable life for himself by staying at the Canadian Department of Public Works. While shy by nature, he is nevertheless a competent engineer and a hard worker. In time, he might have worked his way up to department head and a comfortable annual salary of $4,000. His parents, friends, and colleagues had all encouraged him to stay on, but Blanche refused to let him underestimate his abilities.

Surveyer is only 32, but he has already witnessed great changes in his lifetime. Born in an era of steam-powered engines and gas lamps, he has seen the birth of the automobile and the arrival of electricity to Canada with the construction of its first hydroelectric plants. So much has changed in Surveyer's life already, but the pace of transformation does not concern him. He believes wholeheartedly in the ability of technology and innovation to improve the lot of humanity. It is a time when everything seems possible.

WHAT'S TO BECOME OF ARTHUR?

Arthur Surveyer was born into a well-to-do family in Montreal on December 17, 1878. He spent a comfortable childhood alongside his five brothers and sisters in a spacious home in an upper-class district of the city. His father, Louis-Joseph Surveyer, was a successful hardware store owner with a keen business sense. His mother, Hectorine Fabre, wrote poetry in her spare time and moved easily within the city's social circles. Unlike his older brother Édouard, whose eloquence was quickly apparent, Arthur was a quiet and introspective child. On a summer day, he was more likely to be found silently daydreaming in his room than outside playing.

Arthur's father was a staunch believer in education and expected his boys to excel in the classroom. As a businessman, he also understood the importance of English. To give his sons all the advantages that fluency in English would provide,

The story of one of the most successful engineering and construction companies in the world begins in a modest office on Saint-François-Xavier Street in Montreal, Canada. The furniture is sparse and has been chosen purely according to necessity. A single drafting table is inclined against the wall. A plain desk with an Underwood typewriter sits nearby. The only thing that the tiny office has in abundance is books. A bookcase rises almost to the ceiling, overflowing with titles of every variety.

It is 1911, and Arthur Surveyer has just gone into private practice. His office has only been open a few months, but the contracts are already starting to trickle in. It was not an easy decision, but he is glad he listened to his young bride, he enrolled them in a school that taught the language from first grade on. Louis-Joseph kept a close eye on their progress from the first day, waking them every morning at 5:00 a.m. to carefully review their English lessons before school. By the time Arthur graduated from Collège Sainte-Marie with a Bachelor of Arts degree in 1898, he was fluent.

During his studies, Surveyer had demonstrated a natural inclination towards the sciences. He had also developed the clear and precise prose style that would later become the hallmark of his project reports. What he had not done, however, was decide on a career path. His older brother Édouard had gravitated naturally to the legal profession, and Arthur's parents wanted him to follow his example. His father saw him as a notary, while his mother hoped he would overcome his shyness and become a trial lawyer.

Arthur would have liked to please his parents, but neither option interested him. He was afraid of public speaking, which ruled out trial law, and he thought life as a notary would be too dull. Having run out of career ideas, he approached his father to see if he could work at his hardware store, but Louis-Joseph flatly refused. He had not sent Arthur to college so that he could count nuts and bolts.

A career path soon suggested itself to Surveyer in conversation with some former classmates who had recently

Arthur Surveyer (top left) and his 1902 École Polytechnique de Montréal graduating class.

At the time, the school was located in a private residence behind the Académie du Plateau.

enrolled at the École Polytechnique de Montréal. Founded in 1873, the École Polytechnique had humble beginnings and was not yet an established university when Surveyer became a civil engineering student in 1898. Its curriculum had expanded to include a variety of applied sciences, but it was still located in a mildly dilapidated private residence behind the Académie du Plateau.

The school's physical appearance was, in many ways, a reflection of the status of engineering in Quebec at the time. It was still a fledgling profession, ranking far behind the more prestigious careers available to French-speaking men in the legal and medical fields. But while the École Polytechnique lacked the full support of the educational community, it had the benefit of enthusiastic teachers who believed in the value of a practical scientific education.

During his time there, Surveyer gradually came to realize that his interest in engineering was not necessarily incompatible with his desire to enter the business world. At the outset of the 20th century, Quebec's industrial sector was developing quickly, which meant good economic prospects for the men who could help design the new factories, powerhouses, and smelters. Sensing an opportunity, Surveyer decided to expand his knowledge of industrial engineering and pursue graduate studies at the École spéciale de l'Industrie et des Mines du Hainaut in Belgium.

MARRIAGE AND A FIRST JOB

By 1904, Surveyer was back in Canada, bringing with him fond memories of Europe and a high opinion of the European engineers he had met. Wanting to put his years of study to the test, he now joined the Canadian Department of Public Works as a junior engineer. It was the same year the Parliament of Canada asked Public Works to prepare an in-depth feasibility study of the Georgian Bay Canal project. Surveyer was told to assist Head Engineer Arthur Saint-Laurent with the challenging assignment.

From the outset, the proposed canal between Montreal and Lake Huron in Ontario had both great supporters and great detractors. Those with a vested interest in southern Ontario wanted the business the canal would bring. Others argued that too much money had been poured into Canada's railways to now turn such a large part of their cargo over to ships.

The Georgian Bay Canal would never be built, but nearly 70 years later historian Robert Legget would call the 600-page feasibility study "one of the finest engineering reports ever produced in the history of Canada." Surveyer may have only played a junior role in its creation, but he was nonetheless proud of his contribution.

In 1909, Surveyer was assigned to Port Arthur in northwestern Ontario to supervise the construction of a dry dock. It was on a trip back home to Montreal to visit his parents later that year that he saw Blanche Cholette again. Surveyer and Blanche had once been sweethearts, and they soon realized their feelings for each other had not faded with time. He still admired her energy and intelligence. She could still see past his shyness and reserve to the honest, kind man within. They were married in Montreal on January 10, 1910.

The newlyweds were soon living in Port Arthur, where Surveyer immediately threw himself back into his work. Blanche tried to make the best of the situation, but she quickly grew bored living in a town that was no more than an industrial port. It was then that she encouraged him to enter private practice. It was not complicated, she told him. He was too talented to remain an employee of Public Works, and she missed her Montreal social life too much to stay in Port Arthur.

By the spring of 1911, Surveyer had found and was renting his first office in Montreal. It was as bare as a monk's cell, but it had the benefit of being next to a telegraph company and in the heart of what was then the city's business district. The time had now come to demonstrate that business and engineering actually made excellent bedfellows. There were just two things he had to do first: find a good partner and improve his knowledge of economics and finance with a correspondence course.

Surveyer-Cholette.

Un très chic mariage avait lieu, ce matin à l'église Saint-Louis, de France. M. Arthur Surveyer épousait l'une de nos plus charmantes canadiennes-françaises, Mademoiselle Blanche Cholette, fille de M. L. E. A. Cholette du Square Saint-Louis.

M. Cholette servait de témoin à sa fille, et M. L. J. A. Surveyer à son fils.

C'est l'abbé W. Hébert, qi bénit l'union. Durant la messe, Mlle R. de Lorimier, chanta avec tout le talent qu'on lui connaît, un délicieux cantique tout plein de bonheur à l'adresse des deux époux. M. P. E. Ouimet interpréta le "Credo" de Faure, et une douzaine de chantres de la Chorale St-Louis de France exécutèrent le magnifique " Sanctus " de Godefroi. MM. Émile Chaput et Jos. Monday agissaient comme solistes.

La marie portait à ravir un cos-

tume de voyage wisteria avec turban de même couleur. Son bouquet see composait de roses blanches et de muguets.

Les cadeaux reçus sont on ne peut plus riches et artistiques.

M. et Madame E. Surveyer, accompagnés des vœux nombreux de leurs amis, sont aprtis, ce matin même jour pour New-York et quelques autres villes américaines

FIRST CONTRACTS

Surveyer had distinguished himself during his seven years at Public Works. He had become an expert in hydraulics by cutting his teeth as a junior engineer on the contentious Georgian Bay Canal project. It was that experience that now made him a good candidate for another equally controversial waterway project.

In February 1912, he was contacted with an urgent request. There was little time, he was told, and much was at stake. The Shipping Federation of Canada needed a report on the effects of a planned diversion of the Chicago Drainage Canal. Surveyer was asked to demonstrate that the diversion would lower the St. Lawrence River to a level that would be fatal to the shipping industry. The Shipping Federation hoped to convince the American Secretary of War to stop the project at a meeting scheduled for March 27. That left Surveyer with a little more than a month to produce the report.

Chicago had a sanitation problem that went back more than half a century. The city's solution had been to build a series of sanitation canals, all of which drained water from Lake Michigan, itself indirectly linked to the St. Lawrence River through lakes Huron, Erie, and Ontario. By 1911, the cumulative effect of Chicago's canals on the St. Lawrence was clear for all to see. It had been a particularly dry summer, and the river's level had dropped more than 45 centimetres below what was considered its extreme low water mark. This was bad enough, but, in February 1912, the Sanitary District of Chicago proposed to draw an additional 283 cubic metres per second from Lake Michigan, the equivalent of an Olympic-sized pool every nine seconds. There was an immediate uproar on both sides of the border. It was at this point that Surveyer was called in.

Surveyer got to work immediately. Fortunately, his familiarity with the hydraulic data already compiled by Public Works helped speed up the process, and he

"La Patrie"
Journal du Peuple

11e ANNÉE—No 244—QUATORZE PAGES

In 1910, Arthur Surveyer and his new bride, Blanche Cholette, moved to Port Arthur, Ontario, where he was supervising the construction of a dry dock.

Montreal Harbour,
circa 1915.

was able to deliver his findings two days before the March 27 meeting. He admitted that the short timeframe made an estimation of the full impact of the diversion difficult, but one thing was abundantly clear: the project would have disastrous effects. The water levels in Montreal Harbour would be "affected throughout the whole navigation season from May to November," he said, as they would be "an average of five inches lower, and during the low water months an average of 10 inches lower, with the possibility of a drop of 12 or 13 inches in an exceptionally low water season." He concluded his report with a warning: the project would likely spell trouble for the shipping industry, since larger vessels would have to limit their cargo to safely navigate the river.

On January 8, 1913, Secretary of War Henry Stimson delivered his highly anticipated ruling on the Chicago Canal project. He said that, while he understood the importance of "preserving the health of the great city of Chicago," it was

clear that the diversion would "materially injure a most important class of the commerce of the nation." It would also seriously affect "the interests of a foreign power." The project could not be allowed to go forward. Case closed.

It was a major victory for the Shipping Federation, and also for Surveyer. Slowly but surely, his expertise was beginning to be recognized.

ENERGIZING GRAND-MÈRE

With the report delivered to the Shipping Federation, Surveyer now turned his attention to growing his business.

He had already succeeded in accomplishing his first two goals: he was fast becoming an expert in economics and cost analysis, and he had found a first partner in Augustin Frigon. The men had met a couple of years before at the first meeting of the École Polytechnique Alumni Association. Frigon was a

bright and imaginative electrical engineer. It had taken him considerable effort to convince Frigon to leave the École Polytechnique's Faculty of Engineering but he had finally prevailed. Surveyer was a man of few words, but those he spoke were carefully chosen and generally convincing.

In the summer of 1912, the new partners rented a small suite of offices at 56 Beaver Hall Hill in what was quickly becoming Montreal's new business district, and Surveyer filed the necessary legal papers to change the firm's name to Surveyer & Frigon. There was now enough space to accommodate a few drafting tables if business continued to improve.

Frigon's timing could not have been better. For the past few months Surveyer had been working to help the city of Grand-Mère, located in central Quebec, decide how to acquire the power it needed for its growing population. Frigon's expertise in electrical engineering would be helpful now that the city had opted to build a power station on the nearby Saint-Maurice River. The Grand-Mère City Council soon asked Surveyer to draw up plans and specifications for the station, and even supervise its construction. It was a major step forward for his young firm.

ARTHUR SURVEYER, I. C
MEM. CANADIAN SOCIETY OF CIVIL ENGINEERS
MEM. ASSOC. INTER. DES CONGRES DE NAVIGATION
MEM. SOCIÉTÉ DES INGÉNIEURSCIVILS DE FRANCE
INGÉNIEUR - CORRESPONDANT EXCLUSIF DE LA
CHAMBRE DES INGÉNIEURS CONSEILS DE FRANCE.

SURVEYER & FRIGON
INGÉNIEURS CONSEILS
EXPERTISES LEVÉS DE PLANS ESTIMATIONS ET PROJETS
RAPPORTS TECHNIQUES ET FINANCIERS

ADRESSE: 56 CÔTE BEAVER HALL
TÉL. UPTOWN 3908

AUGUSTIN FRIGON, I. C
INGÉNIEUR ÉLECTRICIEN
PROFESSEUR A L'ÉCOLE POLYTECHNIQUE
UNIVERSITÉ LAVAL
MEM. CANADIAN SOCIETY OF CIVIL ENGINEERS

CHAPTER 2

THE "COMPLETE" ENGINEER

Arthur Surveyer finds himself becoming a spokesman for the Canadian engineering profession. By 1918, he is sitting on the boards of the École Polytechnique de Montréal, the Canadian Society of Civil Engineers, and the National Research Council of Canada. He has penned articles for the *Revue Trimestrielle Canadienne*, Quebec's first true engineering journal. He has begun giving speeches on topics ranging from financial policy to the art of public speaking. All this activity foreshadows the public figure that Surveyer will soon become. His little engineering office is growing, along with his profile, with an important new contract for B.C. Electric Railway.

Inside the powerhouse at Stave Falls in British Columbia, circa 1920.

By 1915, Surveyer's profile as a consulting engineer was definitely rising. He had succeeded in becoming a known quantity within Canadian government and business circles in four short years. Now representatives from both increasingly sought out his opinion on problems requiring particular care and precision. It was quite an accomplishment considering his aversion to the limelight.

The uncounted hours of hard work and attention to detail had begun to pay off. It also did not hurt that Surveyer was part of a network of École Polytechnique alumni who tended to look out for one another's business interests. He had attended most meetings of the École Polytechnique's Alumni Association since it was founded in 1909. Surveyer usually avoided social gatherings, preferring to send Blanche as his goodwill ambassador, but these get-togethers were different. He could talk shop and maybe even get a tip on a potential job.

It was through the Association that Surveyer became friends with Édouard Montpetit. At the time, Montpetit was teaching Industrial Law at École Polytechnique, and Surveyer and Frigon would sometimes meet up with him at a nearby café for lunch. They would discuss current events and exchange opinions about engineering problems. Sometimes the conversation would turn to the lack of serious French trade journals in Canada available to engineers. They felt a reputable publication could be an effective and much-needed mouthpiece for the profession. The question, of course, was who would produce it? Such a publication required competent writers and editors, well-trained engineers, and even some vision. On a winter evening in early 1915, after again voicing their dissatisfaction with existing sources of information, the men decided to stop waiting and produce their own publication.

The *Revue Trimestrielle Canadienne* appeared in May of that year. Montpetit headed up the editorial board and laid out the publication's dual purpose in the first issue. "We will be successful and our ambitions will be entirely realized if we can, at once, serve the practical needs of engineers while communicating to the wider public the abundance of our resources and the means of putting them to work...."

Surveyer, for his part, wrote an article on the "Control of Public Services by Commissions." While still not widely discussed, it was a subject that would gain prominence in Quebec in 1936 with the creation of a board to keep tabs on the rates charged by private power companies. It was not the last time Surveyer would demonstrate an uncanny ability to foresee coming trends.

The appearance of the *Revue* only pushed Surveyer further into the public eye. The next year, he was sitting on the boards of the École Polytechnique, the Quebec branch of the Canadian Society of Civil Engineers, and the National Research Council of Canada. Now there was no looking back. The young man who had not been able to decide on a career was quickly becoming a spokesman for the engineering profession.

The first issue of the *Revue Trimestrielle Canadienne* in 1915.

The Montreal Daily Star.

VOL. XLVIII., NO. 277   The Weather: FAIR and COLD   MONTREAL, MONDAY, NOVEMBER 20, 1916   PRICE ONE CENT

ENGINEERS ADVISE THAT AQUEDUCT WORK BE STOPPED

COTE AND MERCIER STATE AQUEDUCT WORK WILL GO ON

Heads of Works Department Say They Will Not Be Stampeded

PREFER THEIR OWN ADVICE

Quote New York Engineers from Whom Local Men Differ

There was a conference today between Paul Mercier, Chief Engineer,

ENGINEERS WHO SUGGEST AQUEDUCT WORK BE STOPPED

Arthur Surveyer   H. M. MacKay   Phelps Johnson   Sir John Kennedy

BETTER FOR CITY TO LOSE $5,200,000 NOW SPENT THAN TWICE THAT SUM

Hold That Work if Completed Will Not Do What is Claimed for It Say It Should Never Have Been Started and All Thought of Completing It Should Be Abandoned

"The present project should never have been started, and we are firmly of the opinion that all thought of completing it along the present lines, should be abandoned."

MEN WHO ADVISE CITY TO STOP WORK ON THE AQUEDUCT

In 1916, Arthur Surveyer was part of a group of seven "Ratepaying Engineers" who investigated cost overruns on the Montreal aqueduct project.

THE MONTREAL AQUEDUCT DEBACLE

In 1916, Surveyer was again called upon to help bring order to a situation that had spiralled out of control. The matter was no less controversial than the Chicago or Georgian Bay canal projects, but it was considerably closer to home. The issue concerned an expansion of a municipal waterworks project in Montreal. Surveyer was part of a committee of seven local engineers who were asked to investigate the project's cost overruns and mismanagement.

Since the middle of the 19th century, Montreal had been supplied with water from an open aqueduct. In 1905, with demand for water rising, the Superintendent of the Waterworks Department proposed an expansion of the system to City Council. His plan envisioned enlarging the aqueduct and building a hydraulic powerhouse to provide between 2,000 and 5,000 horsepower. All of this, he assured them, could be done at a cost of $2.1 million.

Work began in 1909, but the Superintendent was back before City Council even before construction was complete. In 1912, he proposed to double the capacity of the intake

W. F. Tye

canal and expand the powerhouse to allow it to produce 10,000 horsepower. The extra electricity, he argued, would supply Montreal with affordable energy for many years to come. The city hired a contractor the following year for the supplemental work, on his assurance that it could be carried out for $1.9 million.

Before long there were whispers in the Montreal press of unforeseen difficulties and cost overruns. The trickle of rumours swelled to a river in November 1915 when *Canadian Engineer* published an article on the project. The authors suspected mismanagement and called for a complete investigation into the expansion. With a full-blown controversy on its hands, the city agreed to let a group of Montreal engineers investigate the project and propose modifications if needed. Surveyer was among the seven "Ratepaying Engineers" who delivered a report to City Hall on November 20, 1916.

The *Report by Ratepaying Engineers* was consistent in its condemnation. Surveyer and his colleagues were dumbfounded that no "complete plans and estimates" had ever been made of such "essential parts of the project as the river intake, the powerhouse or the necessary outlet works ....". If the expansions had been properly evaluated, it would have been clear that the new aqueduct would barely be able to carry enough water to safely generate 6,000 horsepower, never mind 10,000.

Then there was the projected cost of the expansions, which had spiralled well beyond $10 million. The city would end up paying about $108 per horsepower, when it could easily buy the same amount of electricity for between $20 and $30 from a local provider. The report recommended Montreal cut its losses and stop the project immediately.

The city's Bureau of Commissioners was split. As always in such matters, a little pride and a few jobs were at stake. The press even reported that the document had triggered bitter exchanges among some members of the Bureau. Unable to come to a decision, they appointed a new committee to study the case.

The matter was temporarily set aside when the military demands World War I placed on the economy brought construction to a halt anyway. As the years passed, opposition to the project grew, and by 1922 the idea of an expanded power station had been abandoned. It had taken close to six years, but City Council had finally heeded the Ratepaying Engineers' advice.

BUT WILL IT BE PROFITABLE?

Augustin Frigon had enjoyed teaching before he joined Surveyer, and his passion for education had not faded during his years with the firm. It was no surprise then, when, in 1917, Frigon accepted the Chair in Electrical Engineering at the École Polytechnique. Surveyer was losing a good partner, but there were no hard feelings. After all, he was a passionate autodidact and a proponent of education. He respected his friend's decision and wished him well.

PROFESSIONAL ENGINEERS

ON FEBRUARY 14, 1920, ARTHUR SURVEYER AND SOME COLLEAGUES FOUNDED THE CORPORATION OF PROFESSIONAL ENGINEERS OF QUEBEC. AT THE TIME, A UNIVERSITY DEGREE WAS NOT MANDATORY TO BECOME AN ENGINEER IN CANADA. ALL IT TOOK WAS A PERIOD OF ON-THE-JOB TRAINING AND THE SPONSORSHIP OF THREE ACCREDITED ENGINEERS. SOME, HOWEVER, BYPASSED EVEN THESE REQUIREMENTS. THE CORPORATION IMMEDIATELY SET ABOUT ENSURING THAT ALL ENGINEERS WHO PRACTICED IN THE PROVINCE HAD THE NECESSARY TRAINING.

With Surveyer on his own once again, the firm's name reverted back to Arthur Surveyer & Co. He now hired engineers as the need arose, but it would be many years before he would again solicit new partners. At least he had profited from his association with Frigon to broaden his knowledge, something he was always eager to do. When combined with his deep understanding of hydraulics, his improved familiarity with electrical engineering now gave him excellent credentials for hydropower projects.

In August of 1920, Surveyer was asked to combine his knowledge of hydropower plant design with his financial expertise for a single project. The B.C. Electric Railway planned to acquire the Western Power Company of Canada, one of its smaller competitors in British Columbia, but first it wanted to determine the value of its hydropower installations and the profitability of a projected 100,000-horsepower station on the Stave River. A contact at the Engineering Institute of Canada had put forward Surveyer's name as an ideal candidate.

The job was indeed custom-made for Surveyer. He had long believed that "the complete engineer should be able to do more than prepare plans and estimate the costs of building a factory." He felt they should also "be able to estimate the operating costs of the factory and the company's margin of profit."

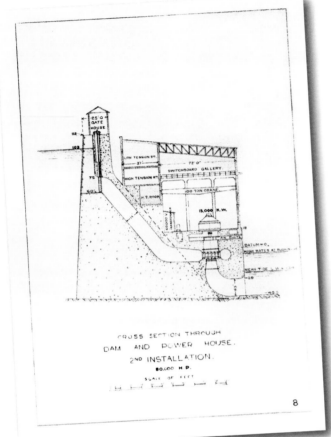

Arthur Surveyer & Co.'s first full-fledged contract outside Quebec was for B.C. Electric Railway. Arthur Surveyer was asked to determine the value of the Western Power Company of Canada and the profitability of its projected hydropower plant on the Stave River in British Columbia.

Surveyer began his study with a trip to Stave Falls. He spent three days inspecting Western Power's existing hydropower plant, as well as the site of the future one. He found that the current plant had been "carefully planned and executed," and that all the hydraulic and electrical equipment was in the "best operating condition." As for the new plant, Surveyer estimated that it would have a peak capacity of 80,400 horsepower, somewhat less than hoped, but still a respectable output for a hydropower station of the time.

After thoroughly examining the numbers and developing a plan of action, Surveyer had no hesitation in recommending the acquisition. "It seems to me that the directors of the British Columbia Electric Railway Company would be well advised to acquire control of Western Power," he wrote. Profit margins for the new power plant would be good, and

there were also obvious strategic reasons for going ahead with the acquisition. B.C. Electric Railway would not only "secure an additional supply of power" but would "consolidate the position of their company" by acquiring a competitor. Assured by his analysis, the company proceeded with the deal.

AN INVITATION FROM INDUSTRY

Surveyer had shown that he was a good multidisciplinary engineer, but that alone did not assure his success. Surveyer sometimes had to rely on grim determination. It was determination that carried him through the depths of the postwar recession, when he again found himself alone and unable even to hire a draftsman or a full-time secretary. It would have been all too easy to throw in the towel. One phone call to Public Works would have done it, but he had not come this far to go back to square one.

By 1921, Surveyer's office on Beaver Hall Hill did not look much different from his first on Saint-François-Xavier Street. Surveyer's only luxury remained a telephone, which brought him some much-needed good news in February. Henning Helin, a Vancouver engineer, phoned to offer him his largest contract to date. Helin explained that he had been hired by Giscome Lumber Company to look into building a paper mill in Aberdeen, Washington, in the United States. He knew a lot about pulp and paper mills, but he needed a good hydraulics man. He had heard Surveyer was one of the best.

It was a great opportunity. Such a large contract would allow Arthur Surveyer & Co. to become a full-fledged engineering office again. It would also mean reaching a pair of milestones: Surveyer would finally crack the industrial sector, and he would do so in an international market. He wanted the contract badly, but as always he betrayed no excitement. "Yes, I have some expertise in hydraulics," he said, with deadpan delivery. "Why don't we arrange a meeting?" The men agreed to discuss the matter further when Helin was in Montreal the following week.

Surveyer told Blanche the good news as soon as he arrived home that night. "I think I have a chance to land the biggest deal of my career," he said with only a hint of a smile. "It's a study for a kraft paper mill in the United States." Surveyer added that a meeting with the engineer who had offered him the work was set for the following week.

Blanche could not believe her ears. "You mean you'll see him in your office?" she asked.

"Well, yes," he replied.

"You can't receive him in that office of yours," she said. "There's nothing in it but a few sticks of furniture. You don't even have a secretary. What will he think of you? You have to make the right impression," she continued. "Leave this to me."

Surveyer eyed her warily. He knew Blanche had excellent business instincts and was gutsy enough to put them into action. He reluctantly decided to leave the matter in her hands and retired to his study to see what he could find on the pulp and paper industry.

The day before the meeting, a large department store delivery truck pulled up in front of Surveyer's office. When he answered the door, the delivery man simply said, "Your furniture." It was only when Surveyer caught a glimpse of Blanche over the man's shoulder that he realized what was going on. "Yes, bring it in," she said, breezing into the office before Surveyer could react.

In came new bookcases, filing cabinets, a small meeting table, curtains, and lamps—everything that a highly successful office of the day would have. When the delivery men left, Surveyer asked how much all of it had cost. "That's not important. Let me take care of that," Blanche answered. "Just get ready for your meeting." Surveyer returned to his pulp and paper research, barely able to conceal his irritation.

The stage was set and all the props arranged by the time Helin arrived. The old furniture had been stuffed into a drafting room and covered up with a screen. Blanche had even hired a babysitter for the day, and was now installed at the new desk to play secretary. At the appointed time, she escorted Helin into the office and went back to her desk where she pretended to type a letter. The meeting went off without a hitch. Helin seemed to have been impressed by the stately decor.

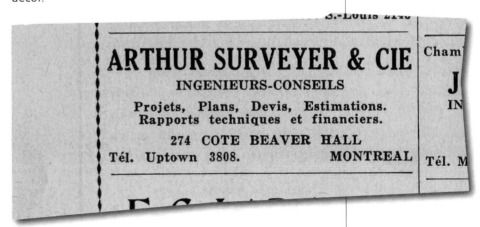

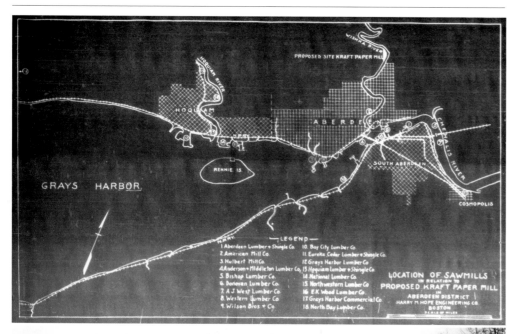

In 1921, Arthur Surveyer & Co. was awarded its first international contract: an engineering and economic study on a proposed kraft pulp mill in Aberdeen, Washington, for the Giscome Lumber Company.

When Arthur Surveyer & Co. was awarded the contract one week later, Surveyer couldn't help but wonder whether the new furnishing had helped seal the deal. Blanche had no doubt. He was talented, yes, but success breeds success.

Surveyer now had the biggest contract of his career on his books. He was new to the sector, but that was no excuse for not filing a detailed and precise project report. Determined to master the subject in record time, he devoured all relevant government reports, statistics, and any library book he could find on the subject. He made trips to the proposed project site in Aberdeen, and consulted experts to ensure he was focusing on the most salient details. There were a multitude of aspects to consider. Was there ample water for manufacturing purposes? Were there good transportation facilities nearby? Would they have access to a competitively priced supply of raw materials? What were the markets like? On May 28, Surveyer reported that the location in Aberdeen met all these criteria.

Now it was up to Giscome Lumber to decide if Aberdeen was indeed the right location. Whatever it decided, Surveyer was glad to have helped the company make its decision in the full light of the facts.

CHAPTER 3

THE **N** AND THE **C**

The Dupuis Frères department store at the corner of Sainte-Catherine Street East and Saint-André Street in Montreal.

Business is booming at Arthur Surveyer & Co. by the early 1920s. Surveyer has relocated to the Drummond Building on Sainte-Catherine Street, where he partners with architect Henri Labelle on major building projects. The new work leads him to hire Georges Chênevert and Emil Nenniger, who quickly prove to be top talents: Nenniger brings innovative engineering techniques from Europe, while Chênevert builds a network of invaluable contacts that help the firm win school and church projects. By 1937, Surveyer must recognize that his recruits have become essential components of his firm, and he makes them partners.

La Patrie

ESSOR REMARQUABLE D'UNE GRANDE INSTITUTION COMMERCIALE CANADIENNE-FRANÇAISE, LA MAISON DUPUIS FRERES LIMITEE

LE BON GOUT ET LE BON SENS ONT PRESIDE A LA CONSTRUCTION DE L'IMMEUBLE DUPUIS FRERES

The 1923 expansion of the Dupuis Frères department store was heralded for its "good taste and good sense" by local newspaper *La Patrie*.

supervision as well as design. There was just one catch—they were slated to begin around the same time in the spring, which meant Surveyer needed more manpower. He called his old friend Augustin Frigon, now the Principal of École Polytechnique, to ask him if he knew of any talented graduates. Frigon had no hesitation in recommending a student in his last year named Georges Chênevert. The kid sounded ideal. He was top of his class, absolutely meticulous in his work, and he came from a family of builders.

The young man who showed up at Surveyer's office for an interview had a compact build, and was dressed and groomed like a matinée idol. Chênevert spoke like a lawyer making a deposition, choosing each word with great care. Surveyer liked the way he seemed to analyse problems from every angle before making a decision, and hired him on the spot.

One and a half months later, Surveyer found himself interviewing another good candidate, although this one had sought him out. The young man had just arrived from Switzerland and introduced himself in broken English as Emil Nenniger. Not knowing anything about the engineering business in Montreal, he had methodically drawn up a list of firms in the city that included Arthur Surveyer & Co. He held a degree in Architecture from the Cantonale School of Technology, but had learned engineering entirely on his own. Surveyer was impressed: the fellow was clearly intelligent and driven. When he discovered that Nenniger had an interest in industrial processes, he was sold.

Nenniger joined Chênevert on the Dupuis Frères project the following Monday. Most of the plans had been drawn up, but there were still issues to resolve. The building would be located on an incline, and the men worked on engineering the 3.3-metre rise between the front and back of the store.

Nenniger and Chênevert were opposites in many ways: Nenniger liked to work quickly and had little patience for protracted discussions. He often sensed the correct answer right away, and would sometimes even work on engineering plans with both hands simultaneously, writing with one and drawing with the other. Chênevert, on the other hand, had what seemed like infinite patience for finer details. He could

I n January 1923, Surveyer rented a suite in the prestigious Drummond Building on Sainte-Catherine Street, Montreal's main shopping thoroughfare. It was a definite step up, and a reflection of his recent run of successful assignments. The office was more spacious than his last and had the benefit of being on the same floor as architect Henri Labelle, with whom he planned to collaborate on some upcoming commercial buildings assignments.

Two were particularly interesting: an expansion of the Dupuis Frères department store and a new warehouse for transportation company, J. B. Baillargeon Express. Both projects were located in Montreal and involved construction

spend hours discussing the minutia of an engineering problem. It was the secret of his uncanny ability to ferret out flaws in design plans.

They did not always agree on how to proceed as they worked, but they found common ground in their exacting standards. The new recruits were soon also helping with the Baillargeon warehouse in the city's east end, the second of the two important contracts.

Both buildings would stand out as examples of sound and elegant design when completed. Dupuis Frères was engineered to be one of the most fire-resistant structures of its kind, with a state-of-the-art sprinkler system and fireproof construction materials (over 4,500 cubic metres of reinforced concrete went into the structure). The building was more than simply practical—it also looked good. On December 15, 1923, the Montreal newspaper *La Patrie* ran an article about the building with the headline: "Good Taste and Good Sense have Prevailed in the Construction of the Dupuis Building."

The Baillargeon warehouse was no less of an elegant fortress. Its 9,200 square metres of floor space was spread out over eight stories, each armed with a set of burglar alarms

and a sprinkler system. Not a single plank of wood was used in its construction to ensure complete resistance to fire. The interior was finished with marble and cement, and even the doors, window frames, and partitions were made of metal. The Baillargeon building was also deemed worthy of a write-up. An article appeared in the April 1924 issue of the *Contract Record and Engineering Review* with a headline that said it all: "A New Warehouse Combining Utility and Beauty."

The firm's new recruits were clearly off to a good start.

A FIRST ACOC CONTRACT

The mid- to late 1920s were years of great industrial expansion in Canada. The postwar recession dwindled into a distant memory as the country experienced one of the greatest economic booms in its history. American companies were investing in Canadian natural resources and manufacturing industries at an unprecedented rate.

Arthur Surveyer & Co. was still busy with civil engineering, buildings, and hydraulics projects, but the call of industry could not be ignored. It built on its Giscome Lumber experience with several studies for the pulp and paper industry between 1925 and 1926, including one for a sulphite pulp mill in Newfoundland. The next year, the firm began its long relationship with the Aluminum Company of Canada (ACOC), a subsidiary of the American Aluminum Company.

In January 1927, Surveyer was asked by Edwin S. Fickes,

the Vice-President of the American Aluminum Company, to evaluate a few different transportation options for a smelter the company was building at Arvida, in the Saguenay region of central Quebec. Surveyer would be working with Olivier Lefebvre, a fellow École Polytechnique graduate.

ACOC had good reasons for choosing the Saguenay region for its second Canadian smelter. Proximity to a power source in the energy-intensive aluminum industry was crucial, and the Saguenay had "power in almost frightening quantities."[1] The region also had a natural river superhighway. Ships bringing in bauxite by way of the Atlantic could travel along the St. Lawrence, then cruise up the Saguenay River. Rounding out the picture was the area's "assured and capable workforce of hundreds who could be trained and developed from the sturdy sons of farm and forest."[2]

ACOC had begun by securing a supply of hydropower in the region in 1925, and, the following year, it bought a company

In 1927, Arthur Surveyer evaluated several possible navigation channels to the Arvida aluminum smelter in central Quebec.

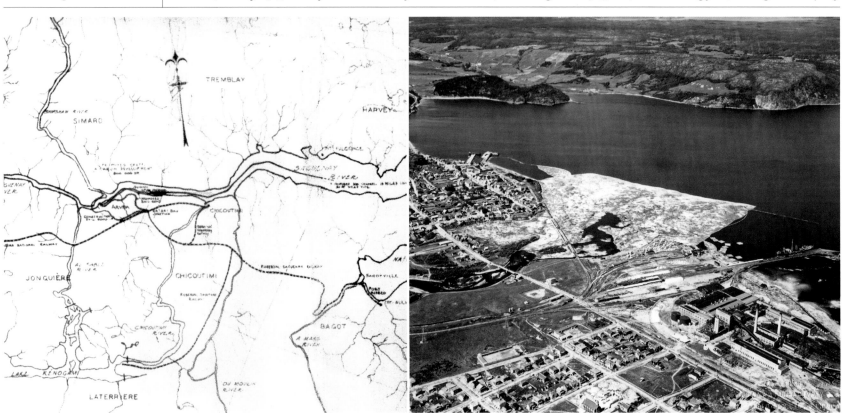

1. Duncan C. Campbell, *Global Mission: The Story of Alcan, Vol. 1*. Montreal, Canada: Alcan Aluminium Limited, 1985-1991. p. 104

2. Campbell, *Global Mission*

that owned convenient port and rail facilities. By then, it had also selected a location for its smelter, named Arvida after its parent company's President, Arthur Vining Davis.

When Surveyer and Lefebvre were contacted by Fickes in early 1927, the third of Arvida's four potlines had just come on line. Fickes asked the engineers to help ACOC choose the best of three transportation options for its smelter's raw materials and finished aluminum. The company was currently using the harbour it had acquired in Port Alfred, but it wanted to know if it would be more practical and economical to abandon it for another in Chicoutimi, or even use a completely new harbour proposed for Arvida itself.

Surveyer and Lefebvre explored each scenario from every angle, weighing the costs against practical constraints. Switching to ports at Chicoutimi or Arvida looked great on a map, but closer inspection revealed they were losing deals for ACOC. While both were physically closer to the smelter than Port Alfred, there were no existing rail facilities that it could use to link them to the smelter. And in order for ACOC's massive ships to access the ports at Chicoutimi or Arvida, several kilometres of the Saguenay River would need to be dredged regularly. In the end, it would cost only half as much to improve and continue to use Port Alfred.

"It is obvious that a project which would nearly double the cost of handling material is not to be recommended," the report concluded. The client eventually took Surveyer and Lefebvre's advice and expanded Port Alfred.

LEAN YEARS

The Great Depression announced itself with dramatic newspaper headlines on October 24, 1929. The New York Stock Exchange crashed, dragging with it many of the world's economies. Canada had been on its way to becoming an industrial powerhouse, but its economy was now on the brink of collapse as investments in such projects all but evaporated.

Arthur Surveyer & Co. was not spared. An investment company Surveyer had set up only a few years earlier failed.

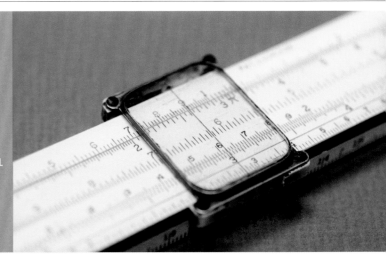

The firm's engineering activities slowed as well. There were still scattered contracts for schools and churches, occasional studies for hydropower, and transmission and distribution projects, but they might not have been enough to keep the firm afloat. Fortunately, Arthur Surveyer & Co. was able to offer something very few other engineering-consulting firms could: expertise in financial appraisals.

In the summer of 1930, Arthur Surveyer & Co. relocated to 1010 Sainte-Catherine Street West, where industrial tycoon Noah Timmins had his offices.

In the spring of 1930, Noah Timmins, the President of Hollinger Consolidated Gold Mines, asked Surveyer to manage his investment company, International Bond and Share. Surveyer was an ideal candidate: he liked to travel and he possessed a rare combination of engineering and financial know-how. The contract would provide more than a sorely needed additional revenue stream; it would also greatly expand Surveyer's business network, bringing him into contact with a number of the world's bankers, company presidents, and ambassadors.

By the summer, Arthur Surveyer & Co. had relocated to a new building on Sainte-Catherine Street, where Timmins had his offices. ACOC was there as well, which allowed the firm to stay in close contact with a major new client and its only real source of industrial work during the Depression. There was a study to examine the effects of fluoric acid fumes at one of ACOC's plants in 1932, followed by another, in 1933, to look into the earnings of Duke-Price, one of its recent acquisitions.

Emil Nenniger used the fixed point method of graphic computation to redesign the Valleyfield Cathedral in the 1930s.

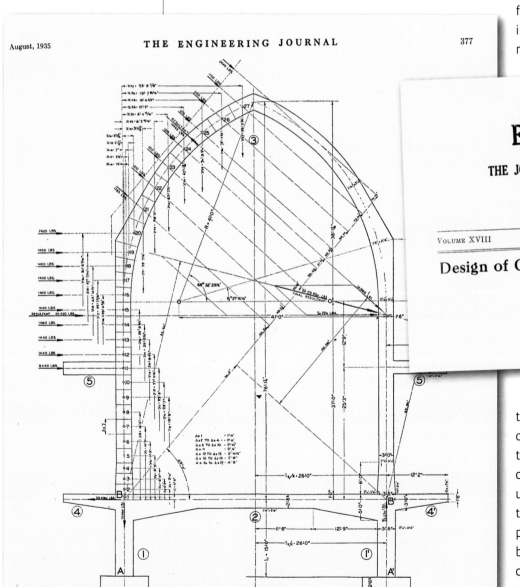

August, 1935   THE ENGINEERING JOURNAL   377

THE

ENGINEERING JOURNAL

THE JOURNAL OF THE ENGINEERING INSTITUTE OF CANADA

Published monthly at 2050 Mansfield Street, Montreal, by The Engineering Institute of Canada, Incorporated in 1887 as The Canadian Society of Civil Engineers.

ENTERED AT THE POST OFFICE, MONTREAL, AS SECOND CLASS MATTER.

THE INSTITUTE as a body is not responsible either for the statements made or for the opinions expressed in the following pages.

VOLUME XVIII   MONTREAL, AUGUST, 1935   NUMBER 8

Design of Continuous Reinforced Concrete Arches by the Fixed Point Method
For the Cathedral, at Valleyfield, Que.
E. Nenniger, A.M.E.I.C.,
Associate, Arthur Surveyer and Co., Consulting Engineers, Montreal.

The following year, Nenniger worked on a contract for the reconstruction of a church in Valleyfield, Quebec. The old cathedral had burnt down, and a decision was made to rebuild it with a fire-resistant combination of reinforced concrete and steel. Nenniger had a flash of inspiration and used an innovative European method unknown in Canada to optimize construction costs. It was known as the fixed point method of graphic computation. Originally developed by Professor Wilhelm Ritter, it allowed engineers to precisely calculate load-bearing capacities graphically, eliminating excess building materials.

Chênevert had some smaller studies for churches and schools. They did not translate into much revenue, but he was slowly building a network of contacts among the clergy and government that would prove valuable in the 1940s and 1950s.

THE PARTNERS

By 1936, there was still little sign of recovery, and the firm often found itself in the red. One of the only contracts that year, an evaluation of the Canadian newsprint industry, came from ACOC.

It was no secret that Nenniger and Chênevert had long wanted to become partners in the firm, and they decided the time had now come to make their case. They reminded Surveyer that they had stuck with him through some very lean years, helping him survive the worst of the Depression with the contracts they brought in.

While naturally cautious, Surveyer did not take long to come to the conclusion that he could ill afford to lose his two best engineers. They had both become valuable specialists: Nenniger in industrial processes and structures, Chênevert in buildings and legal matters. In short, they had earned it.

"I am offering you each 20 percent, but there is no question of changing the firm's name," he told them. He had made that mistake before. "In January, we will find a notary and draft the partnership agreement."

After months of negotiations, a first 10-year partnership agreement was ready on March 11, 1937. There had been many issues to clarify, but all three men were now fully satisfied with the language. Chênevert, always legal-minded and precise, had asked for several passages to be clarified. The only point that had not been open to discussion was the firm's name. Nenniger and Chênevert had accepted that it would remain Arthur Surveyer & Co., knowing there would be an opportunity to revisit the issue in 10 years.

Notary Édouard Cholette assembled the men at his office for the signing. Arranged in a semicircle, each held a copy of the agreement and followed along as Cholette read out the text line by line.

A CHAMPION OF FREE-MARKET CAPITALISM

A PASSIONATE ADVOCATE OF FREE-MARKET CAPITALISM, ARTHUR SURVEYER WAS LEERY OF ANY GOVERNMENTAL INTERFERENCE IN THE PRIVATE SECTOR. IN 1934, HE WARNED THAT PRESIDENT ROOSEVELT'S NEW DEAL WAS LEADING TO A DEVALUATION OF THE U.S. DOLLAR, WHICH WOULD HARM INTERNATIONAL TRADE. IN A SPEECH TO THE CANADIAN INSTITUTE FOR INTERNATIONAL AFFAIRS, HE SAID, "ALL ECONOMISTS AGREE THAT THE MOST IMPORTANT FACTOR IN THE WORLD'S RECOVERY LIES IN THE REVIVAL OF INTERNATIONAL TRADE, AND HERE WE HAVE THE UNITED STATES PURSUING POLICIES WHICH TEND TO ENCOURAGE ECONOMIC NATIONALISM."

Surveyer was nearly 60 and starting to look like the elder statesman of engineering he had become. Such major decisions were never easy for him, but he was nonetheless confident it was the right one. He had quit smoking due to respiratory problems, and much of his time was spent managing International Bond and Share. He knew that if he expected Nenniger and Chênevert to hold the fort, he needed to give them a proper incentive.

At 36, except for his greying hair, Chênevert was identical to the young man who had shown up for an interview all those years ago. His hair was slicked up in a pompadour, and a stylish suit hung on his small, rigidly upright frame. He had been over every line of the agreement, but he was alert to anything he might have missed as he read along. This was one of the proudest moments of his life, but that was no excuse for an oversight.

Nenniger sat beside him, focusing hard on the text from behind his circular glasses. He, too, was 36. His hair had now receded away from his already high forehead, giving him a distinct air of wisdom. Leaving Switzerland for Canada had been a risk, but hard work, talent, and Surveyer's trust had allowed him to reach this point. He was grateful to the older man for giving a foreign, self-taught engineer such an opportunity.

The three partners of Arthur Surveyer & Co. in 1937: Arthur Surveyer, Georges Chênevert, and Emil Nenniger.

The partnership agreement was renewed in 1947 and again in 1957.

"The capital required to operate the said business will be ten thousand dollars ($10,000)," read Cholette, "subdivided as follows: four thousand dollars ($4,000) representing goodwill, three thousand dollars ($3,000) representing the furniture, office equipment and books furnished by the said partners and three thousand dollars ($3,000) representing the working capital."

It was agreed that the two junior partners would devote all their working time to the firm. Surveyer had taken on other commitments but would put in as much time as he felt was needed. He was comfortable now taking on a more supervisory role and leaving most of the day-to-day operations in the hands of these two very capable men.

When Cholette finished reading, the partners got up one at a time to sign copies of the document. They put pen to paper with one eye on the achievements of the past and the other firmly fixed on the opportunities of the future.

No.1367

18th February 1957.

PARTNERSHIP AGREEMENT

between

ARTHUR SURVEYER, JOSEPH GEORGES CHENEVERT and EMIL NENNIGER.

the undersigned Notary for the Province of Quebec practising at the City of Montreal,

A P P E A R E D :

ARTHUR SURVEYER of the City of Montreal, JOSEPH GEORGES CHENEVERT of the City of Outremont, and EMIL NENNIGER of the City of Montreal, all Professional Engineers, and all carrying on business in co-partnership under the name and style of "SURVEYER, NENNIGER & CHENEVERT", W H O DECLARED UNTO THE UNDERSIGNED NOTARY AS FOLLOWS:

That on the Eleventh day of March Nineteen hundred and thirty-seven by Deed executed before E. Cholette, Notary, they entered into a co-partnership agreement (hereinafter sometimes referred to as "Partnership I") for the purpose of carrying on together the business of Consulting Professional Engineers under the name and style above set out;

And after due reading hereof the Parties signed in the presence of the said Notary.

(Signed)   Arthur Surveyer
      "   J.G. Chenevert
      "   E. Nenniger

PART
2 | NEW
HORIZONS

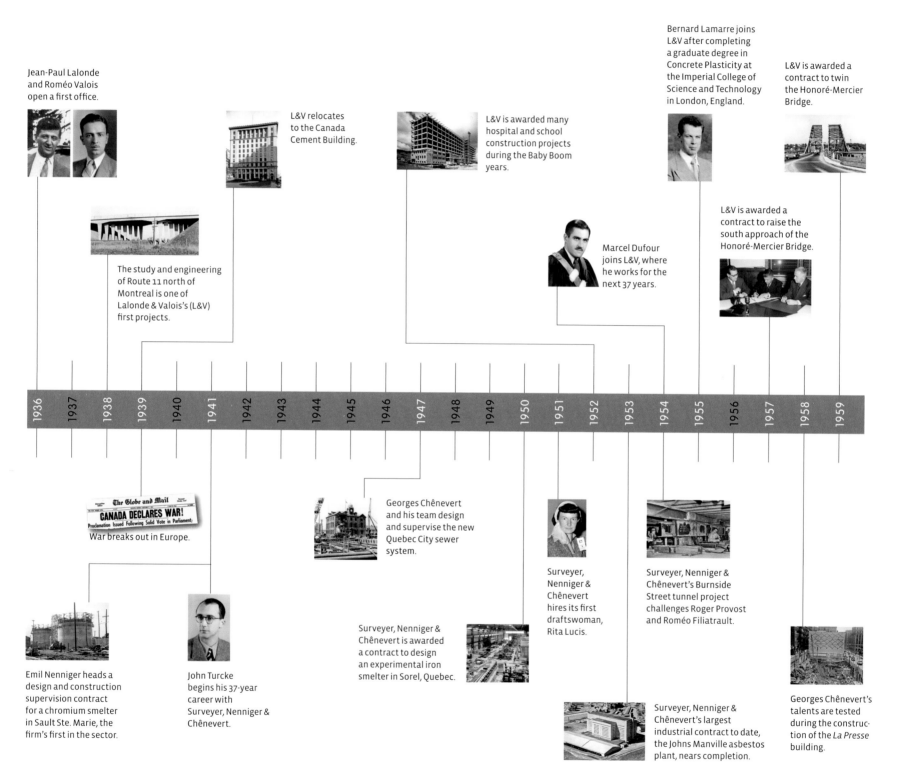

Jean-Paul Lalonde and Roméo Valois open a first office.

The study and engineering of Route 11 north of Montreal is one of Lalonde & Valois's (L&V) first projects.

L&V relocates to the Canada Cement Building.

L&V is awarded many hospital and school construction projects during the Baby Boom years.

Bernard Lamarre joins L&V after completing a graduate degree in Concrete Plasticity at the Imperial College of Science and Technology in London, England.

L&V is awarded a contract to twin the Honoré-Mercier Bridge.

L&V is awarded a contract to raise the south approach of the Honoré-Mercier Bridge.

Marcel Dufour joins L&V, where he works for the next 37 years.

1936 1937 1938 1939 1940 1941 1942 1943 1944 1945 1946 1947 1948 1949 1950 1951 1952 1953 1954 1955 1956 1957 1958 1959

The Globe and Mail
CANADA DECLARES WAR!
Proclamation Issued Following Solid Vote in Parliament.
War breaks out in Europe.

Georges Chênevert and his team design and supervise the new Quebec City sewer system.

Surveyer, Nenniger & Chênevert hires its first draftswoman, Rita Lucis.

Surveyer, Nenniger & Chênevert's Burnside Street tunnel project challenges Roger Provost and Roméo Filiatrault.

Emil Nenniger heads a design and construction supervision contract for a chromium smelter in Sault Ste. Marie, the firm's first in the sector.

John Turcke begins his 37-year career with Surveyer, Nenniger & Chênevert.

Surveyer, Nenniger & Chênevert is awarded a contract to design an experimental iron smelter in Sorel, Quebec.

Surveyer, Nenniger & Chênevert's largest industrial contract to date, the Johns Manville asbestos plant, nears completion.

Georges Chênevert's talents are tested during the construction of the *La Presse* building.

PREVIOUS PAGE
A drawing of the north approach of the Honoré-Mercier Bridge in Montreal, Quebec.

CHAPTER 4

ENTER LALONDE AND VALOIS

In 1936, a long-standing conservative government in Quebec is supplanted by the more liberal government of Maurice Duplessis. Where the previous government had been loath to put the province into debt, the new one has taken it upon itself to dramatically improve Quebec's infrastructure and expand its industries. Jean-Paul Lalonde and Roméo Valois seize this opportunity and open their first engineering consulting office in Montreal. Lalonde & Valois immediately wins a series of design and construction engineering mandates for Route 11 north of Montreal. Other contracts follow in these early years, including a number of assignments for overpasses and bridges.

The Sainte-Thérèse-de-Blainville overpass north of Montreal.

In the fall of 1936, a newly elected Quebec government launched a $50-million transportation infrastructure initiative. It was a declaration that the age of the automobile had arrived. It was also the signal Jean-Paul Lalonde and Roméo Valois were waiting for.

The two engineers had talked about starting their own business since their first meeting at an École Polytechnique Alumni Association dinner in 1933. It was remarkable how well they complemented each other. Lalonde was a stern master engineer who often felt more at ease with a slide rule than with people. He had long dreamed of starting his own engineering firm, but felt incapable of selling himself to prospective clients. Valois, on the other hand, had a good sense of humour and a love of conversation that made him a natural at client relations. He was also fascinated with the nuts and bolts of the engineering business, and had recently penned an article about the new field of "scientific management" in the École Polytechnique's *Revue Trimestrielle Canadienne*. Over dinner, they realized that they would make an unbeatable team.

There were certainly risks involved. Both men had attained enviable positions in the engineering world they would have to walk away from. Lalonde had joined the Montreal engineering firm Eugène Guay straight out of the École Polytechnique in 1926. Within 10 years, he was its Head Engineer and the city's leading expert in reinforced concrete. He had pushed back boundaries, pioneering ways to use the material in foundations, bridges, tunnels, and overpasses. For Lalonde, concrete was the ideal building material. It was as adaptable as sculptor's clay and as durable as mason's stone. Eugène Guay had trusted Lalonde's instincts and given him room to experiment. Lalonde was now 33, with a wife and four young children. It was not going to be easy to leave such a job, or such a mentor.

Scholarships had allowed Valois to earn a Civil Engineering degree at the École Polytechnique in 1930, followed by a master's degree in Engineering Business Administration at the Massachusetts Institute of Technology the next year. Upon his return to Montreal in 1932, he had taught a course in business administration at the École Polytechnique before joining the Montreal Catholic School Commission's (MCSC) Department of Public Works. Valois's blend of business and engineering know-how made him the ideal man for the difficult situation facing the MCSC. With a growing population and the Great Depression in full swing, the school board had to find ways to accommodate a rising number of students without building new facilities. When Valois became its Director in 1934, he oversaw a low-budget refurbishment program that did not compromise on safety or quality. It was quite an accomplishment, and quite a career to drop in mid-stride. Valois was now 30 and, like Lalonde, he too had a young family to support.

But now, the announcement by the Quebec Ministry of Transportation dispelled any doubts Lalonde and Valois might have had. By November 1936, they had saved enough money to rent a modest office in the Dominion Square Building on Sainte-Catherine Street in Montreal and purchase a few essential furnishings. Given how well they got along, and how closely they planned to collaborate, they opted to buy a single large work desk for the office. It was a desk they would share, through thick and thin, for the next 20 years.

Lalonde & Valois's first offices in the Dominion Square Building on Sainte-Catherine Street in Montreal.

Jean-Paul Lalonde

Roméo Valois

A RUNNING START

Now that the government had declared its intention of bringing the province's road network into the 20th century, it needed good engineering firms to carry out the work. Lalonde was fortunate to have already earned the esteem of the newly elected Minister of Transportation, François Leduc. As the former head of the Montreal Concrete Laboratory, he had been witness to Lalonde's innovative work on many of Montreal's tunnels, bridges, and schools.

In December of that year, Leduc asked Lalonde & Valois (L&V) to study and engineer a crucial 43-kilometre stretch of Route 11, at the time a mostly gravel road running north from Montreal through the Laurentians. Municipalities in the region had been petitioning the government to pave the route for close to a decade. Lalonde threw himself into the design of the road, co-ordinating with Alphonse Paradis, the Ministry's Head Engineer, while Valois dealt with Leduc and sought out other prospects.

A couple of months into the contract, L&V saw an opportunity to expand their mandate with the Ministry. They knew that the Quebec government had recently taken over responsibility for eliminating dangerous railway level crossings, and their stretch of Route 11 had three of them. The partners wrote a letter to Leduc asking if they should go ahead

and draw up plans for bridges, tunnels, or overpasses that would take care of the problem.

They soon received a reply from the Minister. "The Route 11 improvement project […] which you have been awarded includes the elimination of three level crossings, including an overpass and a tunnel between Sainte-Rose and Sainte-Thérèse, and an overpass near Saint-Jérôme," wrote Leduc. "You are hereby authorized to prepare these level crossing elimination projects."

Lalonde, a specialist in concrete structures of all kinds, was in his element. He took on the additional work with the help of a geotechnical company L&V had just founded called National Boring and Sounding.

The design of the first portion of Route 11 was finished in May 1937. Having received only positive reviews of L&V's work from Paradis, Leduc now awarded the partners three other sections of the road. By the following year, Lalonde and Valois found themselves working as far north as Mont-Laurier, more than 270 kilometres from Montreal, and responsible for close to 145 kilometres of highway. The new geography presented fresh challenges. As the road moved further north, uneven and rocky terrain sometimes made choosing a route a tricky proposition. National Boring and Sounding proved essential once again by helping to find the best locations for some of the more northern stretches.

Construction of the Sainte-Thérèse-de-Blainville overpass in 1937, and surveying for the Saint-Jérôme overpass in 1938 (right), both north of Montreal.

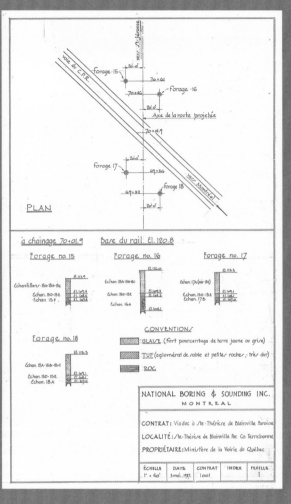

PLAN

à chainage 70+01.9   Base du rail. El. 120.8

| Forage no. 15 | Forage no. 16 | Forage no. 17 |

NATIONAL BORING & SOUNDING INC.
MONTREAL

CONTRAT: Viaduc à Ste-Thérèse de Blainville Paroisse
LOCALITÉ: Ste-Thérèse de Blainville Par. Co. Terrebonne
PROPRIÉTAIRE: Ministère de la Voirie du Québec

ÉCHELLE	DATE	CONTRAT	INDEX	FEUILLE
1" = 40'	3 mai 1937	1001	1

A FIRST SUBSIDIARY

WITH NATIONAL BORING AND SOUNDING, LALONDE WOULD NO LONGER HAVE TO RELY ON THE "SPECIAL" FOUNDATION COMPANIES THAT SOLD SUPPORT PILES AT INFLATED PRICES. MORE IMPORTANTLY, NATIONAL BORING AND SOUNDING GAVE HIM CONTROL OVER THE DESIGN AND THE COST OF HIS FOUNDATIONS. IF THERE WAS ONE THING LALONDE DISLIKED, IT WAS NEEDLESSLY EXPENSIVE FOUNDATIONS.

LALONDE IMMEDIATELY PUT THE SUBSIDIARY TO WORK ON EVALUATING SOIL CONDITIONS WHERE THE SAINTE-THÉRÈSE-DE-BLAINVILLE OVERPASS WOULD BE ERECTED. HE WAS HAPPY TO LEARN THAT BEDROCK LAY RELATIVELY CLOSE TO THE SURFACE, WHICH MEANT SOLID FOUNDATIONS COULD BE BUILT AT AN AFFORDABLE COST.

National Boring and Sounding's first project was a borehole analysis of the soil conditions for the Sainte-Thérèse-de-Blainville overpass.

MEETING MR. DUPLESSIS

L&V completed all work on Route 11 by the end of 1938. In time, it would be known as one of Quebec's most durable and well-designed provincial roads, but, for the moment, Lalonde and Valois were concerned about being paid. Leduc had recently been replaced as the transportation minister following a disagreement with the province's Premier, Maurice Duplessis. The new minister in charge of Transportation was not yet up to speed on the Route 11 file, and the Quebec government was not in a hurry to settle the $100,000 bill.

By now, L&V had several dozen employees and considerable internal expenses. Valois tried numerous avenues to speed up payment, including letters and phone calls. Finally, he decided on a more proactive approach. He knew the Premier took the train from Quebec City to Trois-Rivières every Friday. If he could just arrange to be on the train at the same time, he might be able to get a seat next to him and strike up a conversation. He would then be able to plead his case.

For several weeks in a row, Valois boarded the Friday evening train to Trois-Rivières, and with each trip managed to make his way closer to Duplessis. Finally, with the help of an obliging train conductor, he got a seat right beside the Premier. Duplessis seemed to enjoy talking to Valois, who had a disarming frankness and was always quick with a joke. When the moment was right, Valois detailed the work L&V had done for Route 11. He told the Premier it had been a privilege for their young practice to work on such an important project, but they needed to receive payment soon so as not to fall into debt. By the end of the train ride, Valois had Duplessis's assurance that the matter would be taken care of.

With the Route 11 account settled, the partners could look back with satisfaction at how much they had accomplished in two short years. They had helped build a major provincial road and had eliminated dangerous level crossings by building bridges, overpasses, and tunnels. They had designed several schools and churches, and had founded their first subsidiary.

From where Lalonde and Valois stood, the future looked equally bright. There was no way they could have known that far leaner years were just around the corner.

A SETBACK AND A LEAP FORWARD

Canada's entry into World War II in September of 1939 had a dramatic effect on its economy. The Canadian government passed the National Resources Mobilization Act the following year, placing all human and material resources at the service of the war effort. Canada's war industry consumed nearly all of its steel production. Soon, the metal was available only for domestic purposes by permit.

The scarcity of such a key building material hit the civil engineering sector hard. This was especially true in the case of L&V, which specialized in the design of concrete structures reinforced with steel. Without ready access to the metal, these could not be built.

L&V had by then relocated to a larger office in Montreal's Canada Cement Building to accommodate its more than 90 employees. Now, it became increasingly difficult to hold on to them; many left to find jobs in the war industry, while a number of others enlisted. It was a major setback. The two

men had risked much in deciding to start their own business, only to see their successful run come to a grinding halt a few years after it began. Still, there were glimmers of hope every now and again that helped sustain them. It was during this period that L&V won its first contract for a project outside of Quebec. In 1940, the partners were awarded the design of a military dock in Halifax, Nova Scotia.

By the end of 1942, L&V had been whittled down to only a few employees. Now, more often than not, only Lalonde and a draftsman or two were to be found at the office. Valois's role as a business development specialist was of less use at a time when the practical reality of war made marketing efforts all but futile. Like so many of his former employees, he took a job at a military supply company.

Relief came the following year just as things were looking more desperate than ever. It turned out that all the work Lalonde and Valois had done to eliminate level crossings belonging to Canadian National Railway (CNR) had impressed its Head Engineer, H.A. Dixon. In December 1943, Dixon asked the partners to design all 15 bridges for a new rail line CNR wanted to run through Montreal between its eastern junction and the start of the Bout-de-l'Île line, a distance of 24 kilometres.

Dixon mentioned that the project had a "troubled past," having been deferred for some time due to wartime restrictions, and that CNR was now anxious to get it going. In short, it was a "rush job." Lalonde, who had become an expert in railway grade separations, assured him that L&V would be able to complete the work on time.

The contract breathed new life into L&V. Valois was glad to be able to resign his position as manager at the parachute manufacturing company and return full time to his L&V responsibilities. Now that it looked like the Second World War might end at any time, Valois wanted to re-establish contact with clients before the windfall of deferred contracts arrived. It was not long before it did.

Lalonde & Valois relocated to larger offices in the Canada Cement Building in the late 1930s.

THE TROIKA

Arthur Surveyer & Co. picks up its first contract in the mining and metallurgy sector in 1941 when the firm is asked to design a chromium smelter in Sault Ste. Marie, Ontario. It is also awarded a major sewer system design contract for Quebec City. War breaks out in Europe, sending hundreds of thousands of refugees to Canada's shores. The firm, always on the lookout for talent, regardless of the language or ethnicity of the engineer, profits by hiring many of them. These engineers will form the basis on which the company will later launch its international expansion.

Construction of the Quebec City pumping station in 1946.

The Depression lingered on through the end of 1937, and the market for engineering in Canada continued to limp along with it. Arthur Surveyer & Co. earned $17,218.04 for the entire year. Once rent, office expenses, and salaries had been deducted, a meager profit of $458.02 was left for the partners to share.

Still, a profit was a profit. With things as tough as they were, the employees of Arthur Surveyer & Co. counted themselves lucky to be in the black at all. Nenniger and Chênevert certainly had no complaints. They were visibly energized by their new stake in the firm. Surveyer had given them his full confidence, and they worked harder than ever to reward that trust.

The two junior partners now divided most of the work between themselves. There was some crossover, but it was generally understood that Nenniger headed up industrial projects, while Chênevert oversaw everything that fell within the realm of municipal engineering and hydraulics. Bridges, technically under Chênevert's responsibility, but which Nenniger was a whiz at designing thanks to his mastery of the fixed point method, were still up for grabs.

The division of labour not only reflected their respective interests and abilities, it also helped keep the peace. The men respected each other, but they sometimes had conflicting opinions about how a project should be carried out. Even the hours they kept reflected fundamentally different approaches to working life. Nenniger, in true Swiss style, would arrive at 7:30 a.m. and leave at 4:30 p.m. with clockwork precision. Chênevert kept later hours, showing up sometime after 9:00 a.m., but often staying into the evening. Their schedules aligned in one way, however; both men thought nothing of putting in extra time on weekends.

Surveyer was now less present at the office, although he remained available at all times to his two lieutenants. With considerable prestige connected to his name, he knew he could do more for the partnership through his association with influential commissions and companies. He still devoted time to International Bond and Share, and had also now been named Commissioner-Censor of the Crédit Foncier Franco-Canadien, a pioneering Quebec mortgage and loan company. It was a list of commitments that would only grow over the next decade. Although it seemed his external responsibilities left him with time for little else, all his effort was about to pay off.

THE QUEBEC CITY SEWER SYSTEM

Near the end of 1937, Surveyer was asked to sit on another important commission. This one had been created by Public Works Canada to study a major sanitation problem facing the city of Quebec. The Saint-Charles River, into which it had long pumped its sewage, was becoming a breeding ground for waterborne disease.

The Saint-Charles cut conveniently through the city on its way to the St. Lawrence River, but its level sometimes dropped dramatically in dry season, causing it to stagnate or even reverse. This resulted in the "backing up of sewage all along the banks and the accumulation of solid matter." It was more than just an unpleasant situation; it was quickly becoming a dangerous one.

The commission studied several options, but was ultimately faced with the fact that the system, as designed, was now a hazard. With the health and welfare of the citizens in their hands, its members saw no alternative but to completely overhaul the network. Arthur Surveyer & Co. was given the task of designing and supervising the construction of a modern sewer system.

The new network would have to bypass the convenient but unpredictable Saint-Charles and empty directly into the St. Lawrence. That sounded simple enough, but Quebec's wildly uneven topography made moving large quantities of sewer water across the city problematic. The higher areas near the St. Lawrence could use gravity drainage, but a sophisticated array of pumps and regulators was needed to get water to the river from lower-lying regions to the north.

Arthur Surveyer

In 1937, Arthur Surveyer sat on a Public Works Canada commission to study the sanitation problem in Quebec City.

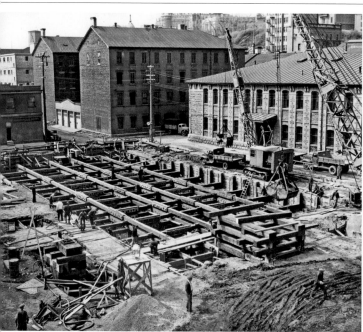

Georges Chênevert's designs for the Quebec City sewer system called for a sophisticated array of pumps and regulators to overcome the city's uneven topography.

Chênevert, too, felt challenged. He finally had a contract whose complexity and scope would test his abilities to the fullest. He knew the devil was in the details, and he was going to make sure none escaped his attention.

CHROME-X

Just as Chênevert was getting started on the Quebec City sewer project, Surveyer was offered an opportunity he had long been waiting for. In 1934, Noah Timmins had created another Hollinger Gold Subsidiary called the Chromium Mining and Smelting Corporation. Timmins passed away two years later, but in early 1938 his son Leo asked Surveyer to help the company decide how best to expand its operations. The plan was sure to involve the construction of a new smelter, and it was understood that Arthur Surveyer & Co. would be asked to handle the design and supervise its construction. It would be the breakthrough into the mining and metallurgy sector Surveyer had long dreamed of.

Leo Timmins believed he had an ace up his sleeve that would help him corner a portion of the chromium market. Martin Udy, the company's Chief Metallurgist, had invented a process that turned lower grade chromite into what he called "Chrome-X." Simply put, Chrome-X could be heated with steel to produce high quality alloys at a lower cost. Timmins just needed to acquire some additional deposits and expand his smelting capacities.

Surveyer was first asked to look into the construction of a new ferrochrome smelter in Quebec. The plant needed to have ready access to a rail network and clean water for cooling the various transformers and furnaces. Other than that, Timmins left it up to Surveyer to determine what would constitute an advantageous location.

Surveyer counted on Nenniger's support and subscribed to all the relevant technical journals in his name. He hit the books as well. At 60, the senior partner was still willing to put in the work needed to acquire expertise in an unfamiliar area; in fact, he took great pleasure in it.

It would be a major challenge, but Surveyer had no qualms about putting Chênevert in charge. At 40, he still had the focus needed to work long hours on a major project and not miss a single detail. All he needed now was to assemble a project team that was able to keep up with him.

Chênevert began by hiring a young engineer by the name of Hector Asselin, an École Polytechnique graduate with a keen eye for detail. He appreciated Asselin's natural caution. Like his boss, Asselin preferred to study all angles of a problem before proceeding. Before long, Chênevert was leaving him in charge when he travelled to Quebec City for client meetings.

Other recruits who were not so exacting would sometimes find working under Chênevert intimidating. He had an uncanny ability to spot even the slightest error in an engineering plan. "What's this?" Chênevert would say pointing to a slope for a drainage or intake pipe that was off by the slightest fraction. "Didn't you verify your calculations?" The Quebec City sewer project team quickly learned to double- and triple-check their figures before presenting them to the boss for approval. But, while working under Chênevert could be nerve-racking, they knew it made them better engineers.

The fieldwork came next. During the winter of 1938, Surveyer and Nenniger made numerous trips to potential locations. They spoke to any relevant official they could find, and noted the pros and cons of each site in exacting detail. By May, they were able to report that the company's requirements were met at locations in Trois-Rivières, Beauharnois, and Arvida. It turned out that Timmins was not quite ready to commit, however.

Two years later, Timmins decided that expanding the company's existing smelter in Sault Ste. Marie, Ontario, where it had developed Chrome-X, would present less of a risk. He proposed to increase its overall furnace output from 8,200 kilovolt-amps to 23,000, effectively tripling its capacity. After studying the numbers, Surveyer concluded the expenditure was "well justified." Timmins was ready to act this time, and, by the spring of 1941, Arthur Surveyer & Co. had its first design and construction supervision contract for a smelter.

Nenniger, who had worked so hard to build up a client base in the industrial sector, took the lead. He had recently hired several engineers, and the Sault Ste. Marie contract now allowed him to continue to build up the firm's fledgling Industrial Division. The first person he called was a young man named John Turcke. He was Swiss, like himself, and held a diploma from the renowned Swiss Federal Institute of Technology in Zurich. Turcke had come by the office a few years earlier in search of a job, but Nenniger had been forced to turn him away.

"I've been studying for eighteen years," the athletic looking Turcke had said. "Now I'd like to know if I can make some money with what I've learned. But for the time being," he had hastened to add, "I'm willing to work without pay."

"Don't worry," Nenniger had answered, impressed by his modest proposal, "you'll be paid here, but do you have any experience with storm sewer systems?" At the time, the only project that needed engineers was the Quebec City job Chênevert was starting up.

The Chromium Mining and Smelting Corporation plant expansion in Sault Ste. Marie, Ontario, during the early 1940s.

John Turcke

The firm's excellent relationship with Alcan helped sustain it during the war years. A red mud treatment plant in Arvida, Quebec, circa 1943, and inside the castings quality control room at Etobicoke Works, Ontario, circa 1944.

"Unfortunately, no."

"Too bad. I really have nothing else to offer you right now, but that could change at any moment." Nenniger had suggested he try to find work at Eugène Guay, another engineering firm, but promised to call him back when he had an opening in his Industrial Division. That time had now come.

Turcke and the other new recruits soon realized Nenniger was an interactive boss. They got used to seeing him strolling stiffly among the drafting tables, a White Owl cigar clenched between his teeth and a slide rule protruding out of his back pocket. This allowed him to lend a hand when one was needed. It also let him see who was doing quality work and who was bringing up the rear. If he saw that a new recruit was making a great effort, he could be forgiving, but a pink slip awaited anyone who repeatedly failed to pull his weight.

THE WAR YEARS

In early 1939, Surveyer took a trip to Europe to explore investment opportunities for International Bond and Share. The conversations he had with business leaders, politicians, and journalists left him with little doubt that another major armed conflict lay on the horizon. By September, World War II had begun.

The British government quickly became one of the biggest clients of Canada's industrial manufacturers. Alcan (formerly ACOC) was among the companies that benefited most. Between 1939 and 1944, its production of primary aluminum expanded from a respectable 75,000 tonnes per year to a colossal 418,000 tonnes, mainly to meet military demand from England.

This was good news for Arthur Surveyer & Co., which had established an excellent relationship with the company since its first contract in 1927. Between 1940 and 1942 alone, it was awarded contracts for an Alcan brucite plant in Wakefield, Quebec, an aluminum sand foundry in Toronto, Ontario, and a red mud treatment facility at its aluminum plant in Arvida, Quebec.

But while Arthur Surveyer & Co. may have benefited from the war industry, the tragedy of the conflict had a profound effect on many of its employees. The widespread destruction and loss of life only reaffirmed Surveyer's deep conviction that it was important to accommodate differences in others.

This belief, also shared by his two partners, helped make Arthur Surveyer & Co. something of a bastion for European engineers during the hostilities. Nenniger would even walk down to Montreal Harbour and hire the shell-shocked engineers as they disembarked. Others, on a tip that Arthur Surveyer & Co. was hiring employees based only on ability, found their way to the office on their own steam. All were welcome, provided they had the necessary skills.

These refugees, many from Germany, Poland, and Hungary, were among the best-trained in their home countries. They also allowed the partnership to operate in languages other than French and English. Arthur Surveyer & Co. was laying the foundation on which it would launch its expansion into foreign markets.

CHAPTER 6

L&V AND THE
ST. LAWRENCE SEAWAY

Lalonde & Valois has more work than it can handle by the early 1950s. The Baby Boom brings with it many new contracts for schools and hospitals, and its engineers work weekends just to keep up. New recruits arrive, including Bernard Lamarre, Marcel Dufour, Jean-Paul Dionne, and André Denis. They join the firm just in time to help it carry out a contract to raise the Honoré-Mercier Bridge, and then another to twin the structure. These jobs establish Lalonde & Valois as a leading bridge design firm in the province, and lay the groundwork for the large infrastructure jobs it will win in the 1960s.

The twinning of the Honoré-Mercier Bridge in Montreal.

Jean-Paul Lalonde

Roméo Valois

Marcel Dufour

By the mid 1950s, L&V was well on its way to becoming one of the most successful engineering consulting firms in Quebec. Its office in the Canada Cement Building had been running at full capacity since the end of the war. There was so much work that all employees were asked to put in six hours of overtime each week, including a few hours on Saturday morning.

The Baby Boom was the main cause of the pace of activity at L&V. The number of children in Quebec had shot up dramatically in the past decade. The increase, when paired with the new requirement that children attend school until age 14, forced the government to build additional schools. Since the end of the war, L&V had participated in well over 125 school construction or renovation projects. The Baby Boom also stepped up the rate of hospital construction in Quebec, and L&V won contracts to build many of the facilities.

Even with so much going on, Jean-Paul Lalonde still found time to closely oversee all of L&V's engineering activities. He was a man who liked to leave nothing to chance. He took notes constantly so as not to forget a single detail. His need to stay on top of things extended to his employees' work, as well. After they had left for the day he would sometimes peek at their designs to see what progress they had made. But while Lalonde was demanding, he was also fair. When an employee worked hard, he was sure to be rewarded.

If Lalonde provided the discipline, Roméo Valois enjoyed supplying a bit of levity. When he arrived at the office, he would often stop by the crowded central drafting room to talk and joke with employees. It was his way of taking the edge off the pressure everyone was under—himself included.

Valois was working harder than ever to stay in touch with a growing list of clients. He seemed to always be en route to some meeting or other. On weekends he might be found playing a round of golf with a government minister or discussing business over dinner with a potential client. At L&V, it was said that Valois knew everyone in Quebec who was capable of awarding an engineering contract. In fact, he knew most of the people they knew as well.

ENGINEERS WANTED

The dream of sailing from the Atlantic Ocean into the heart of North America dates back to the arrival of Jacques Cartier in 1534. The great explorer hoped that what is today called the St. Lawrence River would turn out to be the Northwest Passage. He was sure he had found the fabled route, until he caught site of the violent rapids that began just west of Montreal.

Nearly 400 years would pass before the Canadian and U.S. governments would talk seriously about creating a major North American shipping canal. World War II had underlined the need to allow medium- and large-tonnage vessels to reach the heartland. There were also business interests to consider: larger vessels would be able to transport more goods at a lower cost. In 1954, the two countries finally reached an agreement on a joint project.

The key component was the canal that had to be trenched along the St. Lawrence River all the way to Lake Ontario. As one of Quebec's leading transportation infrastructure specialists, L&V hoped it would pick up some of the associated work. The problem was that the firm was already stretched to capacity with its many school and hospital contracts. L&V engineers were crisscrossing Quebec, overseeing construction work on buildings from Hull, near the Ontario border, to Val d'Or, in the north of the province. The partners felt they could not in fairness ask any more of them. They would just have to find room for new engineers.

In 1954, Lalonde hired a pair of École Polytechnique de Montréal graduates. The first was André Denis, who already had six years of work experience as a structural engineer with B. & H. Metal Industries. The other was a young man named

Marcel Dufour. He held a degree in Civil Engineering, but looked more like a football linebacker than an engineer. When Lalonde noticed that Dufour had a knack for coming up with clever solutions to foundation problems, he sent him to Harvard for graduate studies in soil mechanics.

The next year Lalonde recruited his son-in-law, Bernard Lamarre, into the firm. He had met Lalonde's daughter, Louise, while on a cruise to Europe. From their first meeting, Lamarre had impressed the older man as unusually bright and ambitious. Lalonde had initially approached him about joining L&V in 1954, while he was completing a graduate degree in Concrete Plasticity at the Imperial College of Science and Technology in London, England. It might have been an easy decision had Lamarre's father, Émile, not also wanted his son to work for him. Émile Lamarre owned a construction company in Jonquière, Quebec, and Bernard's expertise in concrete structures would have been valuable to him as well. There were also his father's feelings to consider. He had been his first mentor, and Bernard hated the idea of disappointing him.

In the end, it came down to where the young couple most wanted to settle. After spending two years in London, the slower pace of life in Jonquière was less appealing. L&V, on the other hand, was located in downtown Montreal, a vibrant city in its own right. In the end the newlyweds opted for life in the city.

HONORÉ-MERCIER BRIDGE, TAKE 1

With additional engineers on board, L&V now had the breathing room needed to take on any contracts it was awarded for the Seaway. Of particular interest to Lalonde and Valois were the bridge projects. All four bridges that crossed the St. Lawrence in the Montreal area had to be raised to provide the 36-metre clearance required for large ocean-going vessels.

In January 1957, the St. Lawrence Seaway Authority awarded L&V the design and construction supervision contract to raise the south approach of the Honoré-Mercier Bridge. With the future construction of the St. Lawrence Seaway in mind, it had been designed to allow for the passage of large ships. Unfortunately, at the time, the Seaway had been planned to run along the north shore of the River; it would now flank the south side.

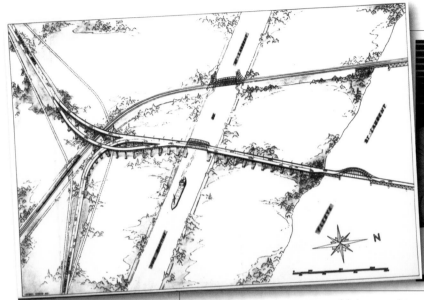

Map of the St. Lawrence Seaway around Montreal.

Jean-Paul Lalonde (centre) signing the contract for the raising of the Honoré-Mercier Bridge at the St. Lawrence Seaway Commission office.

Jean-Paul Dionne

L&V's engineers would be working upstream from Surveyer, Nenniger & Chênevert, which had been awarded a very similar contract for the Jacques-Cartier Bridge. It would be a chance for L&V to demonstrate that it could keep pace with one of Montreal's most prominent engineering firms.

It would not be easy, however. The delicate operation of demolishing and raising the Mercier Bridge's south approach had to be co-ordinated with clockwork precision. L&V would be overseeing the work of several contractors, and each had to finish his job before the next could begin. Time was of the essence. The opening of the canal was set for early 1959, and the St. Lawrence Seaway Authority was adamant about meeting the schedule.

Lalonde made new employee Jean-Paul Dionne the Resident Engineer for the project. He was young, but he already had quite a bit of work experience. More importantly, he seemed to have a natural air of authority that would serve him well in the supervision of such a job. Dionne's first task was to oversee the construction of a temporary approach, since there was no question of shutting down one of Montreal's busiest bridges. A massive rock embankment, including a sidewalk, railings, and electric lighting, was built and opened to traffic on April 11, 1957.

This cleared the way for the demolition of the existing access. But just as one contractor was preparing to dynamite the concrete piers under the south approach, another alerted Dionne to unstable soil conditions at the site. Marcel Dufour, who had been in charge of National Boring and Sounding since his return from Harvard, ordered other boreholes to be drilled. When quicksand was found, L&V had no choice but to redesign nearly half the piers to include deep concrete pilings.

With the Seaway Authority refusing to delay the opening of the canal, the project team began looking for ways to make up the lost time. It did not take them long to find one. The technique they used was known as "sliding forms," an invention whose genius was in its simplicity. The concrete for the piers would be poured into a metal mould that slid up automatically, nearly halving the time it took to erect a pier. The project was soon back on schedule.

SOME SAD NEWS

Just as the project was moving towards a successful conclusion in the summer of 1958, the employees at L&V received some sad news. Jean-Paul Lalonde had suffered a heart attack at home. He was only 55, but the years of relentless work had finally caught up with him. Never one to complain, he faced his health crisis with the same stoicism and determination that had served him so well throughout his engineering career.

Lalonde's doctor told him in no uncertain terms that he had to take several months off to recover. With Valois now also requiring time off for health reasons, the partners needed to appoint someone to take over their duties on a temporary basis. There were a couple of candidates, but only one had the required combination of engineering know-how and salesmanship. In the short span of three years, Bernard Lamarre had risen to become the Chief Engineer of the Structures Department, and had proven himself to be an enthusiastic salesman.

He was only 27, but they were sure he was ready. For the past several years, Lalonde had shared everything he knew about running an engineering business with him. Most importantly, he would have an excellent and seasoned team of engineers behind him.

HONORÉ-MERCIER BRIDGE, TAKE 2

Even before the St. Lawrence Seaway was inaugurated, the Quebec Ministry of Public Works had decided that the Mercier Bridge would have to be enlarged. A twin of the bridge would be built to accommodate Montreal's rapidly rising number of commuters.

L&V's work on the south approach for the St. Lawrence Seaway Authority left Charles Laberge, the Deputy Minister of Public Works, with no doubt that the firm could handle the contract. He contacted Lamarre on December 10, 1959, to tell him that L&V had been selected to design and oversee construction for the southern portion and main span of the twin bridge. No engineering firm had yet been assigned the contract for the north approach in the densely populated

Photos showing the progress of the twinning of the Honoré-Mercier Bridge, between August 1961 and September 1962.

Inside the work chamber at pillar number 3A on May 5, 1961.

municipality of LaSalle. That section fell under the jurisdiction of the Ministry of Transportation.

Bernard Lamarre and the Mercier Bridge team were ecstatic, but felt it would be extremely disappointing if they were not awarded the contract for the northern section as well. Successfully designing an approach through dense residential and industrial zones would provide L&V with the ultimate calling card for future transportation projects.

Lamarre wasted no time in drafting a letter to Antonio Talbot, the Minister of Transportation. "Since the study for the new bridge project must be carried out concurrently with that of the approach on the north side in LaSalle, and as the construction of these approaches is under your responsibility, it

is our honour to offer you our firm's professional services." Not knowing how well Talbot knew L&V, Lamarre added that it had highly competent personnel who were ready to proceed immediately. As it turned out, Talbot had already been considering L&V for the contract. By May 1960, the firm had a lock on the entire job.

By then, National Boring and Sounding had finished studying the riverbed. Its geologists reported that conditions would make it necessary to separate the two new lanes from the existing ones over the St. Lawrence. They would split into a V shape and be close to 50 metres apart when they touched down in LaSalle at the north end. It would be an unusual design, but L&V assured the government that it would be elegant nonetheless.

With the geotechnical issues resolved, André Denis, the Chief Engineer of L&V's Metallic Structures Department, began designing the twin bridge itself. He knew there was little room to manoeuvre when it came to the overall look (it was a twin, after all), but why not improve on some of the individual components?

Denis suggested that the deck of the twin bridge be made of prestressed concrete, for example. Invented some years earlier, the technique involved using concrete deck slabs fastened together internally by steel cables. It had many advantages over the traditional method of placing a steel joint between slabs. Drivers would experience a smoother ride, and the deck would adjust more easily to temperature changes, limiting cracks and saving on repairs.

The construction of the south approach and main bridge went seamlessly. As expected, however, the north approach required special care. It was important to preserve the residential character of LaSalle, so L&V planned to use sunken highways wherever possible. While this solved the aesthetic problem, the engineering involved was not quite as cut-and-dried. Certain parts of the road would have to be squeezed between existing buildings.

In September of 1962, Bernard Lamarre received a call from the Chief Engineer at the Ministry of Transportation, Arthur Branchaud. He said that the Seagram distillery company was worried that the construction of a sunken road would cause damage to its warehouse. The building was only 4.5 metres from the path of the road and contained an estimated $40 million worth of whisky. Branchaud said that Seagram was threatening to litigate if its wall collapsed.

Lamarre immediately called Dufour, whose geologists at National Boring and Sounding had determined there would be no damage to Seagram's warehouse during construction. He trusted his friend's judgment, but the repercussions of even a slight error could be enormous. He wanted Dufour's assurance that the warehouse would not collapse.

"Our calculations are good," said Dufour. "We have nothing to worry about."

Dufour nevertheless decided to err on the side of caution and install sensors at several locations in the soil to monitor water levels. He also had the contractor erect a retaining wall, just in case. In the end, the construction of the road went off without incident. While he had been confident, Dufour could not help but feel relieved.

The new and expanded Mercier Bridge was opened to traffic in the fall of 1964. It was a great accomplishment, but by then L&V had already set its sights on other, even larger contracts. The "Quiet Revolution" had begun in Quebec, and with it would come the province's first megaprojects.

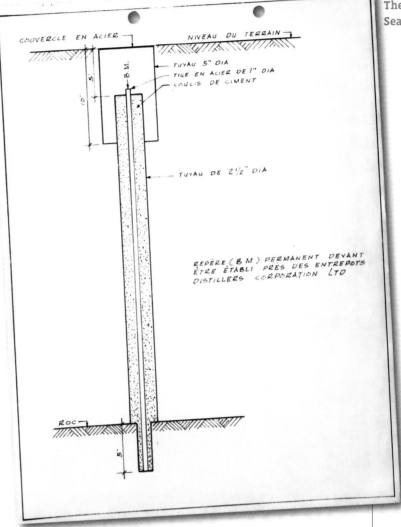

The retaining wall built for Seagram's warehouse.

CHAPTER 7

SURVEYER, NENNIGER & CHÊNEVERT

Discussing plans for the Quebec Iron and Titanium plant in Sorel, Quebec: Jack Hahn (far left), Emil Nenniger (third from left), and Georges Chênevert (second from right).

In 1947, a second partnership agreement is signed. Arthur Surveyer has now agreed to change the name of the firm to reflect those of all three of its partners. Surveyer, Nenniger & Chênevert, as it is now known, proceeds to carry out several major projects in the 1950s, including a smelter for Quebec Iron and Titanium in Sorel, and an asbestos mill in Asbestos. These years also see the firm win two jobs that will become legendary in the annals of Montreal building projects: the *La Presse* newspaper building expansion and a tunnel extension through the Drummond Court Apartments.

By the spring of 1946, the partners had begun discussing the terms of a new 10-year agreement. It was clearer than ever to Arthur Surveyer that he had made the right decision. Nenniger and Chênevert had proven themselves capable managers, taking up the slack and carrying the partnership forward into new sectors. He could not deny that Arthur Surveyer & Co. was now as much their firm as it was his. He was ready to make concessions.

After considerable discussion, Surveyer agreed to relinquish some of his share of the profits. His portion would fall from 60 to 40 percent, with the 20 percent difference split between Georges Chênevert and Emil Nenniger. Surveyer also agreed to make the partnership's name more inclusive. All three partners would now be represented.

The question of whose name would come second proved to be a more difficult decision for Surveyer, however. The issue dragged on for months. Both Nenniger and Chênevert felt their name should follow Surveyer's. He had still not come to a decision about the firm's name when the partners gathered in the office of notary Édouard Cholette on November 28 to finalize the agreement. It was just the sort of decision that he found so hard to make, but now he could no longer avoid it.

After a brief discussion, Surveyer decided that Nenniger's name would be second. Why he chose as he did was never made clear, but on December 31, 1946, the firm officially became known as Surveyer, Nenniger & Chênevert.

In the late 1940s, Surveyer, Nenniger & Chênevert designed and supervised the construction of the first aluminum highway bridge ever built.

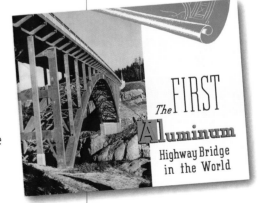

The FIRST Aluminum Highway Bridge in the World

THE TWO TEAMS

The wartime industrial boom transformed Nenniger's team. Several months before the partnership agreement was finalized, he had taken his expanded Industrial Division and relocated to the prestigious Sun Life Building on Metcalfe Street. They moved right into Alcan's offices on the sixth floor.

The move seemed like a logical one. The offices at the Dominion Square Building had become too small for all the partnership's activities, and Alcan was by far Nenniger's most important client. The firm was currently working with them on a first-of-its-kind aluminum arched bridge in Arvida, Quebec. It was a special job for Nenniger, who took pleasure in designing challenging structures. Alcan hoped the bridge would demonstrate the versatility of aluminum as a structural material.

The physical separation of the two teams was short-lived, however. In 1948, Surveyer rented the spacious 10th floor of the Keefer Building on Sainte-Catherine Street to reunite his 100-odd employees. He had never been fully comfortable with having the two teams in different locations, and hoped that reassembling the divisions would further strengthen the synergies between them.

This pencil sketch of the Quebec Iron and Titanium smelter in Sorel, Quebec, by Lili Rheti, showcases the artist's talent for capturing the spirit of large construction projects.

A view inside the smelter.

At Keefer, each partner had a private office, and their teams were split into two large drafting rooms linked by a corridor. Team Chênevert, composed mainly of French Canadians, occupied the east side, while Team Nenniger, sometimes referred to as the United Nations for all the different nationalities of Europeans who worked there, was on the west.

The friendly rivalry between the two division heads inevitably trickled down to their employees, but there was more than enough goodwill to keep things civil. If anything, the rivalry inspired each team to excel and work harder to win and successfully execute contracts. When one team was doing well, the other could not help but feel a bit of pressure to perform. This surely must have been the case for Chênevert's team in the early 1950s, when it sometimes seemed as though Nenniger was announcing a major new contract every month.

INDUSTRIAL PURSUITS

Nenniger's string of important contracts began in 1950, when his division was awarded the design of an experimental iron smelter in Saint-Joseph-de-Sorel, Quebec. The client was Quebec Iron and Titanium Corporation, or QIT for short. The company had been formed a couple of years earlier by New Jersey Zinc and Kennecott Copper with a very specific goal: develop a process to extract iron and titanium dioxide from solid ilminite ore mined in the north shore region of Quebec. It had never been done before, and certainly not with the electric furnace process that QIT was trying to perfect.

By now, Nenniger had built up a crack team of industrial engineers that included the many European refugees he had hired during the war. One of them, an employee by the name of Jack Hahn, was asked to handle the electrical engineering for the furnaces.

Hahn was a small and energetic German refugee who had only narrowly escaped Nazi persecution. Upon arriving in Canada in 1939, he had managed to scrounge a living doing odd jobs. There had been numerous obstacles to overcome, but he had been resolute in his determination to become an engineer. Nenniger had hired him in 1945 while he was still a student at McGill University in Montreal.

Hahn designed QIT's enormous electric furnaces, brick by brick. Heat control was a particular concern. He spent months just fine-tuning the movement of the carbon electrodes in the furnaces. The slightest miscalculation could result in disaster. If a furnace was not precisely regulated, the product might become inconsistent. Explosions of superheated slag were another concern, but Hahn could always count on Nenniger's support. The boss still prowled among the rows of drafting tables offering help to whomever needed it. Hahn appreciated Nenniger's input, although he could have done without the smoke from his cigars.

As the project was entering its second year, Nenniger's division landed another milestone contract. This one came from the Johns Manville Corporation, which mined and refined asbestos. Surveyer, Nenniger & Chênevert was asked to design and supervise the construction of a new mill in Asbestos, Quebec.

Nenniger at first had to turn down the job when the President of Johns Manville called to offer it to him. His division was already overloaded, and Surveyer had agreed that sacrificing quality on several jobs just to take on one more was unacceptable. In the days following the call, Nenniger racked his brain to figure out how to accommodate Johns Manville, but concluded there was no way he could hire enough men in time. The problem soon sorted itself out when a contract for a zinc smelter was put on hold.

The Johns Manville project was the largest industrial contract Surveyer, Nenniger & Chênevert had ever won. The firm would have to redesign and rebuild its asbestos mill from scratch, as well as manage the complexities of construction. Hahn, who had done an admirable job on the Sorel contract, was made Project Manager.

Johns Manville was acting mainly out of health concerns for its workers. The filtering system for the asbestos fibres was far from adequate, and the structural integrity of the building itself was in question. The sifters at the old wooden

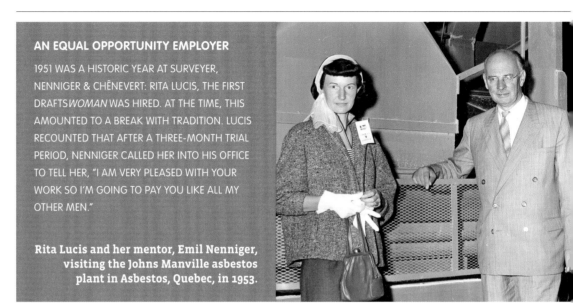

Rita Lucis and her mentor, Emil Nenniger, visiting the Johns Manville asbestos plant in Asbestos, Quebec, in 1953.

mill in Asbestos had a tendency to shake the entire building when they came into alignment. When Nenniger and Hahn made a first inspection of the mill, they were astounded by what they found. The vibrations grew stronger as they went up each successive floor. By the time they reached the top, the structure was shaking so violently they could barely stand up.

"This can't be safe," an alarmed Hahn said as he braced himself against a wall.

"Certainly not," Nenniger replied.

Fearing for their safety, they hastily made for the stairs.

Walter Stensch, the division's Chief Structural Engineer, was given the job of designing a new, more solid mill out of reinforced concrete and steel. Stensch was another German refugee Nenniger had hired during the war. He had begun as a wide-eyed office boy in 1943. When Nenniger saw that he had calculation abilities that rivaled his own, he decided to mentor him and sponsor his engineering studies.

When the project was approaching completion in the spring of 1953, Nenniger chartered a bus and took his entire department on a field trip

Walter Stensch

Jack Hahn

Aerial view of the Johns Manville plant in Asbestos, Quebec.

Emil Nenniger and his team on a field trip to the Johns Manville plant in 1953.

to the mill. He felt it was important that his staff see the end result of their hard work. Nenniger's employees had a lot to be proud of. The reduction in dust was dramatic, and the building was efficiently and solidly designed. It was the most modern site of its kind in the entire Western hemisphere.

24
Une visite à l'imposante usine moderne d'Asbestos

Des ingénieurs conseils montréalais ont conçu les plans d'une usine géante pour la plus grosse mine d'amiante au monde.

par Eugène Lafond
envoyé spécial de la "Presse"

Asbestos, 27. — En parcourant les Cantons de l'Est on a vraiment l'impression qu'une vaste partie de cette région repose sur un lit d'amiante. Une zo-nehouse de 60 milles, s'éten-... -bestos, four-

nique moderne assurant le plein rendement, un produit de haute qualité, sans négliger les principes de sécurité et d'hygiène. La vieille usine de traitement était donc dé-modée, mais le projet d'une nou-velle usine devait prendre une telle envergure, exigeant une mise de fonds de plusieurs millions, que la compagnie se devait d'en confier l'exécution à des techniciens ré-tés. Elle a donc retenu les ser-ces des ingénieurs conseils Sur-yer, Nenniger et Chênevert, de ontréal, qui compte un personnel e plus de 150 techniciens.

C'est en compagnie de MM. E. enniger, l'un des ingénieurs asso-iés, J. Hahn, ingénieur du projet 'Asbestos et E. N. Gougeon, ingé-ieur de projets ainsi que d'une rentaine de techniciens qui ont travaillé pendant plus de trois ans à la préparation des plans que le représentant de la Presse est allé samedi dernier visiter l'imposante structure de la plus grande usine du genre au monde.

Usine des plus moderne

La nouvelle usine de traitement où l'on extrait la fibre de l'amiante tirée de la mine Jeffrey est une

Asbestos Plant Opened By Premier Duplessis

By FERNAND RENAULT
The Star's Quebec Correspondent

ASBESTOS, Que., Sept. 30 — Premier Maurice Duplessis today opened the new Johns-Manville fibre mill.

All operations in one section of the 14-storey steel-and-con-crete mill were thrown into gear when the Premier pressed a but-ton.

This new mill, replacing the present mills which are becoming obsolete, is described by com-pany officials as "the most im-portant single project in Johns-Manville's expansion during the past decade."

Commercial mining of asbes-tos in Canada began in 1876. To-day, Canada produces 65 per

Thetford Mines and here in As-bestos.

Karl V. Lindell, vice-president of the company and general man-ager of its asbestos fibre division, said the new mill "incorporates the most modern facilities for the milling and production of high quality asbestos fibre."

The mill is aimed at providing better quality asbestos at a lower cost.

It is the first of two buildings that will eventually make up the entire mill. The second building is expected to be ready for use in the spring of 1956.

When completed the mill will have a yearly production cap-acity of 625,000 tons of asbes-

NEVER SAY NEVER

While Chênevert's team was overshadowed by Nenniger's industrial contracts in the early 1950s, the second half of the decade would change all that. By the mid-1950s, Chênevert's division was hard at work on a pair of contracts that would become legendary in the annals of Montreal building projects.

In 1953, the Executive Committee of the City of Montreal asked Surveyer, Nenniger & Chênevert to study the possibility of running Burnside Street (now De Maisonneuve Boulevard) through the Drummond Court Apartments. The city at first proposed to demolish the building, but its owner lobbied to have a passageway run through the obstructing north wing in-stead. The Executive Committee agreed, but to "avoid any tie-ups, legal or otherwise," it decided to buy the building from the owner for a dollar and sell it back once the work was completed.

Chênevert put two of his best young engineers on the contract. Roger Provost, a structural specialist who had joined in 1946, was asked to plan the job. Provost was mild-mannered, with a natural talent for engineering. There was a certain understated elegance to him that translated into his engineering work. His project reports read like literature, and he was able to come up with ingenious solutions to delicate problems. Just what was needed for Drummond Court.

The construction itself would be supervised by recently hired engineer Roméo Filiatrault. Chênevert had been instantly impressed by his drive and energy. He had confidence to spare and knew how to relate to people, a crucial trait for a good construction manager.

Filiatrault had actually been on the verge of leaving Surveyer, Nenniger & Chênevert before Drummond Court came along. He had walked into Chênevert's office and told his boss that he was bored stiff by the sort of projects he was being assigned. He was going to look elsewhere to satisfy his appetite for challenges, he said. Not wanting to lose such a promising engineer, Chênevert offered to put him on Drummond Court. "I think this will challenge you," he said with a smile.

The first step involved clearing the bottom two levels of the north wing of all but their support columns. Then it was time to prepare a new series of columns to bear the weight once the old ones were demolished. The transfer of the load, which required powerful hydraulic jacks, was all the more delicate because tenants were still living in the building. Every possible precaution was taken, including designing the new columns so they could bear twice the required weight.

In the end, the heart-stopping procedure went off without a hitch. The movement of the building after the transfer was completed was less than a millimetre. Given the scale of the operation and the number of variables, that was just about perfect.

Chênevert won the second contract just as Drummond Court was getting under way. This one posed an entirely new set of problems. In fact, at first Surveyer had not wanted to touch it because of the risks involved.

Montreal's main French-language daily, *La Presse*, wanted to broaden its circulation and increase its number of printing presses. On March 15, 1955, Chênevert delivered a report that outlined three choices: the newspaper's current building on St. James Street in Montreal could be renovated, a completely new location could be found, or a second building could be built next door.

The board of directors rejected the first idea, saying that the building was just too small to meet its needs, even with significant renovations. The second possibility was ruled out, as well. The board categorically refused to leave the neighbourhood: it was located in the heart of the action, right next to City Hall, the Stock Exchange, and Montreal Harbour. It was no surprise, then, when they voted for the third option,

Roger Provost
Roméo Filiatrault

A delicate manoeuvre: preparing the building for the load transfer, demolishing the columns, and the completed Burnside Street tunnel under the Drummond Court Apartments.

Construction of the
La Presse building between
1957 and 1958.

even though Chênevert's report warned that a nearby underground river would hinder construction.

Surveyer tried every means to get *La Presse* to consider building in a new location across town. Construction of a large building in such wet soil conditions was almost certainly going to be more trouble than it was worth, he cautioned. Besides, with modern publishing techniques, it was no longer necessary to be right downtown. It was no use; his efforts were in vain.

Surveyer's misgivings proved well-founded. On the first day of excavation, the crew had to contend with a 120,000-volt underground cable that ran a half-metre from the foundation line for the new building. One of the city's main power arteries, it had to be carefully protected before excavation could continue. Trenches were dug around the line with shovels, and tightly fitted piles were inserted to keep it from being damaged.

As expected, the biggest challenge proved to be soil conditions. Water seeped in continuously as the ground was excavated, causing the clay walls to collapse. Despite their best efforts, the construction crew could not keep the site dry. With the project rapidly falling behind schedule, Chênevert called in a well-known American geologist named Arthur

Casagrande to help sort out the problem. He came to the worksite and spent some time walking around in its puddles. The way he saw it, Chênevert had two choices: "When you've got both feet in the water, either you get out or you wear boots. I think you are going to be needing boots."

The "boots" that Casagrande was referring to was the ICOS method, invented by the Italian firm of the same name. A row of wells would be drilled about one metre apart, while bentonite, a kind of slurry, was pumped in to maintain their integrity. Another series would then be drilled between those wells using the same technique. The process would be repeated until a single continuous wall was formed. When concrete was later pumped down into the wells to replace the bentonite, the result would be a watertight barrier inside which the foundation could be poured. It worked like a charm.

The project ended up costing considerably more than expected due to unforeseeable difficulties, but the foundation held beautifully. Chênevert's engineers could not have known at the time that they would soon be using the ICOS method once again for the largest contract they had yet been awarded. Surveyer, Nenniger & Chênevert was about to enter the mega-dam business.

THE CHANGING OF THE GUARD

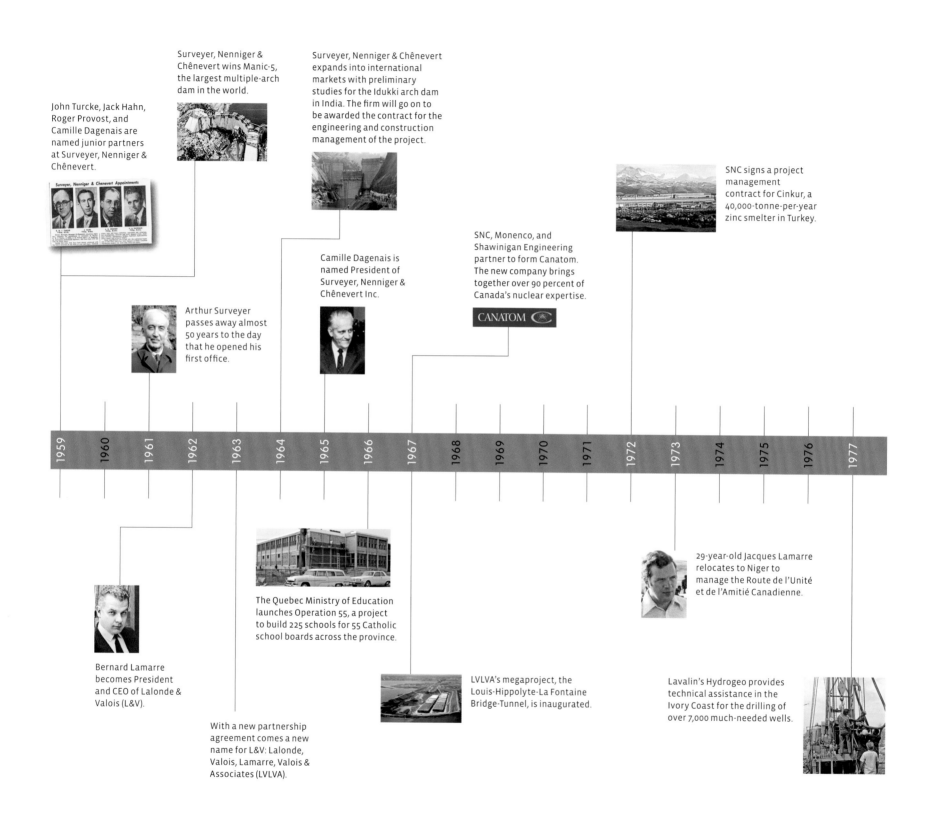

John Turcke, Jack Hahn, Roger Provost, and Camille Dagenais are named junior partners at Surveyer, Nenniger & Chênevert.

Surveyer, Nenniger & Chênevert wins Manic-5, the largest multiple-arch dam in the world.

Surveyer, Nenniger & Chênevert expands into international markets with preliminary studies for the Idukki arch dam in India. The firm will go on to be awarded the contract for the engineering and construction management of the project.

SNC signs a project management contract for Cinkur, a 40,000-tonne-per-year zinc smelter in Turkey.

Arthur Surveyer passes away almost 50 years to the day that he opened his first office.

Camille Dagenais is named President of Surveyer, Nenniger & Chênevert Inc.

SNC, Monenco, and Shawinigan Engineering partner to form Canatom. The new company brings together over 90 percent of Canada's nuclear expertise.

1959 1960 1961 1962 1963 1964 1965 1966 1967 1968 1969 1970 1971 1972 1973 1974 1975 1976 1977

Bernard Lamarre becomes President and CEO of Lalonde & Valois (L&V).

The Quebec Ministry of Education launches Operation 55, a project to build 225 schools for 55 Catholic school boards across the province.

29-year-old Jacques Lamarre relocates to Niger to manage the Route de l'Unité et de l'Amitié Canadienne.

With a new partnership agreement comes a new name for L&V: Lalonde, Valois, Lamarre, Valois & Associates (LVLVA).

LVLVA's megaproject, the Louis-Hippolyte-La Fontaine Bridge-Tunnel, is inaugurated.

Lavalin's Hydrogeo provides technical assistance in the Ivory Coast for the drilling of over 7,000 much-needed wells.

PREVIOUS PAGE
A drawing showing one of the Louis-Hippolyte-La Fontaine Bridge-Tunnel's 32,000-tonne segments and the technique used to sink it down to the riverbed.

CHAPTER 8

PROJECTS, PROJECTS, PROJECTS

The Louis-Hippolyte-La Fontaine Bridge-Tunnel under construction in the St. Lawrence River.

The Quiet Revolution arrives in Quebec in the 1960s. It is a time of great social and economic upheaval. For engineering firms like LVLVA, it is an opportunity to pit their expertise against some of the most ambitious Canadian infrastructure projects ever conceived. The charge is led by Bernard Lamarre, now the President of LVLVA, his partner, Jean-Pierre Valois, and the firm's associates: Gaston René de Cotret, Jean Croteau, Jean-Paul Dionne, André Denis, and Paul Roberge. Among the most high-profile contracts won during these years are the Louis-Hippolyte-La Fontaine Bridge-Tunnel project and the Ville-Marie Expressway, both components of the Trans-Canada Highway.

By 1961, Jean-Paul Lalonde and Roméo Valois were actively preparing the ground for their retirement.

Lalonde was proud of all he had achieved during his engineering career. Quebec was now dotted with his bridges, tunnels, schools, and hospitals, all of them proof of concrete's innate versatility and strength. And, of course, there was the firm he had helped build and the many engineers he had taken under his wing. But Lalonde's illness had afforded him ample time to reflect on his life, and he had emerged a changed man. He wanted to spend more time with his family and travel while he still could.

Valois, too, could look back with satisfaction on a long and productive career. The human element had always mattered to him. Why not share a laugh with colleagues and clients while building a successful business? He had proven that the two were not incompatible. He might have continued on, but he could not imagine himself working without Lalonde. Looking back over the last 25 years, Valois felt that they had been more like a happily married couple than business partners. If Lalonde was going to retire, then his time had come too.

The founders could not have walked away if they did not feel the firm was in good hands. Bernard Lamarre had done a fine job of filling in for them over the last three years. He had maintained Lalonde's exacting standards for engineering work, while building up a network of contacts to rival Valois's own.

It had not been easy. Many of the decision makers in the provincial government were of his father's generation and preferred to deal with men their own age. But young Lamarre was willing to do what it took to get that crucial first meeting.

Bernard Lamarre

Jean-Pierre Valois

Sometimes that had even meant staking out the underground corridor that linked the Quebec Parliament Building with the Ministry of Transportation for passing politicians.

Those like Marcel Dufour, who had known Bernard Lamarre in university, were not surprised by his insatiable appetite for work. While still a student, Lamarre had discovered that every extra hour of effort he put in was like compound interest. If you worked 10 percent harder than the competition, he realized, your capital would double in seven years. Lamarre wanted a return on his investment in half that time, so he resolved to work at least 20 percent harder.

By March of 1962, Jean-Paul Lalonde and Roméo Valois needed no further demonstration of Lamarre's ability to lead Lalonde & Valois (L&V) and named him President and CEO. To allow him to concentrate more on engineering activities, Valois brought in his son, Jean-Pierre, to head up marketing. Tall and dapper, he bore a striking resemblance to his father, and shared his facility with people. The founders hoped that Lamarre and the younger Valois would develop the same dynamic that had worked so well for them.

LALONDE, VALOIS, LAMARRE, VALOIS & ASSOCIATES

Through the end of 1962, L&V's lawyer, Émile Colas, worked to finalize a new partnership agreement. A flamboyant and aggressive solicitor, Colas had been hired in 1960 following his dazzling defence of the Aboriginal people of Kahnawake during the St. Lawrence Seaway project.

Colas had been told to prepare the necessary legal work to make Lamarre and Jean-Pierre Valois the firm's new partners, allotting each a 25-percent stake. The remaining 50 percent would be divided between the five chief engineers, who would become associates. The founders would now be "consultants," with no ownership stake in the firm.

Lalonde and Valois had no reservations about expanding the circle of ownership to include the chief engineers. They had all redoubled their efforts to support Lamarre during a difficult time of transition. As a result, the founders' absence had barely been felt. In fact, the firm had grown considerably.

The most senior of the engineers was Jean Croteau. Hard working and keenly intelligent, he had been with L&V since 1948, and was now Chief Engineer of its Public Works Department. Croteau had proven invaluable on the Honoré-Mercier Bridge contract, where he had overseen the delicate relocation of power, rail, and telephone lines during construction of the north approach in LaSalle.

Gaston René de Cotret, the Chief Engineer for the Municipal Department, was the next in line of seniority. Always elegantly dressed with distinctive horn-rimmed glasses, he had been a quiet but reliable presence at L&V since 1951. He now had several successful projects under his belt, including a state-of-the-art filtration plant in Jonquière, Quebec.

There was André Denis, the talented Chief Engineer of the Structural Steel Department. He had produced elegant and economical designs for the Honoré-Mercier Bridge. With Denis on side, L&V was able to compete head-to-head against omnipresent Dominion Bridge, the top bridge-building firm in Canada at the time.

Jean-Paul Dionne was another deserving employee. He had been in charge of the firm's Construction Supervision Department since 1958. His role was becoming increasingly important as project management opportunities began to present themselves.

The fifth new associate was Paul Roberge. A highly trained concrete specialist, he had assumed responsibility for the firm's Structures Department when Lamarre took over from the founders. Roberge was a dynamic presence in the office. Fuelled by caffeine and creativity, he had already worked several minor miracles with concrete.

In March of 1963, the founders, new partners, and associates gathered in the conference room at the Belmont Building in downtown Montreal, which L&V had occupied since 1959. The air of anticipation was palpable as Colas read out the new terms. As agreed, Bernard Lamarre and Jean-Pierre Valois would now control all aspects of the firm. The chief engineers would continue to have responsibility only for their departments, but they would now negotiate and sign their own contracts.

There had also been considerable discussion around the firm's name. Obviously a new one had to be found. In the end they opted for Lalonde, Valois, Lamarre, Valois & Associates, or LVLVA for short. It was a mouthful, but it had the advantage of reflecting the firm's storied past while representing its new partners and associates.

Jean Croteau

Gaston René de Cotret

Jean-Paul Dionne

Paul Roberge

Lalonde, Valois, Lamarre, Valois & Associates' offices at 615 Belmont Street in Montreal.

LALONDE, VALOIS, LAMARRE, VALOIS & ASSOCIÉS
INGÉNIEURS-CONSEILS

BERNARD LAMARRE, ING.P.,M.SC.
JEAN CROTEAU, ING.P.
ANDRÉ DENIS, ING.P.
PAUL ROBERGE, ING.P.,D.I.C.

JEAN-PIERRE VALOIS, ING.P.
GASTON R. de COTRET, ING.P.
JEAN-PAUL DIONNE, ING.P.

615 RUE BELMONT
MONTRÉAL 3

CONSEILLERS
JEAN-PAUL LALONDE, ING.P.   ROMÉO VALOIS, ING.P.,M.SC.

THE LOUIS-HIPPOLYTE-LA FONTAINE BRIDGE-TUNNEL

In the summer of 1960, a new Quebec government led by Jean Lesage set out to radically transform the province. The Premier promised to revamp its aging infrastructure and modernize its education and medical systems. Historians would later call it the "Quiet Revolution." For Quebec's engineers, it would be a golden age.

One of his first decisions was to allow the extension of the Trans-Canada Highway through Quebec. Unlike his predecessor, Maurice Duplessis, Lesage saw many reasons for giving the project the go-ahead. Montreal was set to host Expo 67, and the Trans-Canada would provide better access from all corners of the country. There would also be the obvious benefits to commerce from improved infrastructure. If that were not enough, the federal government was willing to foot up to 90 percent of the bill.

There was never any doubt that the highway would run through the island of Montreal, but not everything about the project was as easy to define. By early 1962, engineers at the Quebec Ministry of Transportation had still not decided whether to build a bridge or a tunnel at the southeastern end of the city where the St. Lawrence River split around Charron Island. Both options looked overly expensive. A bridge would have to be high enough to allow for ocean-going vessels to pass beneath it. A bored tunnel, on the other hand, would need to be unusually deep to get under the thick layer of alluvium south of Charron Island.

When Per Hall, the President of the engineering firm Per Hall & Associates, heard about the government's dilemma, he called Lesage's office to arrange a meeting. Hall and his Vice-President, Armand Couture, had just finished an innovative bridge-tunnel in Vancouver. Instead of boring the tunnel though the bedrock, its segments had been prefabricated and sunk into a trench in the riverbed. They brought along a film of the construction so that the Premier could see first-hand how practical it was.

Couture narrated as the grainy images of the project flickered by. At the end of the film, he proposed running a 457-metre bridge from the South Shore to Charron Island, and a 1,368-metre segmented tunnel from there to the island of Montreal. There would be no need for a massive bridge over Montreal Harbour, and the deep layer of alluvium and sand south of Charron Island would not be a problem. Lesage thought it was a brilliant idea and particularly liked that such a tunnel could be built using local materials and labour.

In November 1962, Per Hall, L&V, and the Montreal engineering firm Brett & Ouelette were retained to design and supervise construction of the Louis-Hippolyte-La Fontaine Bridge-Tunnel. The members of the consortium chose their top engineers for the project's Technical Committee. Per Hall elected Armand Couture, Brett & Ouellette volunteered Roger Nicolet, and L&V was represented by Bernard Lamarre.

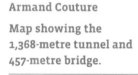

Armand Couture

Map showing the 1,368-metre tunnel and 457-metre bridge.

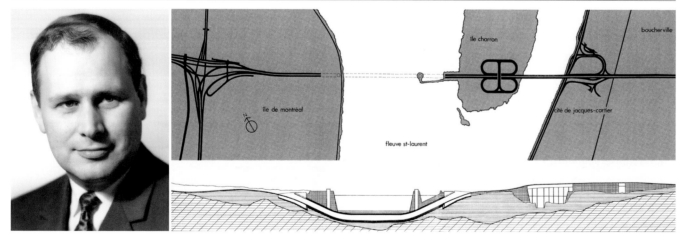

A WORKSITE IN THE RIVER

By the fall of 1963, local newspapers were abuzz with talk of the massive worksite in the St. Lawrence River. A dry dock the size of 10 American football fields had been pushed out into the current from Charron Island, leaving just enough room for ocean-going vessels to squeeze by. The tunnel's seven 32,000-tonne concrete segments would be cast there.

Couture, who had headed the design work of the tunnel, enjoyed seeing his gigantic creations come to life. It had been his idea to use prestressed concrete instead of heavier and more costly reinforced concrete. He had also streamlined the design of the components by scaling down the tunnel's ventilation system. The original plans had called for two ventilation corridors, one to draw in air and another to evacuate fumes. Couture realized that the movement of constant traffic would create an air current that made the second corridor redundant. Some members of the Technical Committee had been skeptical, but he succeeded in proving his point by having a life-sized replica of a segment built out of plywood.

May 6, 1965, marked the start of the most delicate phase of the project. A series of powerful pumps began filling the dry dock with water. Inside, the gigantic tunnel segments had been sealed at either end so they would be buoyant enough to be tugged into position. The next stage would see them sunk with ballast while divers and powerful hydraulic jacks ensured they hit their mark to within millimetres.

Couture and Lamarre looked on as the seven segments rose slowly in the water like a fleet of ocean liners. Over the last three years, the two men had formed a close friendship. Lamarre had come to consider Couture one of the finest technical minds he had known. Where most saw problems, Couture saw only solutions. For his part, Couture had developed a high regard for Lamarre's leadership skills and his ability to co-ordinate complex technical mandates.

After being built in a dry dock in the St. Lawrence River, the seven massive 32,000-tonne concrete segments were tugged into position and sunk. Divers used hydraulic jacks to position them to within millimetres of their mark.

AN INVITATION

The Québec Department of Roads invites you to a special preview showing of the new

LOUIS-HIPPOLYTE LAFONTAINE BRIDGE-TUNNEL

on Saturday, March 11th from 5:00 p.m. to 11:00 p.m. and Sunday, March 12th from 10:00 a.m. to 11:00 p.m.

Bilingual guides in free special buses will conduct public tours of the Bridge-tunnel on Saturday and Sunday only. The Bridge-tunnel is closed to normal traffic until Monday, March 13th at 1:00 p.m.

SEE IT FIRST!

Bring the family, park the car, ride the buses for a visit to the new, exciting Louis-Hippolyte Lafontaine Bridge-Tunnel.

SPECIAL PARKING FACILITIES:

For Montréal visitors— Métro Station—Frontenac at junction of Ontario and d'Iberville.

For South Shore visitors— Spancrete Company Parking lot bordering Route 3 (or Autoroute 20)

QUÉBEC DEPARTMENT OF ROADS

At the inauguration in March of 1967, Quebec Premier Daniel Johnson verbalized what so many were thinking: "This structure is much more than meets the eye. It is first a monument to the boldness, creative genius, and exceptional skill of all those who participated in designing and building it," he said. "This project is proof that our engineers, contractors, technicians, industrialists, and workers are no longer content to be disciples, but have risen to the rank of masters."

The Ville-Marie Expressway cut through the core of downtown Montreal.

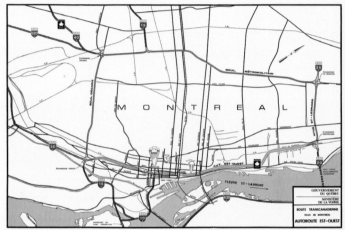

THE VILLE-MARIE EXPRESSWAY

As the La Fontaine Bridge-Tunnel neared completion, LVLVA received some bad news about another Trans-Canada Highway project it was working on.

In the fall of 1963, the firm had been awarded a contract to design the Ville-Marie Expressway, an eight-kilometre stretch of the Trans-Canada that ran through the downtown core of Montreal. Since then, a team led by Eugène Claprood, which included Gaétan Boyer for geometry and Bernard Lamarre's brother Pierre for structural design, had been working overtime to thread its six lanes around, under, and over major roads and towering buildings.

In the summer of 1966, as the finishing touches were being put on the Expressway's highly complex preliminary designs, the new Daniel Johnson government decided to cut Quebec's massive transportation budget, starting with the Trans-Canada Highway.

The project team was devastated: years of meticulous and innovative engineering had gone into the designs. Bernard Lamarre was equally dismayed, but after reflecting on the matter for a few days, he decided to push ahead at LVLVA's cost and complete the plans. "One day someone will decide to finish this highway and we will be ready with the plans," he assured them.

Lamarre breathed a great sigh of relief when Robert Bourassa was elected Premier of Quebec in January 1970. His campaign slogan had been "100,000 Jobs," and he hoped to create most of them through infrastructure projects. Michel Bélanger, the Secretary of the Treasury, was given the task of finding those projects. One of his first calls was to Claude Rouleau, the Deputy Minister of Transportation. Rouleau recalled that LVLVA had been working on the Trans-Canada at one time, and offered to call Bernard Lamarre to inquire about the plans.

"You want plans? Claude, I have at least $110 million worth of plans ready to go," Lamarre said. "We never stopped working on them, and even went ahead and designed the other sections as well."

Within a couple of days, the plans and specifications were delivered to the Ministry of Transportation, and Bourassa had found quite a few of his promised 100,000 jobs.

PROJECT MANAGEMENT BREAKTHROUGH

In the fall of 1966, Bernard Lamarre saw an excellent opportunity to expand LVLVA's repertoire of services. The Quebec Ministry of Education had launched Operation 55, a project to build 225 schools for 55 Catholic school boards across the province, but things were not going well. After two years, only a handful of buildings had been finished, and most had gone over budget. The government realized that it needed a project management firm to oversee the initiative, and Lamarre wanted LVLVA to be that firm.

The problem was that LVLVA did not have project management expertise. Few Canadian engineering firms did. Among all his contacts, Lamarre knew of only one person who was qualified to do that kind of work in Quebec. His name was Yves Maheu, and he was currently overseeing the construction of a building LVLVA had designed in Montreal. Maheu was bright and driven, and had an innate sense of what materials and services should cost. If Lamarre could convince him to join LVLVA, they would stand a good chance of winning the contract.

Lamarre called Maheu to make him an offer, but for once his powers of persuasion failed. Maheu said he liked his current job, and the idea of moving to Quebec City to work alongside career bureaucrats did not appeal to him.

Determined not to let the contract slip by, Lamarre spent the next two months combing through Quebec's engineering profession for someone with Maheu's expertise. Time was running out: he had learned that the Ministry of Education was going to hire a firm from the United States if it could not find one in Canada.

A CONCRETE MASTERPIECE

WITH A TOTAL SURFACE AREA OF 23,105 SQUARE METRES, PLACE BONAVENTURE WAS COMPARABLE TO A SMALL INDOOR CITY. DESIGNED BY PAUL ROBERGE, IT CONTAINED A HOTEL, A MOVIE THEATRE, EXHIBITION HALLS, OFFICE SPACE, SHOPS, BOUTIQUES, RESTAURANTS, AND BARS. THE ENTIRE 17-STOREY BUILDING WAS MADE OF REINFORCED CONCRETE, INCLUDING THE EXTERIOR WALLS. WHEN IT WAS COMPLETED IN 1967, IT WAS BY FAR THE LARGEST CONCRETE BUILDING IN WORLD.

When Lamarre's search ended in disappointment, he knew he had to convince Maheu to join LVLVA. He decided to appeal to his sense of pride.

"So Yves, are you certain that you are not willing to go to Quebec City?"

"Yes, I haven't changed my mind, Bernard," Maheu answered.

"I'm sorry to hear that," Lamarre said. "You know, the government is going to bring in an American firm if it can't find one to manage their project here. I think that would be a shame since we have the expertise." Like Lamarre, Maheu was proud to be a Quebec engineer. He was proud of the growth of the profession in the province over the last 50 years. The idea of importing expertise that he himself had made him reconsider and accept the offer.

Before Maheu arrived, the Ministry of Education had drawn up a budget for each school that contained only the total amount for the entire project. As a result, the architects, who had final authority over the plans, had tended to include costly design flourishes at the expense of air-conditioning and heating systems.

Jacques Lamarre (right) with a colleague at Manic-5.

The 1966 extension of Queen Elizabeth High School in Sept-Îles, Quebec, was one of many school projects the Quebec Ministry of Education awarded LVLVA.

Yves Maheu

Maheu immediately established new standards. From now on, everything from geological studies to electrical work would be allotted its own budget. But he knew it was not enough to simply tell architects and engineering firms how much they had for their part of the project. The new budgets also had to be respected. In the future, any project whose budgets were exceeded would be immediately stopped.

Once Maheu had put cost control measures in place, he focused on quality and schedule. Up to now, each school project had been supervised by one team in Quebec City. Maheu recommended assigning individual engineers to the different school districts. They would be able to closely monitor the quality of designs and ensure construction moved ahead.

Bernard Lamarre's younger brother Jacques was one of several LVLVA engineers chosen for the project. Bernard had just convinced him to leave Janin Construction, where he had been building diversion tunnels for the Manic-5 hydropower project in northern Quebec. With his boundless energy, large build, and baritone voice, the younger Lamarre had an unforced air of authority that his brother thought would be useful on Operation 55.

In the summer of 1967, Jacques packed his bags and went to meet Maheu in Quebec City. He was put in charge of three districts, which together required over 30 schools. He had enjoyed his job with Janin, but this was exactly the sort of work he had gone into engineering to do. He liked project management, and above all, craved responsibility.

MANIC-5

The majestic Manic-5 multiple-arch dam taking shape in northern Quebec.

Surveyer, Nenniger & Chênevert is growing quickly. Before the 1960s arrive, four new partners are named: Camille Dagenais, Jack Hahn, John Turcke, and Roger Provost. The new additions to the firm's management have bold ideas that butt up against those of its senior partners. Meanwhile, the firm is starting work on Manic-5, the largest multiple-arch dam in the world. SNC makes use of a revolutionary new technology called the computer to accelerate its calculations on the dam. Arthur Surveyer will not live to see the completion of the structure, passing away in April of 1961, almost 50 years to the day that he opened his first office.

In the spring of 1954, Camille Dagenais walked into Georges Chênevert's office in the Keefer Building. The 34-year-old was tall, with slicked back hair that threw his high forehead and intense eyes into relief. He had been hired only a few months earlier, but he never hesitated to speak his mind. Dagenais had heard that the Quebec government planned to build a massive hydropower development, and he wanted to be part of it.

Chênevert listened patiently as Dagenais made his case. He was interested, of course, but everyone knew those jobs tended to go to major engineering firms with recognized expertise in the field. Refusing to see that as an obstacle, Dagenais suggested Chênevert contact Hydro-Québec directly. What was there to lose?

The province had created Hydro-Québec in 1944 to nationalize its power production. One by one, power companies like Montreal Light, Heat and Power were being absorbed into the public utility. But unlike neighbouring Ontario, which had nationalized its electricity in 1906, Quebec decided not to keep the engineering arms of the companies it acquired. As a result, it contracted out major jobs to private engineering firms.

Dagenais wanted Surveyer, Nenniger & Chênevert to be one of them. He had long dreamed of working on a mega-structure, something that would stand as a testament to the ingenuity and imagination of man. He still remembered the first time his father had taken him for a drive over the Jacques-Cartier Bridge in Montreal. Young Dagenais had been awestruck by its sheer size, its enormous steel girders and massive bolts. When his father told him that engineers had built the bridge, he made up his mind to become one.

With Dagenais sitting nearby, Chênevert put in a call to Raymond Latreille, a former École Polytechnique classmate

In the fall of 1954, Camille Dagenais led a team that conducted preliminary studies of the Megiscan, Outardes, and Manicouagan rivers in northern Quebec.

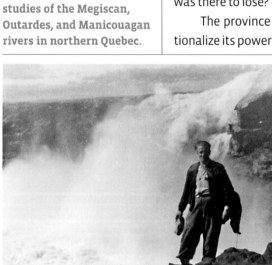

who was now a commissioner at Hydro-Québec. It would be a shame, Chênevert told him, if no local engineering firms were involved in the project. Latreille, it turned out, felt just as strongly about the issue, and soon persuaded Hydro-Québec's Chairman, L.-Eugène Potvin, to give Surveyer, Nenniger & Chênevert a shot. In the fall of 1954, Dagenais was made Resident Engineer for a preliminary study of the Megiscan, Outardes, and Manicouagan rivers in the north of the province.

DRAMA AT DE LA CACHE

In the spring of 1958, Dagenais took a giant step closer to his dream of working on a major structure when Hydro-Québec asked his team to evaluate possible dam sites on the Manicouagan. They would not be starting right away, however. First, over 25 tonnes of equipment would have to be hauled into the virgin region, including two massive diamond drills and a tractor.

It was a logistical puzzle. A road was being planned under the supervision of Roméo Filiatrault but would not be finished for several years. For now, the only means of transportation were the Norseman and Beaver single-engine planes that took passengers from Baie Comeau to Lake De la Cache. The remaining eight kilometres of dense bush and wildly uneven terrain had to be portaged or covered by tractor.

Dagenais entrusted the job of co-ordinating the operation to Bernard Arsenault, one of his most resourceful land surveyors. With no other options, Arsenault decided to take the equipment apart and fly it up to De la Cache using a Norseman. The pilot was reluctant when he learned of Arsenault's plan. Such heavy cargo would force him to fly at a precariously low altitude, and he did not relish the idea of landing with a full payload on a frozen lake so late in the season. Arsenault finally convinced the pilot to go along with the plan by performing borehole tests on the ice to prove it was thick enough to bear the weight.

The operation took four days. When the last flight touched down at De la Cache, a relieved Arsenault called Dagenais in Montreal to tell him the mission had been a resounding success. It was a call he would soon regret making. An hour later, he learned that the last shipment had broken through the ice of a lake while en route to Manicouagan.

Arsenault called Dagenais back to ask him what he should do. Dagenais liked to give his men responsibility, but the more he gave them, the more accountable they were when something went wrong.

"Bernard, you're in charge of the operation," Dagenais answered. "I'm here if you need my help, but I expect you to figure out a way to get the equipment out of there."

Forced to improvise once again, Arsenault and his team rigged a large tripod with a pulley system and placed it over the hole in the ice. A diver hired for the occasion positioned himself under water while a foreman named Arthur Dufour directed the procedure from atop the tripod. He was ideal because he weighed no more than 120 pounds, and every additional ounce made the operation riskier.

It was slow and tedious work, but after seven days, the equipment was out. Arsenault happily called Dagenais to tell him the detailed studies of the Manicouagan would soon be able to begin.

Bernard Arsenault at work in the Baie Comeau office in August 1955.

A tripod with a pulley system was placed over the hole in the ice so that a diver could recover the equipment.

THE NEW GUARD

A third partnership agreement between Arthur Surveyer, Emil Nenniger, and Georges Chênevert was signed on February 18, 1957. But by then, a new generation of leaders was growing restless. Like Nenniger and Chênevert before them, Jack Hahn and Camille Dagenais had begun to feel that their contribution should be formally recognized. They too wanted to become partners.

Hahn was now Head of Engineering for Industrial Processes. He had led important projects for Atlas Steel, New Jersey Zinc, and Johns Manville, but his ambition had moved beyond individual assignments. He was increasingly interested in the big picture: business development.

Charismatic and driven, Dagenais had impressed everyone since his arrival in 1954. He had shown he possessed the traits of a natural born leader during the Megiscan, Outardes, and Manicouagan studies. In the depth of a virgin wilderness, he had managed to inspire deep loyalty in his team, encouraging them to fight through giant populations of voracious insects and bitter cold. Like Hahn, he too had a vision of what the firm could become.

The Montreal Gazette,
January 16, 1959.

They felt there were others whose contribution needed to be acknowledged, like John Turcke, now Head of Engineering for the Structural Department. He had helped make the firm a top supplier of pulp and paper expertise, and had led its first major manufacturing project, a factory for electronics giant RCA. He was also universally respected for his fair-mindedness and honesty. If anyone deserved to become a partner, it was Turcke.

To round out the group, Dagenais and Hahn brought in Roger Provost. Everyone knew he was a top-notch structural engineer. He was also the firm's peacemaker, and it was crucial to have one at the top of any organization.

Negotiations with the partners began in mid-1958. Surveyer was now 79 years old and in ill health, so Nenniger and Chênevert represented him at the table. From the start, they were aware that they held few cards. Dagenais, Hahn, Turcke, and Provost were now the heart of the firm, responsible for most of its day-to-day operations. If they left, a number of projects would come to a grinding halt and important prospects would fall away. Nenniger and Chênevert could not deny that time had marched on, leaving them dependent on the skills and ambitions of these younger men.

On January 1, 1959, Dagenais, Hahn, Turcke, and Provost became the firm's new associates. Nenniger and Chênevert were now "intermediate" partners, while Surveyer remained the sole senior partner. It was a massive and sudden leadership change. There were now three generations of partners at the helm, with three different visions of the firm's future.

GEOLOGICAL SURPRISES

On October 2, 1959, Surveyer, Nenniger & Chênevert was awarded a contract to design and supervise the construction of a massive multiple-arch dam at waterfall No. 5 on the Manicouagan River (it would soon simply be known as Manic-5). Behind it would swell the largest hydropower reservoir in Canada.

The firm had Quebec Premier Daniel Johnson to thank. Unlike some of his predecessors, he felt local engineering offices deserved a shot at Hydro-Québec's big contracts. How else were they going to build up expertise?

Surveyer, Nenniger & Chenevert Appointments

E. W. J. TURCKE
P.Eng., B.A.Sc.

J. HAHN
P.Eng., B.Eng.

J. R. PROVOST
P.Eng., B.A.Sc.

C. A. DAGENAIS
P.Eng., B.A.Sc.

Messrs. **Surveyer, Nenniger & Chenevert,** consulting engineers, announce the appointment as associates of Messrs. E. W. J. Turcke, J. Hahn, J. R. Provost and C. A. Dagenais, all well known professional engineers, who have been with the firm for many years.

During this time, they have been closely connected with the firm's activities in the fields of pulp and paper, chemical plants, light and heavy industries, appraisals and valuations, site investigations, filtration and sewer disposal plants, municipal services, expressways, bridges, highways, hydro-electric power plants and technical reports.

These appointments are in line with the continuing expansion of this firm which has been engaged in major Canadian engineering projects for more than thirty-five years.

Supporting Surveyer Nenniger & Chênevert would be French dam experts Coyne & Bellier. It was on their recommendation that Hydro-Québec had opted for a multiple-arch dam instead of a concrete gravity dam. While the latter seemed appropriate to the site, a multiple-arch dam would be a spectacular demonstration of Quebec's new-found confidence.

The news was greeted with cheers up at Manicouagan, where Surveyer, Nenniger & Chênevert's geologists were finalizing their studies. Leading them was Sam Charalambakis, a former geology professor from Greece. Dagenais had just convinced him to leave H. G. Acres and join his team. Charalambakis spoke little English or French, but had an amazing ability to determine geological conditions with a glance at surface topography. He would need every ounce of his talent for Manic-5; the site turned out to be full of geological surprises.

One of the first was a deep V-shaped gravel-filled gorge that snaked up the centre of the riverbed. In early 1961, Hydro-Québec and Surveyer, Nenniger & Chênevert opted to use an ICOS wall to seal it at the upstream cofferdam. A series of closely fitted wells would be filled with concrete to create a watertight barrier. It was the same technique that had saved the *La Presse* newspaper building eight years before, but here, it would be used on an unprecedented scale.

The second hurdle appeared in early 1963. On the recommendation of American geological consultant Ed Burwell, a trench had been dug along the foundation to check for irregularities in the bedrock. The investigation had revealed evidence of sand-filled fissures under the lower right bank—not unlike the fractures that had brought down the arch dam at Malpasset in France only years earlier. They seemed to be as wide as 30 centimetres in places, and who knew how deep they were?

Charalambakis needed someone who could assess the scale and depth of the fissures. Claude Poulin, one of his geologists, volunteered his brother, Rock.

"The guy has spent the last seven years locating half-inch threads of precious metals at mines in Abitibi," he said. "He'll surely be able to map foot-wide fissures."

Rock Poulin at first expressed reservations when Charalambakis called to offer him the job. He had worked hard to make a good career for himself in mining. Besides, he knew nothing about dams.

"That's exactly why we want you," Charalambakis said. "We need a geologist who sees the rock from the bottom up, not the top down."

In the spring of 1964, Poulin, a five-foot-four dynamo, became Manic-5's Resident Geologist. He immediately began

Sam Charalambakis (on the phone) and his colleagues using a camera to conduct geological observations at Manic-5.

A plaster model of the dam is tested in Montreal.

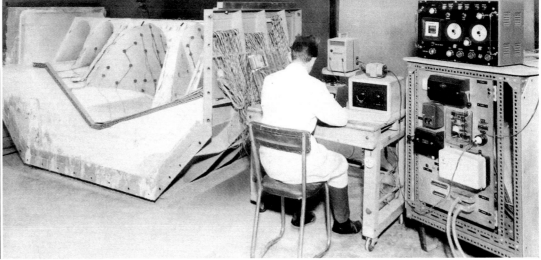

Lili Rheti's sketch of the first concrete being placed for Manic-5 at the absolute bottom of the gorge, finally located 46 metres below the riverbed.

An intricate system of cables and buckets was used for concreting at Manic-5.

blasting was needed. "It's simple," he told the dynamiters. "Call me when there is no more red."

With the major geological hurdles out of the way, concreting kicked into overdrive. An intricate system of cables and buckets had been strung high overhead to bring the 2 million cubic metres of concrete needed for the dam from a nearby plant that had been designed by Surveyer, Nenniger & Chênevert. With each fresh bucket, the dam's 13 arches slowly took shape. From a distance the structure began to resemble a Moorish castle. From up close, it was simply breathtaking.

EXPANSION OR OPERATIONS?

Now that the firm had seven partners, it was important that each have a defined role, otherwise, they were liable to step on one another's toes. In April 1959, Nenniger became Head of Operations, assisted by Turcke and Provost. Chênevert took over Development and Promotion, assisted by Hahn and Dagenais. Surveyer was still in charge of the "general conduct of the firm."

Hahn and Dagenais wasted no time in moving the firm into new markets. In the fall of 1959, they oversaw the acquisition of its first subsidiary, a printing company called Ozal (later renamed Reprotech). The following year, a soil analysis firm called Terratech was created, and a marketing office with the name SNC International was opened in New York. Hahn had received a letter from an American client addressed to Surveyer, Nenniger and *Chevrolet*. It had been good for a laugh at the office, but there was nothing funny about a client who could not remember your name. Hahn thought it best to use SNC south of the border.

The two development champions also began travelling to drum up business abroad. Dagenais took a trip to South America sponsored by the Canadian Department of Industry and Commerce. Soon afterwards, Hahn left for Asia on a similar mission.

investigating the fissures using techniques from the mining sector. The results confirmed Charalambakis's fears. Some areas that had already been excavated had to be blasted down as much as another metre.

Each additional excavation was greeted by howls of protest by those who were trying to control costs. Tired of constantly debating the need for re-excavations, Poulin grabbed a can of red paint and drew large Xs wherever additional

HYDRO PROJECTS LARGE AND SMALL

MANIC-5 STOLE ALL THE HEADLINES, BUT SURVEYER, NENNIGER & CHÊNEVERT ALSO WORKED ON SEVERAL SMALLER HYDROPOWER PROJECTS LIKE THE RAPIDES-DES-ÎLES DAM AND POWERHOUSE IN SOUTHWESTERN QUEBEC TO SUPPLY POWER TO LOCAL INDUSTRY. WHEN HYDRO-QUÉBEC AWARDED THE FIRM THE CONTRACT IN JANUARY 1965, IT WAS ADAMANT THAT THE FACILITY BE UP AND RUNNING BY OCTOBER 1966. MARCEL CÔTÉ'S TEAM EMPLOYED SEVERAL INNOVATIONS TO SUCCESSFULLY FAST-TRACK THE PROJECT.

Turcke, meanwhile, was left to hold down the fort in Montreal. By September, he was finding it difficult with all the talk of expansions and acquisitions. Every meeting of the partners now dragged on interminably with discussions of new business development ventures. "We don't even have time to solve mundane problems related to running the firm, like hiring new engineers," he complained. He had even had to turn down a project for a tire factory for lack of staff.

The situation came to a head at the end of the year when some clients began grumbling about delays. Surveyer had mostly been supportive of the push for development, but this was unacceptable. He felt the need to remind the partners what their first commitment was.

"As you know, we have worked for 50 years to build up the reputation of our firm," he said. "But a handful of dissatisfied customers could tarnish that reputation in a few short months." Surveyer's opinion, always measured and sober, still carried enormous weight. They all agreed that something needed to be done to ensure current clients always came first.

After discussions, the partners resolved that, "in principle, Surveyer, Nenniger & Chênevert should favour expansion insofar as each possibility can be discussed at the time it arises and a decision arrived at." In other words, they would ensure they kept existing customers happy while looking for new ones.

A SEVEN-HEADED MONSTER

In August of 1960, while flipping through an issue of *Business Week* magazine, Hahn came across an article that described how a consultant named Douglas Russell had helped save an architectural firm. Its six partners had been incapable of getting along, but Russell got them talking again.

Hahn did not think Surveyer, Nenniger & Chênevert was about to collapse, but there were undeniable similarities. He circulated copies to the partners with a brief note: "I found this article interesting enough to make copies for each of you."

Surveyer was fascinated with the article and called a meeting on the subject. Now 81 and afflicted with emphysema, he generally spent no more than a few hours a week at the office, and always in the company of his nurse. Surveyer wanted the partners to sort out their communication problems now, while he was still around.

"Jack has distributed this article, and I think it may hold the answer to some of the difficulties we are currently facing," began Surveyer. His voice, which had always been soft, had now dwindled to little more than a whisper. "I think we should have him in and see what he recommends for us."

The consultant arrived at the offices of Surveyer, Nenniger & Chênevert on April 10, 1961. One by one, the partners met with him in private to speak about their expectations, ambitions, and frustrations. Some had great burdens to get off their chest, while others simply expressed concern about the direction of the firm. Within two days, Russell had heard more than enough to render a verdict.

"I regret to have to tell you that your firm is a seven-headed monster," he began. "If you don't succeed in understanding one another, I give you less than two years. You're going to go under."

The partners were stunned. Yes things were bad, but could they really have degenerated to that point? Russell explained that the problem was not the structure of the firm, but a total lack of communication. He left them with several suggestions about how to better share information among themselves.

It was a wake up call for everyone. All agreed that the firm had to come first. They resolved to talk to one another more, share information, and, most importantly, listen.

THE PASSING
OF ARTHUR SURVEYER

On April 17, 1961, only a week after Russell had delivered his disquieting verdict, Arthur Surveyer passed away at his home, surrounded by his wife and children. It was almost 50 years to the day that he had opened his first office.

His many accomplishments were reflected in the obituaries that appeared in the press. He was called a "man of broad culture and great qualities of heart and mind" in *La Presse*. *The Montreal Gazette* said that the city had "lost more than an eminent engineer in the death of Dr. Arthur Surveyer; it has lost a mind whose views, disciplined by an engineer's training and experience, looked upon many other aspects of Canadian life with precision and independence."

The passing of the firm's great founder signaled the end of an era: there was no doubt that the time of small engineering projects and slide rules was coming to an end. Engineering was being transformed by the first hints of globalization and the introduction of powerful new technologies like the computer.

On a hot July morning, barely three months after Surveyer's death, a massive IBM 1620 mainframe was hoisted by crane up to the top floor of the Keefer Building. Walter Stensch watched nervously from among a crowd of spectators as it rose. It had taken Stensch a while to convince the partners to pay the $4,000 per month it would cost to rent the machine. Now that they had agreed, he was hoping the floor would bear its weight.

Some colleagues doubted it would. "Hey Walter, what goes boom, boom, boom, boom, boom, boom, BANG!?" they teased. "It's the sound of your computer falling through the Keefer Building and hitting the basement!"

Turcke had been one of the first at Surveyer, Nenniger & Chênevert to see the potential in computers. The previous year, he had sent Stensch and fellow engineer René Landry to IBM's Montreal office to calculate the stresses on Manic-5. It was expensive at $30 per hour, but no human could work through equations with 20 variables so rapidly.

IBM's computer had helped Stensch accelerate the design work on the dam. In the end, that was enough to convince the partners that it was a sound investment.

Arthur Surveyer

SNC's first computer, an IBM 1620, was hoisted by crane to the 10th floor of the Keefer Building on Sainte-Catherine Street in 1961. From left to right: Guy Beaudin, Douglas Duncan, Walter Stensch, Roméo Filiatrault, and Jack Hahn.

The Keefer Building in downtown Montreal.

LAMARRE VALOIS INTERNATIONAL

Work progressing on the Dahomey (now Benin) land transportation project in 1967.

Bernard Lamarre suspects the boom in Quebec's construction market will come to a crashing halt before the end of the 1960s. He takes preventive measures by founding Lamarre Valois International to pursue contracts abroad. A first study is won in Dahomey in 1967, followed by an important contract for the Route de l'Unité et de l'Amitié Canadienne in Niger. The contract gets off to a difficult start in 1971, threatening to sideline LVLVA's international ambitions. To head off disaster, Bernard Lamarre names his younger brother Project Manager for the job. Jacques Lamarre's surprising success earns him a reputation as one of the firm's "firemen."

Yves Beauregard

One of Lamarre Valois International's first projects was a comprehensive land transportation study in Dahomey (now Benin), West Africa, which resulted in improvements to over 600 kilometres of roads.

E ven during the headiest days of the Quiet Revolution, when contracts seemed to be falling from the sky, Bernard Lamarre had foreseen the end. At the rate that major projects were being constructed, he knew a time would come when there would be almost nothing left to build in Quebec. Unless LVLVA had other markets to turn to, he reasoned, the firm's growth would hit a wall sometime in the late 1960s. So, in 1963, during the height of the Quebec construction boom, Lamarre and Jean-Pierre Valois created Lamarre Valois International.

Looking out at prospective markets, the partners saw that the best opportunities lay in French Africa. Canada had no colonial past, and LVLVA could offer the region North American technology in its own language. All they needed was someone who knew the region well enough to help them get a foot in the door. Lamarre's list of contacts once again yielded a promising candidate: Yves Beauregard, a classmate from his days at École Polytechnique who was now working for the United Nations where he oversaw international development projects.

Lamarre booked a flight to Cameroon, where Beauregard was stationed. During their meeting he peppered him with questions about the international engineering market, the pitfalls and the best opportunities. He asked about the inner workings of development agencies, and how best to win contracts. By the end of the talk, Lamarre knew he had the man for the job.

Beauregard was posted to Senegal in early 1964 as the President of Lamarre Valois International. Progress was slow at first, but things began looking up just as Quebec's engineering market went into the tailspin Lamarre had predicted.

In early 1967, Lamarre Valois International teamed up with Vancouver transportation specialists Norman D. Lee & Associates, to carry out a transportation study in Dahomey (now Benin). Beauregard had told Lamarre there were two ways a Canadian firm with no international experience could win contracts abroad: it could work with a Canadian development agency, or join forces with a firm that had international credentials, like Norman D. Lee.

The project was intended to help the West African country modernize its transportation system, but the most important component was a large-scale training program, whereby hundreds of locals would be instructed in the finer points of equipment purchasing and road maintenance.

Dahomey and the World Bank were pleased with the project, but it yielded few profits. The firm had made the mistake of negotiating the contract in American dollars, and currency fluctuations had cut into its fees. It was a hard lesson, but the financial disappointment was more than offset by the exhilaration of having successfully completed a first international project.

THE ROUTE DE L'UNITÉ ET DE L'AMITIÉ CANADIENNE

In 1969, Beauregard introduced Lamarre to the President of Niger. It was a fruitful meeting that revealed much to him about the needs of the West African country. He learned the Nigeriens were interested in improving their roads and wanted to start with a 430-kilometre highway between the towns of Gouré and N'Guigmi in the south.

When Lamarre returned to Canada, he contacted Paul Gérin-Lajoie, the President of the Canadian International

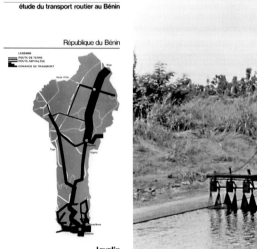

Development Agency (CIDA), to see if he was interested. It turned out to be just the sort of development project Gérin-Lajoie was looking for. The year before, Canada's Prime Minister, Pierre Elliott Trudeau, had given him instructions to shift the focus of the country's development programs from Asia to French Africa.

The Route de l'Unité et de l'Amitié Canadienne, as the project came to be called, was considered a fool's errand by some European firms with experience in Africa. They doubted the project team could get adequate water and materials, let alone build a road in the middle of the desert. Bernard Lamarre saw things differently. Dahomey had taught LVLVA a few things about working in Africa, and CIDA would be there to guarantee financing, one of the riskier aspects of doing business in a developing country.

The Route de l'Unité did not get off to a good start when LVLVA's project team arrived in early 1972. Only a handful of the team members had ever ventured outside Quebec, and they now found themselves living in a tiny base camp in the middle of the African desert. Many had difficulty adjusting to the extreme heat and barren landscape. There were also the very real difficulties of building a road in the desert that the Europeans had warned of. The vibrations of the power generators caused them to sink into the sand, and the sophisticated North American graders (levelling trucks) broke down in the harsh African climate.

Bernard Lamarre followed the project with increasing concern. By the spring of 1973, he had become exasperated with its snail-like progress. Three project managers had given up before even one kilometre of road had been completed. Each had come back utterly defeated, saying that the project was impossible and the people unmanageable.

Lamarre realized LVLVA was facing a moment of truth. He had expected difficulties, but outright failure was not an option. Either the firm succeeded in Niger, or it would have to rethink its international ambitions. He called his younger brother Jacques into his office.

"Everything is going extremely badly in Niger," he said. "CIDA is threatening to take us off the project and never give

INROADS IN DISTANT LANDS
NICK LEE, A SURVEYOR FOR THE NEW SUBSIDIARY PHOTOGRAPHIC SURVEYS, WAS THE FIRST LVLVA EMPLOYEE SENT TO NIGER FOR THE ROUTE DE L'UNITÉ PROJECT. IN LATE 1971, WITH AN ARMED GUARD AND A DRIVER, LEE CHARTED A PATH FOR THE ROAD THAT WOULD RUN AS CLOSE AS POSSIBLE TO WATER SOURCES AND CONSTRUCTION MATERIALS.

us another one. One of us has to go over there and sort things out. Will you go?"

Jacques was 29 with a wife and two young children. Uprooting them would not be easy, but then his wife, Céline, had always supported his career. He was sure she would agree to accompany him if he explained the importance of the project.

In the summer of 1973, Lamarre and his family arrived in Niger's capital, Niamey, and then took a five-hour flight in

Jacques Lamarre (second from left) in Niger with General Kountché, who became president of the country in 1974, and Jean-Pierre Goyer, the Canadian Minister of Supply and Services.

a DC-3 to the isolated work camp in Gouré. The situation was indeed as bad as he had been told. In the sunburned faces around him, Jacques could see the hopelessness that sets in when a project seems doomed.

At his first meeting as Project Manager, Lamarre sought to reset everything to zero and make a fresh start. "We need to create a proper base for this project," he began. "First, we are going to repair the equipment, and then we are going to start being honest and open with one another."

It took weeks to get the equipment running properly again. The sand was cleaned out of the generators and crushers, then they were placed on more solid concrete foundations. The instruments of the graders were reinforced and protected from the blowing sand and extreme heat.

Once the hardware was in order, Lamarre worked on bringing more accountability into the mix. "We have had a terrible time meeting the schedule for this project," he said. "You are going to tell me what is the minimum that you will be able to achieve in a week. I leave it up to you, but remember, this is your minimum, so there is no excuse for not doing it."

To Lamarre's surprise, not only did the team members begin meeting their work commitments, they began surpassing them by a large margin. He treated the local workers the same way and got the same results. It was so simple, he realized: be well organized, treat people fairly, get realistic commitments from them, and hold them to their word.

Things were soon moving forward again. Even the medical trailer, staffed by only one nurse and stocked with an assortment of over-the-counter medications, began to run like a well-oiled machine. It was soon treating 50 people a day, most of whom were locals who had nothing to do with the project.

The following year, with 105 kilometres of road completed, Jacques was called back to Montreal. His surprising success on the Route de l'Unité had earned him a reputation as one of the firm's "firemen." Now he was needed to unblock an important project for the Montreal Olympics.

His replacement in Niger was Pierre Ranger. He had been hired in 1966 by Jean-Paul Dionne on a probationary basis. After three months, Dionne had taken him on full time without reservation. Ranger had spent the last seven years cutting

Construction of the Route de l'Unité et de l'Amitié Canadienne, 430 kilometres of road between the cities of Gouré and N'Guigmi in Niger.

his teeth supervising road and bridge contracts throughout Quebec. Dionne could think of no one better to carry on the work in Niger.

Two years later, Ranger and the project team had taken the Route de l'Unité from 105 kilometres to 430. A modern road had been built in the middle of the desert. In the engineering world of the time, it was a feat akin to pulling a rabbit out of a hat.

With a foothold in the African market, Lamarre Valois International now sent representatives to two other promising regions. Frank Sutcliffe took on responsibility for the Caribbean and South America, and Jean Gagnon began overseeing marketing activities in Asia. It was the nucleus of the global network that would soon help establish LVLVA as one of the most international engineering firms in the world.

WELLS, WELLS AND MORE WELLS

The Route de l'Unité became an instrument of development for Niger, but the 44 wells drilled to supply the project team with water were of even greater interest to the locals. Each time a well appeared, they would move closer to it to access the precious resource.

Marcel Dufour, the head of the LVLVA subsidiary National Boring and Sounding, had taken note of the great popularity of the wells. In 1972, he attempted to buy a small Ontario well drilling firm called International Water Supply. The acquisition looked great on paper, but the firm's management was unmoved by Dufour's grandiose plans for conquering Africa's well-drilling market. After several failed rounds of negotiations, Dufour opted to build a well-drilling company from the ground up instead.

In August 1973, Dufour created Hydrogeo. A former manager at International Water Supply named Jean Gauvin became its President and first employee. He immediately set out to build a team that would be equal to Dufour's lofty ambitions.

After several smaller mandates, Hydrogeo won a major contract in the Ivory Coast in June of 1976. Aware that economic development and access to clean water went hand in hand, the country had founded a state-owned company called Forexi to improve its water supply. One of its first contracts was to drill 7,200 wells, mainly in rural regions. Hydrogeo was hired by CIDA to provide Forexi with technical assistance.

Gauvin was posted to the country as the project's first Technical Director. When he fell ill a few months later, he was replaced by José de Carvalho, another former International Water Supply employee. Dufour had persuaded him to take the job when it looked like Gauvin would have to come back to Montreal for medical treatment. Gauvin's illness had prevented him from giving Forexi his full attention, and the company was now plagued by inefficiencies.

"This will be a booming business in Africa, but if we're going to take advantage of those opportunities, we have to get things running smoothly in the Ivory Coast," Dufour told de Carvalho. "I promise you'll have my full support."

When he arrived in January 1977, de Carvalho quickly realized that the difficulties Forexi was having were the result

An offical visit by President Kountché of Niger to the project site. Facing him are José de Carvalho (centre), representing contractor International Water Supply, and Pierre Ranger for Lamarre Valois International.

of poor training and substandard equipment. The bedrock in the region was deep and the holes had a tendency to cave in before casings could be inserted. Without proper drilling machines and the right know-how, the job was almost impossible.

Using a $5-million line of credit from CIDA, de Carvalho went shopping in Canada for state-of-the-art equipment that would solve the problem. He purchased pneumatic drilling machines as well as steel casings that could be rapidly inserted into the holes to keep them from caving in.

With the new equipment en route for Africa, de Carvalho then proceeded to weed out unproductive workers and ensure promising ones were properly trained and supervised. For that he enlisted the help of new team members like André Béland, a hydrogeologist and top-notch supervisor.

Things soon improved dramatically, and CIDA took note in its report on the project. "In evaluating the mission, we can affirm that, a little more than five years after its creation, Forexi has attained a remarkable level of organization, and that its technical execution capacity is impressive." CIDA went on to say that it was "largely thanks to Hydrogeo."

CHAPTER 11

SNC ABROAD

SNC rides its success on Manic-5 all the way to India for the Idukki arch dam. The project is the firm's first contract outside North America and a major profile raiser. Back home, a series of consultants are invited to help the firm resolve tensions between its management. The decade draws to a close with Camille Dagenais being named President and CEO of SNC Enterprises, an incorporated company with employees as its shareholders. Share ownership serves as a powerful incentive for the firm's managers, who proceed to go out and win major industrial projects in Turkey and Algeria.

The Idukki arch dam in Kerala State, India.

In 1963, two new partners were named, bringing the total to eight. From left to right: Jack Hahn, Roger Provost, Georges Chênevert, Emil Nenniger Jr., Emil Nenniger, Roméo Filiatrault, John Turcke, and Camille Dagenais.

Raymond Surveyer

In 1963, two new partners were brought in to balance out the power dynamic at Surveyer, Nenniger & Chênevert: Roméo Filiatrault, the well-liked Director of Personnel, and Emil Nenniger Jr., who, like his father, excelled in industrial processes.

Arthur Surveyer's son Raymond was also moving up the ranks. He may not have been a partner, but he had the inborn clout that came from being the founder's son. He had joined in 1961, with the intention of tending to his father's legacy.

Unfortunately, adding more cooks to the kitchen only caused further complications. It was soon clear that increasing the number of leaders, no matter how talented, was not the solution. What was needed now was a single, unquestioned chief.

Later that year, following discussions with the partners, Jack Hahn called Douglas Russell to see if he would return. Russell said he was tied up with other commitments, but suggested Hahn contact a management consulting firm called Leadership Resources. There was a good corporate psychologist there named Richard Ericson who might be able to help.

In January of 1964, Ericson became their last hope. Over the next four months, he conducted interviews with the partners and department heads, gave presentations, and handed out copious reading assignments. Slowly, he began to piece together a picture of what was ailing Surveyer, Nenniger & Chênevert.

On May 8, he gathered the partners together in the conference room to deliver his preliminary report, and it was not good. Ericson said that problems had been allowed to go unresolved for too long, and that old personal tensions among the firm's management and employees had only been exacerbated by phenomenal growth.

The upside was that he found deep reserves of loyalty among those he had interviewed. "Most of the people with whom I have spoken have offered various examples of evidence of their pride in being associated with the firm," Ericson said. But he hastened to add that their goodwill was not inexhaustible. "Urgent action is required to ensure your firm does not begin bleeding its talent."

Desperate to resolve the situation, the partners were willing to go along with any solution that Ericson proposed. But when he suggested T-Groups (Training Groups) for the firm's entire top management, they were no longer so sure. The latest fad in corporate psychology, T-Groups involved heart-to-heart discussions meant to foster mutual understanding. For a group of logically minded engineers, that was about as appealing as an ice bath.

Ericson probed to see what the partners thought of the idea. Nenniger Sr. and Chênevert did not want to participate. Turcke and Dagenais were unsure if it would help, while Hahn, Filiatrault, Provost, and Nenniger Jr. were silently apprehensive. No one was eager to endure such an arduous exercise, but then they had run out of options.

What followed would be remembered by some as a crucial turning point in the history of the firm, and by others as the most gruelling ordeal of their lives. The T-Groups were meant to tear through their tough exteriors to the common humanity of each man. The participants were encouraged to tell their life stories, reveal their vulnerabilities, and share their most secret dreams.

Many were surprised by what they learned about their colleagues during these bare-all discussions. Hahn told the harrowing story of his midnight escape from Germany at the beginning of the Second World War. Turcke revealed that he had come to Canada from Switzerland to prove that he could succeed on his own, without the support of his wealthy and overbearing parents.

The most difficult sessions were the no-holds-barred peer critiques, where participants were encouraged to get everything off their chests. One evening, several months into the T-Groups, Dagenais, a highly self-disciplined and reserved man, thought he had endured all he could take and came to within a hair's breadth of pulling out. He was not alone; Filiatrault and Hahn were also close to the breaking point. All had to marshal reserves of inner strength to push on.

Ericson gave everyone a short break to lick their wounds before starting them on D-Groups (Development Groups). Now that they had gotten to know each other better, it was time to choose a leader to give the firm badly needed direction.

On a cool morning in September of 1964, the partners gathered in a small meeting room at the Tom Wheeler Club in Mont-Tremblant, Quebec, for the first D-Group meeting. Moments later Ericson walked in and, without saying a word, drew a large triangle on an easel at the front of the room. He wrote "Friendly Helper" at the top, "Tough Battler" at the lower left point, and "Logical Thinker" at the bottom right.

"These," he explained, "are the three types of leadership. Each of you will have your own triangle like this. One at a time, the others will place a sticker on the spot that best describes you."

John Turcke went first, putting one sticker somewhere on each of his colleagues' triangles. Dagenais went next, then Hahn. Soon each man had completed the exercise, and it was time to examine the findings. There were few surprises. Soft-spoken and mild-mannered Provost was a Friendly Helper. Filiatrault fell into the same category, although some of his stickers were in the Tough Battler corner. Turcke and Nenniger Jr.

TIME	WEDNESDAY	THURSDAY	FRIDAY	SATURDAY	SUNDAY	MONDAY	TUESDAY
	SURVEYER, NENNIGER AND CHENEVERT Partners' Retreat, August 19-25, 1964 AGENDA						
8:00 to 9:00	ARRIVE AT	* * * * * Dialogue: Provost and Ericson	* * * BREAKFAST * * * * * Dialogue: Filiatrault and Ericson	Dialogue: Nenniger Jr. and Ericson	* * * * * Dialogue: Hahn and Ericson	* * * * * Dialogue: Turcke and Ericson	* * * * Dialogue: Dagenais and Ericson
9:00 to 10:30	LODGE AND SETTLE IN ROOMS	T-Group	Enacting SNC Role-Play Simulations	T - Group	Group Dynamics Observation Session	T - Group	Preliminary Exploration of Long-range SNC Problems
10:30-10:45		* * * * *	* COFFEE	BREAK * * *	* * * * * *	* * * *	* * * *
10:45 to 12:00	Opening General Session	T-Group	SNC Simulations (Continued)	T - Group	Group Dynamics Observation Session	T - Group	Preliminary Problems Exploration (Continued)
12:00 to 1:30	* * * *	* * * * *	* * LUNCH * *	* * * * *	* * * * *	* * * * *	* * * *
1:30 to 3:00	Discussion of Partners' "Values and Goals"	Role-Play Simulation	T - Group	RECREATION ACTIVITY	T - Group	Evaluative Discussion: "What have we learned?"	Concluding General Session
3:00-3:15	* * * * *	* * * * *	COFFEE	BREAK * * *	* * * * *	* * * * *	CONFERENCE ADJOURNS
3:15 to 4:30	"Values and Goals" Discussion, Cont'd.	Creating Role-Plays from SNC data	T - Group	RECREATION ACTIVITY	T - Group	Evaluative Discussion: "To what must we yet attend?"	
4:30 to 7:30	* * * * DINNER	AND	RECRE	ATION	* * * * *		
7:30 to 9:30	DIALOGUES: (1) Jack and Camille (2) John and Romeo (3) Roger and Emile	DIALOGUES: (1) Jack and John (2) Camille and Emile (3) Roger and Romeo	DIALOGUES: (1) Jack and Roger (2) Camille and John (3) Romeo and Emile	OPEN FOR APPROPRIATE WORK (TO BE DECIDED)	DIALOGUES: (1) Jack and Romeo (2) Camille and Roger (3) John and Emile	DIALOGUES: (1) Jack and Emile (2) Camille and Romeo (3) John and Roger	
Before Bed-time	* * * *	* * * Entries	in Your	"Retreat Diary"	* *	* * * * * *	

The gruelling T-Groups schedule for the week of August 19, 1964.

were generally Logical Thinkers, while Dagenais and Hahn were clearly seen as Tough Battlers.

Everyone knew that the demands, pressures, and challenges of the engineering world required leaders who would not give up and would grind through the most difficult obstacles. It was no surprise, then, when the partners voted unanimously to make Dagenais, a very tough battler, leader at one of the last D-Group sessions in February of 1965. He was more than simply determined, however; he also inspired confidence—something that the firm needed now more than ever.

It had been a tough lesson in corporate dynamics. They had learned the hard way that a firm that could not renew itself internally would be forced to resort to drastic measures to do so. But though they were bruised by the ordeal, they knew they had done the right thing. Finally, for the first time in close to a decade, it felt like hope had returned to Surveyer, Nenniger & Chênevert.

EXPERTISE FOR INDIA

In the summer of 1963, as concreting was starting on Manic-5, Jack Hahn received a phone call from a contact in Vancouver. Bill Waymark, a former consultant with the engineering firm T. Ingledow & Associates, was looking for a Canadian engineering company with expertise in arch dams.

Waymark said he had contacts at the Central Power & Water Commission (CPWC) in New Delhi. He had learned that the CPWC planned to build a massive concrete arch dam in the state of Kerala in southwest India. If Surveyer, Nenniger & Chênevert was interested, he would make the necessary introductions.

While performing preliminary studies in 1964, Frank Tordon (far left) was amazed at the dense tropical jungle and the wild elephants roaming the river's edge.

Waymark had contacted the right man: Hahn was eager to expand into international markets. With the expertise that the firm had acquired on Manic-5, the Indian hydroelectric sector was an ideal first choice.

Camille Dagenais accompanied Waymark to India to meet R.P. Nair, the Chief Engineer at the Kerala State Electricity Board. Nair had heard of the multiple-arch dam Surveyer, Nenniger & Chênevert was building on the Manicouagan, and was eager to talk shop. It did not take long for Dagenais to convince him that they were capable of carrying out his project as well.

By mid-January 1964, Geotechnical Engineer Frank Tordon was in India to perform preliminary studies with the help of a local team. One of the first Canadians to ever set foot in the region, he was amazed by what he found. The Idukki gorge descended into dense tropical jungle. Wild elephants roamed the edge of the river and monkeys frolicked in the hibiscus. The annual monsoons had forced the local tribe to build its shacks high in the trees. It was unlike anything he had ever seen.

Tordon soon realized that under the site's exotic surface lay a solid foundation of granite. His findings were included in a report alongside the upbeat financial data collected by the firm's new subsidiary, Systems, Operations Research and Economic Studies (SORES). In January 1965, Surveyer, Nenniger & Chênevert was awarded the design and construction supervision contract for Idukki.

It was the firm's first major international contract, and the first time it would be designing a concrete arch dam on its own. Dagenais, a fervent believer in the value of consultants, made arch dam specialists like André Géhin of France and American Frank Nickell available to his team. There was only one condition: "You can take all the advice from them you want," he told his engineers, "but they cannot design the dam."

For that, the firm had Bob Griesbach and Serge Valent. The greatest challenge they faced was an enormous rock knob on the left bank of the gorge. The protrusion was precisely where the dam had to go, but the cost of levelling it was deemed prohibitive. Finally, after checking with

the consultants and the firm's Chief Dam Designer, Walter Stensch, the engineers decided to rotate the axis of the dam to avoid it altogether. It was an unorthodox solution, but they were sure it could be done safely.

A PROBLEM AND A SOLUTION

In January 1968, a geological team led by Rock Poulin arrived in India to conduct detailed tests on Idukki's gorge. The geologist would again have to be the bearer of bad news when his investigations uncovered an unforeseen problem. In November that year, Poulin noticed a small patch of vegetation on the underside of the infamous rock knob. That suggested a fissure deep enough to be fed with a constant supply of water. Subsequent tests confirmed his fears.

He knew how the news would be received in Montreal, but this was not information he could sit on. The Idukki region had more than its share of earthquakes, and a strong tremor might one day dislodge the knob, sending it crashing into the dam.

Poulin immediately telexed Dagenais, who insisted on flying to India to investigate the situation for himself. If Poulin was right, then initial investigations had overlooked it. "Show me this crack," Dagenais grumbled to Poulin when he disembarked from the plane. "I want to see it with my own eyes."

The geologist went over his new data with Dagenais and took him up to the rock knob. It was soon obvious that he was right, but with concreting under way, dynamiting the boulder would be far too risky. The only option was to permanently wedge it in place with a series of precisely engineered support columns.

When Poulin drove Dagenais back to the airport, he got a discreet pat on the back. "Good job," Dagenais whispered before boarding the plane, "but make sure that knob doesn't fall on the dam."

The job of overseeing the implementation of designs went to Marcel Tremblay, the Chief Engineer from Manic-5. Burly and highly

Local manual labour at Idukki, and high-tech calculations being performed by Gordon Gerry (left) and Walter Stensch in Montreal.

Rock Poulin at Idukki (also sometimes referred to as Idikki).

In 1968, with concreting on the dam under way, Rock Poulin discovered a fissure on the underside of the rock knob. A series of precisely engineered support columns were designed to permanently wedge the knob in place.

Marcel Tremblay

competent, Tremblay took on tremendous responsibility as the on-site Project Manager for Idukki. Because communication was slow and decisions often needed to be made without delay, he and his team had to be almost completely self-sufficient.

The lack of regular contact with Montreal also had the unexpected benefit of bringing the members of the project team closer together with their Indian counterparts. They relied on one another to navigate the myriad ups and downs that made up the day-to-day reality of project life. As a result, mutual respect quickly grew between them.

Tremblay certainly felt that working in India made him more sensitive to other cultures. "On long jobs abroad you have to learn to work, co-operate with, and accept a different type of human being, a completely different way of thinking, a different society," he said in the October 1974 edition of the internal newsletter.

A NEW TEAM

In April 1965, while Idukki was still at the studies stage, Dagenais was named President of SNC Inc. With the help of Hahn and Turcke, he had finally convinced Nenniger and Chênevert to create an incorporated company. The senior partners had not been ready to dissolve the partnership, however. For now, SNC Inc. and the partnership would have to coexist.

Dagenais wasted no time in creating a parallel management team for the incorporated company. He made Hahn Vice-President of Planning and Marketing, Turcke Vice-President of Engineering, Filiatrault Vice-President of Personnel, Provost Assistant to the President, and Nenniger Jr. Director of Technical Development.

Dagenais' Executive Committee also included some standouts who were not partners, like Jean-Paul Gourdeau, the new Vice-President of Operations. Chênevert had hired him in 1961 to build up the firm's Municipal Department, which specialized in sewer systems and water pollution studies. He had since demonstrated iron-clad integrity and a willingness to do what was needed to ensure that his projects were successful. Dagenais had been eyeing him for the top operations job for some time.

Another was Dick Balfour, the new Vice-President of Construction. Hahn had recently brought him over from Brown & Root to help the firm develop an engineering, procurement and construction (EPC) capability. In an EPC contract, an engineering firm took on responsibility for the entire project. Balfour knew the key to success in the EPC world was to accurately estimate costs, and he had already found a pioneering expert in the field, a young man by the name of Ted Papucciyan.

Dagenais now had a team that suited his vision of the company. The only thing standing in the way was the old partnership structure. One of the main advantages of incorporation was the ability to put profits into development, but the persisting partnership agreement made that impossible. Something had to give.

THE "SNC BIBLE"

On June 2, 1966, Dagenais distributed a highly confidential report to the members of his Executive Committee, composed of Hahn, Turcke, Filiatrault, and Gourdeau. He called it the *Special Report by the President to the Executive Committee Members*. The outline for the document had come to him in a flash of inspiration while on a fishing trip in northern Quebec. With nothing to write on, he had hastily sketched his ideas on his paper lunch bag. It was an inauspicious beginning for a text that would eventually become the famous "SNC Bible."

It was obvious that each of its 32 pages had been forged in the fires of SNC's recent difficulties. "As we have learned at SNC, success in the long run can only be achieved with the help of all," Dagenais wrote. "Low morale, lack of co-operation, and a lack of trust and confidence will eventually destroy the organization."

Dagenais never wanted to see the company teeter on the precipice again. The solution, as he saw it, lay in a new set of rules, which he outlined in four "Creeds," 10 "Policies," and an all-encompassing Code of Ethics. Ironically, the new rules were actually a formalized version of the old principles long espoused by Arthur Surveyer.

They addressed the need to balance maximum profits with the best interests of clients, employees, and suppliers. They touched on the importance of loyalty, integrity, competence, and of respecting the dignity of each member of the firm. They insisted that the selection

Jean-Paul Gourdeau

Dick Balfour

Dagenais' *Special Report by the President to the Executive Committee Members,* a.k.a. the SNC Bible.

Dagenais' fishing-trip jottings put SNC on course to success

nding the US economy. 'We have tablished ourselves in three of the regions pinpointed in our ten-sterplan and set up offices in New e says. 'The US is going to be ortant to us. After all, it is the ngineering market in the world just down the road.'

ng on his career from his le 39th-floor office in Complexe Desjardins, ays: 'Mine is a very interesting s a very risky business, a very business, but it's not the business.

ople make more money with hat are not as complex as e that fellow Colonel Sanders money with his Kentucky n than we do. But money ng — a lot of people do be the best. We may not be ut we want to get there.

ose,' confides Dagenais, recent vacation in Fort re his 24-year-old son beat hardly a fair match since

ughts of retiring? 'I don't ays retiring from certain onds cautiously. 'I've om different jobs that he presidency of the nsulting Engineers of Canadian Nuclear I'm still very heavily rnational Commission I'll be running for the November.'

er's principle that level of incompet-'I maintain that you of incompetence if e thing. Find other e best at and you

and promotion of personnel be based solely on performance and qualifications, and that SNC always provide services and products of the highest quality.

Dagenais felt that the sky would be the limit for SNC if everyone played by these rules. In four short years, he envisioned doubling the company's profits by expanding across Canada. But conquering the domestic market would just be a first step. The ultimate goal was to make SNC the biggest and most successful engineering company in the world. Period.

The *Report* contained something else, which had nothing to do with the future and everything to do with the past. Buried within its pages was a radical solution to the impasse over the partnership. In a section called "Some Comments re: Present Partners of SNC," Dagenais proposed a way of ending the deadlock. He suggested allowing the current partnership agreement to lapse when it came up for renewal. The equity of Nenniger and Chênevert would then be purchased by a new holding company, and they would be invited to become consultants.

He realized that while this was "an ideal solution from an organizational point of view, it might not be so from a human viewpoint." To make sure the process was as respectful and gentle as possible, Nenniger and Chênevert would be encouraged to offer "suggestions as to their further ownership and contribution to the firm."

SNC ENTERPRISES

While negotiations with Nenniger and Chênevert were under way, Dagenais checked off another item from his *Report*: he restructured the operations of SNC Inc. according to sectors of expertise (commercial, hydroelectric, industrial). The firm had previously been organized by disciplines (mechanical, electrical, structural), but such a system was impractical for larger engineering firms. The new structure would group everyone who worked on the same kinds of projects under a single manager. That way, when the company grew as Dagenais expected it to, each division would be able to oversee its own projects. It was a major change that caused some apprehension, so Dagenais launched a company-wide tour to explain the advantages of the new structure.

On April 11, 1967, after 10 months of negotiations, Nenniger and Chênevert were finally persuaded to terminate the partnership agreement. Dagenais deeply regretted having to force them out, but he saw no other way. As he had written in his *Report*, "No organization can survive not facing the truth, the reality of things, and doing what must be done, however difficult, for the good of all, and not a few." He was glad they had at least agreed to stay on as consultants.

With the partnership dissolved, Dagenais was able to create the holding company he had envisioned. During the last week of May 1967, SNC Enterprises Ltd. acquired the equity of all the former partners and began redistributing it to new employee shareholders.

Dagenais insisted the distribution be done systematically, according to criteria in his *Report*. Shareholders, it said, had to fall into one or more of six categories: they had to be administrators, salesmen, entrepreneurs, idea men, public figures, or at least have a good reputation that allowed them to obtain and hold clients. If they passed that test, they then had

EPC AMBITIONS

SNC ACQUIRED PENTAGON CONSTRUCTION IN 1969 TO BUILD UP ITS EPC LUMP SUM CAPABILITY. PENTAGON HAD EARNED A SOLID REPUTATION IN EASTERN CANADA AS A HEAVY CIVIL WORKS CONSTRUCTION CONTRACTOR CAPABLE OF DELIVERING QUALITY PROJECTS ON TIME.

Pentagon was awarded the construction contract for the town of Fermont in northern Quebec, including its wind-shielding wall.

to demonstrate leadership qualities like courage, judgment, integrity, and dedication. Dagenais proposed a list of 50-odd employee shareholders who, he felt, met those standards.

The largest portions of shares would go to the 12 members of SNC Enterprises' new board of directors. SNC may have only been a medium-sized private company, but Dagenais still felt a board was essential to ensure proper transparency and accountability. He would become the first Chairman, with Hahn, Turcke, Filiatrault, Gourdeau, Balfour, Raymond Surveyer, and several others as board members. He was

adamant that the board have real power and vowed to implement their collective decisions.

It had been a period of dizzying change at SNC. In the space of only seven years, the company had rocketed through its adolescence and reached early maturity. Somehow, while the breathtaking changes were occurring, the company had found the time to relocate its 650 employees to more spacious offices at 1500 De Maisonneuve Boulevard West, in Montreal. The Keefer Building, and the partnership, had both now become chapters in SNC's history.

SNC executives in 1968. From left to right: Roméo Filiatrault, Raymond Surveyer, Roger Provost, Camille Dagenais, John Turcke, Jean-Paul Gourdeau, and Guy Beaudin.

AGE OF THE ATOM

Completed in 1971, Gentilly 1 was the first nuclear power station built in Quebec.

Pierre Fortier

Alex Taylor

A fierce debate raged within Quebec government and business circles during the 1950s and 1960s. One side argued that the province was blessed with a massive hydropower potential that begged to be tapped. The Manicouagan-Outardes hydropower development was under way, and there were several other watercourses equally suited to power generation, such as the legendary La Grande River. Clearly, hydropower could meet Quebec's energy needs for many years to come.

The other side, whose most vocal spokesman was economist and future Quebec premier Jacques Parizeau, saw the great potential in nuclear power. They suggested building a series of generators all along the St. Lawrence River. This would put them closer to consumption areas, cutting the cost and avoiding myriad complications of transmission.

Jean-Claude Lessard, the new President of Hydro-Québec, was swayed by the nuclear argument. Above all, he liked the idea of having access to diverse sources of power. In 1966, the utility signed an agreement with Atomic Energy of Canada Limited (AECL) for a 250-megawatt nuclear test plant at Gentilly near Trois-Rivières. AECL's expertise was limited to reactors, however, so the Crown corporation hired SNC and Montreal Engineering (Monenco) for all the mechanical, thermal, structural, and electrical work.

Gentilly's experimental reactor would use light water instead of heavy water to transfer heat from its core to its turbines. Heavy water had the great benefit of slowing down neutrons accelerated by nuclear fission, but it was not cheap. If AECL's light-water prototype was proven stable, there would be considerable cost savings for Hydro-Québec.

SNC's Project Manager on the job was Pierre Fortier, an Athlone Fellow who had obtained a diploma in Nuclear Power from the Imperial College of Science and Technology in London, England. He already had several excellent young engineers on his team, including René Godin and Pierre Lebrun, but he did not have anyone who knew much about the large steam generators used in nuclear plants. Given Gentilly's highly experimental design, Fortier thought it wise to find one quickly.

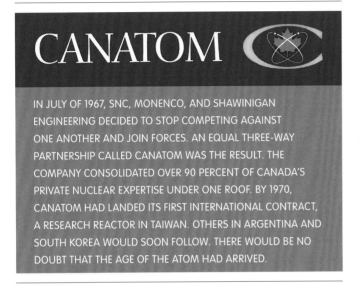

IN JULY OF 1967, SNC, MONENCO, AND SHAWINIGAN ENGINEERING DECIDED TO STOP COMPETING AGAINST ONE ANOTHER AND JOIN FORCES. AN EQUAL THREE-WAY PARTNERSHIP CALLED CANATOM WAS THE RESULT. THE COMPANY CONSOLIDATED OVER 90 PERCENT OF CANADA'S PRIVATE NUCLEAR EXPERTISE UNDER ONE ROOF. BY 1970, CANATOM HAD LANDED ITS FIRST INTERNATIONAL CONTRACT, A RESEARCH REACTOR IN TAIWAN. OTHERS IN ARGENTINA AND SOUTH KOREA WOULD SOON FOLLOW. THERE WOULD BE NO DOUBT THAT THE AGE OF THE ATOM HAD ARRIVED.

Alex Taylor had been making a name for himself in Britain's nuclear sector when Fortier paid him a visit in 1966. Nuclear plants were suddenly all the rage and Taylor had already been approached by several firms from North America, but Fortier was able to offer him something that few of the other companies could. At SNC, Taylor would be a shareholder of a company he was helping to build. Within 72 hours, everything had been arranged, including transportation.

AN OPENING IN ALGERIA

In the spring of 1968, Jack Hahn, the Vice-President of Development, and Marcel Sicard, the head of the department, were discussing where and how to expand. Hired in 1961 from Federal Pacific, Sicard had a broad and affable face that was a good indication of his nature. Like all excellent marketing men, he was skilled at client relations because he genuinely liked people.

Hahn and Sicard were desperate. There were few contracts in Quebec since the glut of the Quiet Revolution. In 1965, SNC had entered into a partnership in Ontario with the engineering firm W.A.H. Filer, but that province was proving equally challenging. They needed to find new markets outside North America.

"What about Algeria?" Hahn said, pulling his pipe from his mouth—he had taken up smoking a pipe many years before to combat the fog from Nenniger Sr.'s cigars.

"Yes, they have pretty much cut off ties with France since the revolution," Sicard mused. "Maybe they would be interested in North American technology offered in French."

In the spring of 1969, Sicard secured a contract to help the Algerians evaluate tenders for cement plants from several European firms. It was an important symbolic victory, but barely enough to raise morale back in Montreal. The company was gradually, but inexorably, sliding into the red. By the end of the year, SNC Inc. had recorded a loss of $63,340. There was now more pressure then ever to secure international contracts.

It was on a trip to Algeria to examine the tenders that summer that Sicard saw an opening and took it. A representative from Algeria's Société Nationale des Matériaux de Construction remarked that the cement plant that was currently being studied would be too small for their purposes. Sicard managed to convince the government to let SNC build another, larger facility. The new one, to be known as Meftah, would produce 1 million tonnes of cement each year and be almost fully automated.

Sicard looked into getting financing from the Canadian government, but it was not interested. In the end, Algeria, flush with oil money, decided to pay for the project itself. For the first time, SNC would be on its own in the international arena.

One of the greatest challenges on the project proved to be the procurement of equipment. Most of it was shipped in from Europe and Japan, but the industrial boom in Algeria had jammed up the country's ports, causing interminable

In 1970, following the signing of the Meftah contract in Algeria. From left to right: Paul Huybrecht, Marcel Sicard, Gunter Schoof, and a representative from the Algerian Ministry of Industry.

With its highly automated dry process and its production capacity of 1 million tonnes per year, Meftah was trumpeted as one of the world's most modern cement plants at the time.

Anwar Thomas in front of Meftah's pre-heating and feeding unit.

could then be transferred to smaller boats and unloaded at a nearby fishing port. From there heavy haulage trucks would do the rest.

Already up to his eyebrows in delays and complaints, the Customs Director had no time for such wild ideas. "Impossible, we don't do that kind of thing," he said, barely acknowledging Thomas' presence. "You will just have to wait like everyone else."

delays. When the first cargo ship arrived in the summer of 1971, the captain was told that it would take up to six months to clear customs. The entire project was suddenly in jeopardy: Project Manager Paul Huybrecht knew the boats would simply turn around if they were not allowed to unload their cargo soon.

Huybrecht sent Anwar Thomas, the project's resourceful Technical Director, to the port to try to work out an arrangement with the Customs Director. Thomas quickly came up with a solution: he would ask the Director to set up a temporary customs office near the project site. The equipment

With the project hanging in the balance, Thomas had no choice but to play hard ball. "That's unfortunate," he said. "I will have to inform the Industry Minister that his project will be late, and that we are not responsible because you refused to let us have our equipment." When the Customs Director learned that Meftah was part of a national cement plant construction program, he changed his tune and agreed to Thomas' plan.

With the procurement issue resolved, construction proceeded smoothly, and the plant was commissioned a few years later. At the inauguration, the President of Algeria, Houari Boumediène, praised SNC for building such a remarkable facility on time and within budget. It was an excellent start to a relationship that would prove increasingly important to the company.

ZINC IN TURKEY

SNC had now turned its attention to the international market in earnest. In 1971, SNC International, which had been no more than a blip on the corporate radar since 1959, opened a second office in London, England. Lionel Cook, a former vice-president at T. Ingledow & Associates, was put in charge of the office.

While Cook looked for opportunities in Europe, important inroads were being made in a new market. In the fall of 1972, Gaétan Lavallée, SNC's Vice-President of Mining & Metallurgy, signed a project management contract for Cinkur, a 40,000-tonne-per-year zinc smelter in Turkey. Brilliant and offbeat, Lavallée had an enigmatic way of thinking, but he brought home the goods. He had won the project against a slew of international competition largely thanks to the sophisticated zinc refinery SNC had recently built in Valleyfield, Quebec, for Noranda.

Turkey had no existing zinc industry, so Cinkur included an important transfer-of-technology component. SNC agreed to supervise local engineering firms hired by the client and train them if necessary. Offices in Istanbul and Ankara were subcontracted for the structural and mechanical work.

By the summer of 1973, engineering was more than 50 percent complete, and the first shipment of Canadian materials was set for the end of the year. Things seemed to be going well, but on a routine inspection trip to the Ankara office, structural engineer Maxime Dehoux discovered problems. He realized that most of the engineers from the local firm were recent university graduates with zero experience, and the work they were producing was not up to scratch. Dehoux refused to approve the latest drawings and called Montreal to request assistance.

John Turcke, now the Vice-President in charge of Quality Assurance, soon arrived to assess the situation. When he had been given the new assignment in 1967, Turcke had eagerly hit the books to find out what were the best industry practices

Lionel Cook

Gaétan Lavallée

Nine million tonnes of Canadian equipment was shipped to Turkey for the Cinkur zinc complex in Kayseri.

Montreal Project Manager Gerald Gray (left) and Vice-President, Quality Assurance, John Turcke, with the award of excellence given by the Association of Consulting Engineers of Canada for the Cinkur zinc complex.

in quality assurance. He had emerged from his investigations with one golden rule: incorporate quality from the very start of a project. Clearly, this was a case that proved the point.

"Well, you're right, Maxime," he said, shaking his head as he looked over some of the most poorly engineered plans. "This is completely unacceptable. Don't worry, we'll send you the help you need." A week later, a team of six engineers and six draftsmen reported for duty in Ankara to oversee the design work on a permanent basis.

The corrected plans soon arrived at the construction site, located below snow-capped Mount Erciyes near Kayseri. SNC's project team, which included Joe Polfer, Dhiru Shankar, Gilles Hudon, and Tom Crawley, were charged with more than simply creating a smelter; they were helping to give birth to a new industry. With no existing zinc smelters in Turkey, the project team was erecting the infrastructure and training personnel for an entire sector. SNC would even operate the plant for three years to ensure a smooth transition to Turkish staff.

In the space of a decade, SNC had transformed itself from a purely Canadian engineering company to a contender in the international engineering market. It closed out 1973 with 24 percent of its revenues coming from international projects, with 1974 looking even more promising. Now Dagenais was thinking bigger than ever: why not aim for 30, 40, or even 50 percent in international revenues?

The world had suddenly become a far smaller place for SNC.

A HELPING HAND

SNC NIGERIA JOINED SNC INTERNATIONAL'S NETWORK OF OFFICES IN 1975. IT WAS THE FIRST TIME THAT A CANADIAN ENGINEERING COMPANY HAD ENTERED INTO A PARTNERSHIP WITH A FOREIGN STATE FOR THE PURPOSE OF TAKING PART IN ITS OVERALL DEVELOPMENT. THERE WERE MANY PROJECTS ON THE HORIZON IN THE COUNTRY, INCLUDING A BROAD RURAL DEVELOPMENT PROGRAM THAT COVERED WATER, POWER, AND HOUSING.

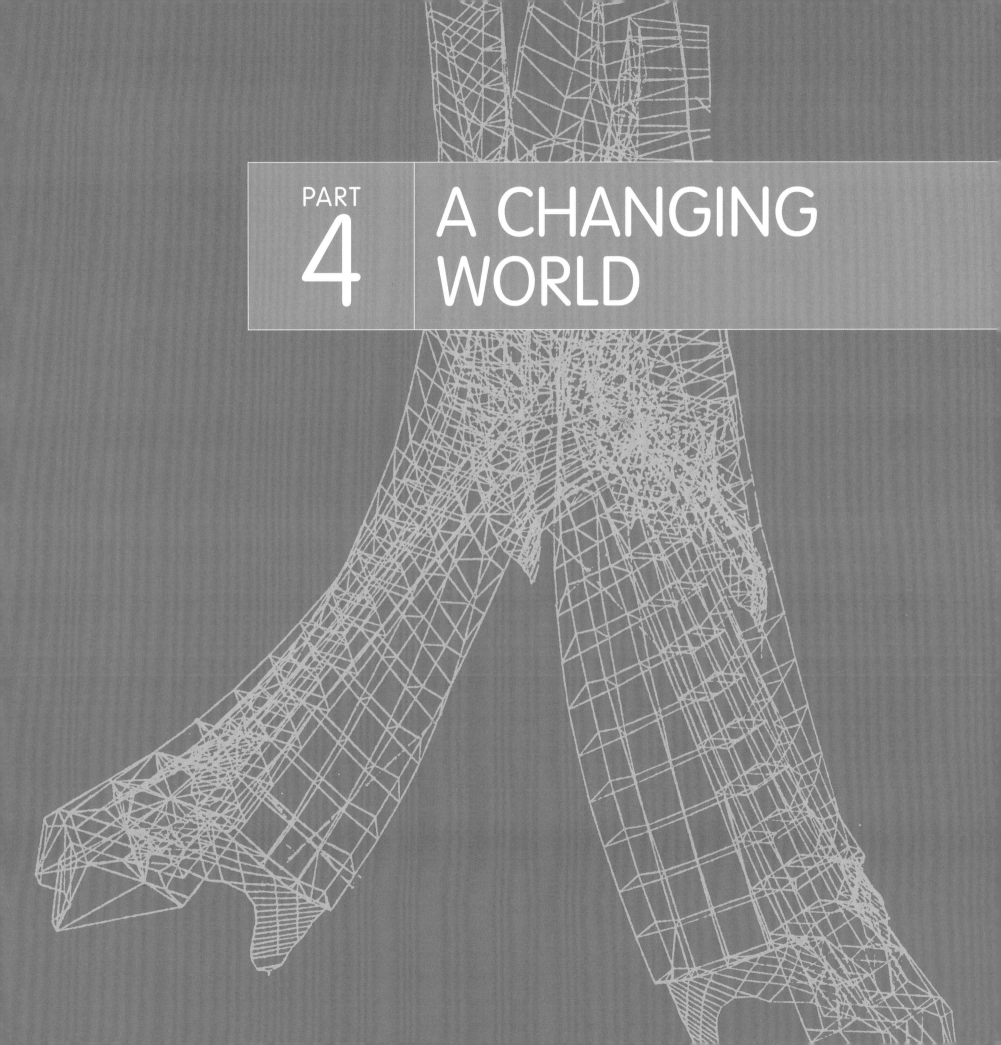

A CHANGING WORLD

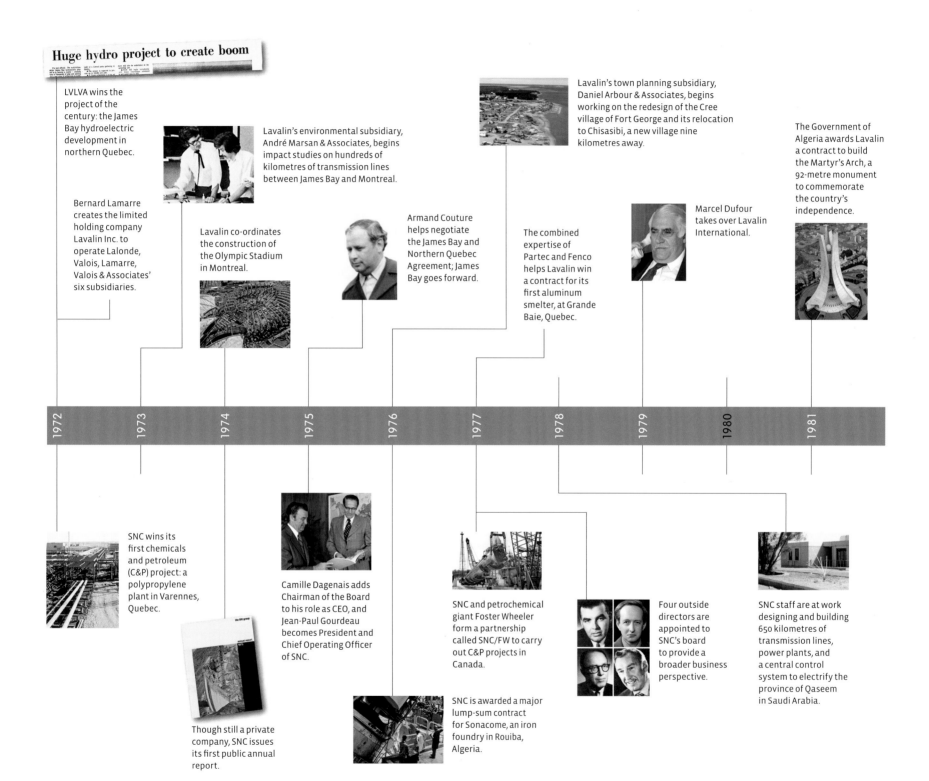

Huge hydro project to create boom

LVLVA wins the project of the century: the James Bay hydroelectric development in northern Quebec.

Bernard Lamarre creates the limited holding company Lavalin Inc. to operate Lalonde, Valois, Lamarre, Valois & Associates' six subsidiaries.

Lavalin's environmental subsidiary, André Marsan & Associates, begins impact studies on hundreds of kilometres of transmission lines between James Bay and Montreal.

Lavalin co-ordinates the construction of the Olympic Stadium in Montreal.

Armand Couture helps negotiate the James Bay and Northern Quebec Agreement; James Bay goes forward.

Lavalin's town planning subsidiary, Daniel Arbour & Associates, begins working on the redesign of the Cree village of Fort George and its relocation to Chisasibi, a new village nine kilometres away.

The combined expertise of Partec and Fenco helps Lavalin win a contract for its first aluminum smelter, at Grande Baie, Quebec.

Marcel Dufour takes over Lavalin International.

The Government of Algeria awards Lavalin a contract to build the Martyr's Arch, a 92-metre monument to commemorate the country's independence.

1972   1973   1974   1975   1976   1977   1978   1979   1980   1981

SNC wins its first chemicals and petroleum (C&P) project: a polypropylene plant in Varennes, Quebec.

Camille Dagenais adds Chairman of the Board to his role as CEO, and Jean-Paul Gourdeau becomes President and Chief Operating Officer of SNC.

Though still a private company, SNC issues its first public annual report.

SNC and petrochemical giant Foster Wheeler form a partnership called SNC/FW to carry out C&P projects in Canada.

SNC is awarded a major lump-sum contract for Sonacome, an iron foundry in Rouiba, Algeria.

Four outside directors are appointed to SNC's board to provide a broader business perspective.

SNC staff are at work designing and building 650 kilometres of transmission lines, power plants, and a central control system to electrify the province of Qaseem in Saudi Arabia.

PREVIOUS PAGE
A three-dimensional computer model of the Martyr's Arch.

CHAPTER 12

THE PROJECT OF THE CENTURY

The James Bay project's LG-3 dam in northern Quebec.

At the start of the 1970s, the Quebec engineering world is abuzz with talk of a gigantic hydropower development around James Bay. Several local engineering firms contend for the contract, including SNC and LVLVA. In a surprise upset, LVLVA secures the job by joining forces with Bechtel. Following the win, LVLVA is incorporated under a holding company called Lavalin, and Armand Couture, a new associate in the firm, heads up the Environment, Transportation and Native Affairs portfolios for James Bay. Couture will take part in the negotiations that bring the Aboriginal people of the region onside in 1975 with the James Bay and Northern Quebec Agreement.

On April 30, 1971, Quebec Premier Robert Bourassa dropped a bombshell of good news on 9,500 Liberal Party workers at Quebec City's Coliseum. Standing under a high-powered light show, he announced that the long-anticipated hydro-electric development at James Bay was finally going ahead.

He called it the project of the century, and the numbers backed up his claim. The first phase alone would marshal 100,000 workers to the most remote regions of the province and add 5,000 megawatts to its energy grid (soon increased to 10,000). Quebec's topography would forever be transformed by the project's eight mega-dams, 700 kilometres of roads, and over 5,000 kilometres of transmission lines. Hydro-Québec's President, Roland Giroux, eagerly jumped on board. The utility had begun investing in atomic energy, but it now set aside its nuclear ambitions and prepared to undertake the titanic task of managing James Bay.

Bourassa had other ideas in mind. That summer, the Liberals tabled Bill 50. The legislation would create the Société de développement de la Baie James (SDBJ) to oversee all natural resource projects in the region. A subsidiary called the Société d'énergie de la Baie James (SEBJ) would then be launched to directly manage the James Bay project. Hydro-Québec would not have control over the project.

The Montreal Star

ENTERTAINMENTS TV-RADIO NEWS and REVIEW WEEKEND

TODAY: Cloudy
TOMORROW: Showers
146 PAGES

SATURDAY, MAY 1, 1971

103rd Year, No. 102

PRICE FIFTEEN CENTS

Jobs, mineral wealth, power to eventually pour from James Bay

Huge hydro project to create boom

It's now official. The multi-billion-dollar James Bay hydroelectric proj... ... a reality — creating... ...up to 125,000 new jobs.

night at a Liberal party gathering in Quebec.
● The project is expected to pro-... ...to get under way in 1973.

ment will also be undertaken at the sprawling site.
● Work will begin immediately with heavy construction scheduled to get under way in 1973.
...made no mention... electric power... was to be

Aerial view of Nottaway River where Hydro-Quebec is to build a control dam and a large diversion canal.

Staff Photo by Bill Robson

la presse

le plus grand quotidien français d'Amérique

Montreal, samedi 1er mai 1971 87e année, no 101, 160 pages, 11 cahiers

DERNIÈRE ÉDITION 25¢

Bourassa confirme le projet au coût de $6 milliards

La baie James: défi et avenir du Québec

...mention by the ...money to pay for ...no mention of ...any of the elec-...duced.
...amatic announce-..., 9,500-seat sports ...with 3,000 Liberal ...who had paid $5 to

...months there have ...ensive meetings, dis-...otiations about the ..." he said.
...now has recom-

DETAILS, Page 2

...of the James Bay area. ...and the jobs won't ... The people here have ...ence of large-scale de-...now that.
...ess of dense forest, with ...of lakes and a few ...Indians as its main in-...ll not change quickly ei-...vast that even the diver-...rivers, the construction ...anals and power stations ...nge its appearance in any ...ay.
...he people of the region, ...d by broken promises and ...economy, the decision to

See AREA, Page 2

The press had a field day trying to deduce Bourassa's motives. They wondered if the Premier felt the project was simply too massive for the utility. Perhaps it was political. It was known that some top Liberals suspected Hydro-Québec of being a "cosy nest of separatists."

Whatever the reason, Giroux hit the roof. "Listen, Robert, you can do what you want, but I will never accept that the SEBJ remains outside our control," he said to the Premier. "If you don't change your mind, you're going to have a terrible fight on your hands."

The fight Giroux predicted took place at the National Assembly in Quebec City. The political opposition called the SEBJ a second Hydro-Québec and vowed to resist Bill 50 with every means at its disposal. Weeks of raucous debate and obstruction tactics ensued. Finally, on July 14, 1971, a heavily modified version of the bill limped into law. Bourassa got his SEBJ, but Hydro-Québec would now be its majority shareholder.

THE BATTLE FOR JAMES BAY

By September, Bourassa had named Pierre Nadeau, an executive with the Industrial Acceptance Corporation, to head the SDBJ. He would hold sway over a resource-rich dominion twice the size of France. Already, there were grand plans for mining and lumber projects scattered across his desk, but the first order of business was, of course, the project of the century. Nadeau made a key decision early on: the province would be best served if its management was entrusted to competent firms with local know-how.

That was good news for SNC, Monenco, and Janin Construction, which had joined forces to offer a total management solution for James Bay. Never in his career had Camille Dagenais wanted a project so badly, but this was about more than his own ambitions. James Bay, he felt, was a chance for SNC to perfect its management skills on a project of unprecedented size.

Nadeau seemed to favour the SNC-led consortium, but his influence over the project was fading fast. When the SEBJ was created in December 1971, Hydro-Québec was given 70 percent of the shares as promised. By January, Giroux had picked up the rest, arguing it would be best for tax reasons if Hydro-Québec owned the SEBJ outright.

James Bay was firmly under Giroux's control now. From the start, he had insisted on the benefits of bringing in a world-class project management firm to gain the confidence

Quebec Premier Robert Bourassa (left) discusses plans for James Bay with Armand Couture.

of financial institutions. Not everyone agreed it was necessary, but Giroux wanted internationally renowned Bechtel on board.

At LVLVA's headquarters, Bernard Lamarre had been watching events unfold with bated breath. He was still disappointed over Janin's eleventh-hour decision to pull out of a consortium with LVLVA to join SNC and Monenco, but he saw that all was not yet lost. If Giroux was going to Bechtel, he reasoned, then Hydro-Québec would need a significant amount of local know-how and LVLVA could provide it.

In the spring of 1972, Lamarre made his move and went to meet Giroux. "I think I know what you are thinking," he said. "I offer to be the local partner, which will allow you to associate with Bechtel. We do not want direct control of the project, but would only supply our expertise to the SEBJ."

Giroux had not made any promises, but it soon turned out that Lamarre had played his hand perfectly. On September 22, 1972, LVLVA signed a contract to supply 70 percent of the SEBJ's personnel, with Bechtel Quebec and the utility itself furnishing the remainder. In the engineering world of the day, it was like winning the jackpot several times over.

Among the thousands of men and women LVLVA would supply to the project, Hydro-Québec wanted at least one of its top decision makers on the SEBJ's Management Committee. Lamarre could think of no one better suited to the job than Armand Couture, his former colleague from the Louis-Hippolyte-La Fontaine Bridge-Tunnel project.

When work on the bridge-tunnel finished in 1967, Lamarre had invited Couture to join LVLVA as its Vice-President of Technology, Economy and Transport. It was a sprawling portfolio that reflected the 37-year-old's broad interests and abilities. Couture's responsibilities at the SEBJ would be equally wide-ranging. As a member of its Management Committee, he would be handed the all-important Environment, Transportation and Native Affairs portfolios. First, however, he would co-chair the committee charged with defining the final size and shape of the project of the century.

LAVALIN INC.

James Bay catapulted LVLVA into the big leagues. It would be sharing the responsibilities for the most ambitious project in Quebec's history with one of the biggest engineering firms in the world. Lamarre understood that a special set of rules applied to companies that operated at that level. Megaprojects were risky, but there would be no appetite for risk if the firm's top management stood to lose their shirts.

In August 1972, as contract negotiations for James Bay were wrapping up, Bernard Lamarre created a limited holding company to operate LVLVA's six subsidiaries. Coming up with a name for the new entity was almost too easy. It turned out that the ideal one had been in use for close to a decade. The telex code for *La*marre *Val*ois *In*ternational had always been Lavalin, so why not go with that? It was just as easy to pronounce in French as it was in English, and it was already the firm's calling card abroad, where Lamarre was now more focused than ever.

The firm's transition to a corporation coincided with a reshuffling of its top management. Armand Couture and

LALONDE, VALOIS
LAMARRE, VALOIS
& ASSOCIÉS, INC.
EXPERTS-CONSEILS   CONSULTANTS
GROUPE LAVALIN
615, RUE BELMONT, MONTRÉAL   H3B 2L9
TÉL. 871-3861   TÉLEX LAVALIN MTL 01-26401

Marcel Dufour had now become associates, joining Gaston René de Cotret, Jean-Paul Dionne, and Paul Roberge. André Denis, the metallic structures specialist, had withdrawn. Jean Croteau, the head of Public Works had too, although he stayed on to help reorganize the company. Lamarre told Croteau that he wanted the different divisions and subsidiaries to have a certain amount of autonomy under Lavalin Inc., but he also expected them to pool their expertise for individual assignments.

While increased size brought great opportunities, it also created administrative challenges for Lamarre. Like his mentor, Jean-Paul Lalonde, he wanted to know everything about the company he ran. But as Lavalin expanded, reaching into new markets and taking on increasingly complex projects, he needed to devise ways to keep information flowing into his office.

New hires were sometimes surprised to learn that a copy of all company correspondence went directly to the President. Lamarre also reserved the right to pick up the phone and call any employee directly to ask a question. To monitor projects and prospects, he created a technical committee. Beginning religiously at 8:30 a.m. every Friday morning, the meetings provided a regular window into the intricacies of the company's operations.

But if Lamarre was Lavalin's all-knowing leader, most of the company's employees considered themselves lucky to work under his rule. Lavalin went to great lengths to make them feel valued. It was part of Lamarre's management philosophy, which he summed up with the phrase, "a happy employee is a productive employee."

At Lavalin in the early 1970s, employees at the Montreal office were

A LAVALIN INSTITUTION

LAVALIN'S TECHNICAL COMMITTEE VETTED PROPOSALS AND WORKED WITH ENGINEERS AND PROJECT MANAGERS TO RESOLVE PROBLEMS BEFORE THEY SNOWBALLED INTO CATASTROPHES. MANY A PROJECT IN DIFFICULTY WAS PUT BACK ON THE RAILS, AND MANY AN ENGINEERING PLAN WAS REFINED AND OPTIMIZED. BEFORE LONG, THE TECHNICAL COMMITTEE WOULD BECOME AN INSTITUTION AT LAVALIN AND AN EFFECTIVE SAFEGUARD AGAINST THE RISKS INHERENT IN THE ENGINEERING AND CONSTRUCTION WORLD.

treated to free coffee and snacks in the cafeteria. Those expecting a baby were given Lavalin's "Benoit Prize," a bonus of $1,600, named after the child of the award's first recipient. Soon, Lavalin would launch a free daycare service for its employees, sparing no expense to make it the "Cadillac of childcare facilities."

Lamarre even extended his philosophy to his employees' physical work environment. Engineering, he liked to say, was fundamentally a creative pursuit, and inspiration was as important as technical ability. In the late 1960s, LVLVA began

One of Bernard Lamarre's favourite art acquisitions, *Bleu,* by Serge Lemoyne.

By 1977, Lavalin held so many works that Léo Rosshandler was hired to manage its collection.

purchasing artwork from living Canadian artists to adorn its employees' offices. By 1977, the company held over 75 works and even had its own curator, Léo Rosshandler, a former president of the Société des musées québécois. The artists of those works benefited greatly from Lavalin's support, while their paintings provided an inspiring environment for the company's engineers as they designed cutting-edge plants and infrastructure.

Ciaccia wanted to do more than settle the James Bay question. He saw the negotiations as an opportunity to resolve most of the longstanding claims by Quebec's Aboriginal peoples. To do so, however, Quebec would have to be ready to make real concessions. Some would be concrete, involving payouts and new rights. Others would be symbolic, like Ciaccia's decision to hold talks with the Indigenous peoples of James Bay on their own territory. It was bold, considering that past negotiations had often been rocky, degenerating at times into yelling matches and near fistfights.

The moment of truth arrived in late 1974. The venue was a school auditorium on the Cree island-village of Fort George. Couture and Ciaccia took the stage before a crowd of anxious villagers. With the help of an interpreter, they described the

A LANDMARK AGREEMENT

The news that the James Bay project was going ahead came out of the blue for the Aboriginal people of the region. They immediately sought an injunction against the project to protect their ancestral hunting grounds. On November 15, 1973, to the surprise of all, Quebec Superior Court Judge Albert Malouf granted them one. He said the government had failed to consult the Aboriginal people of James Bay, and the project could not proceed until their concerns were heard. Within a few days, Bourassa's fabled project of the century—and about 4,000 workers—had come to a halt.

Malouf's decision was soon suspended by the Quebec Court of Appeal, but it was clear that the Aboriginal people of James Bay could no longer be ignored. The government quickly assembled a negotiation team led by former Canadian Indian Affairs Assistant Deputy Minister, John Ciaccia. One of its senior members would be Armand Couture, the SEBJ's head of Native Affairs.

social benefits of hydroelectricity, but ideas were often distorted or lost in translation.

One of the issues that generated the most acrimony was LG-1, the dam that would be closest to Fort George. At one point, a young woman in the audience could no longer contain her anger. "I don't care what you say," she shouted. "You had better move the LG-1 dam. We don't want it here. If you build it, we are going to take our guns and shoot at it."

The first meeting at Fort George was tense, but Couture and Ciaccia sensed a faint undercurrent of acceptance in the audience. All they had to do was cut through the fear and misunderstanding. At the next meeting they were joined on stage by their Cree counterparts. It was a way of showing the people of Fort George that they were partners in the process.

Negotiations continued over the next year. With each passing month, the two sides inched closer together on the most contentious issues—the many millions needed to fund Aboriginal autonomy, the annexing of large portions of the territory for their use, and, importantly for the Cree of Fort George, the relocation of the LG-1 dam farther away from their village.

Finally, on November 15, 1975, the second anniversary of the Malouf ruling, the James Bay and Northern Quebec Agreement was signed. It recognized two key principles: the importance of preserving the traditional way of life of Aboriginal peoples, and the right of Quebec to use the territory's resources to meet the needs of its entire population.

The Cree island-village of Fort George was the venue for the discussions that led to the signing of the James Bay and Northern Quebec Agreement in November 1975.

Following the signing of an agreement in principle for the James Bay project. From left to right: Quebec Premier Robert Bourassa; the Grand Chief of the Grand Council of the Crees, Billy Diamond; the Deputy Premier of Quebec, Gérard Lévesque; and Cree Chief Robert Kanatewat.

MONTREAL-MATIN, VENDREDI 16 NOVEMBRE 1973

...louf donne raison aux Indiens

LES TRAVAUX A LA BAIE JAMES!"

Une grande victoire pour les Indiens

par Bernard RACINE

LE CHEF GROS-LOUIS
"C'est la première fois que l'homme blanc donne raison aux Indiens."

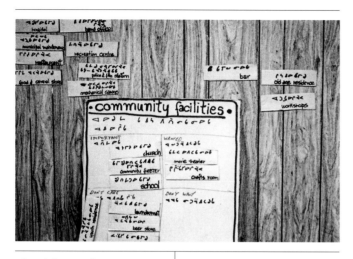

The citizens of Fort George were heavily consulted during the project to redesign and relocate their village.

Herb Goldman

Marie Lessard

Years later, Matthew Coon Come, the Grand Chief of the Grand Council of the Crees, would praise the Agreement as a massive step forward for his people.

"Under the terms of the Agreement, we gained what we had never had before: control of education through the Cree School Board, control of health and social services, control over the government of our lands, a strong voice in the approval of new projects in the territory, rights with respect to the resources of the land… and guarantees of major and important participation in the development of subarctic Quebec."

MOVING FORT GEORGE

The James Bay and Northern Quebec Agreement earmarked substantial sums for improving the Aboriginal villages in the region, but the elders of Fort George had other ideas.

With the population rapidly outgrowing their island home, they decided to use their share of the funds to relocate. In 1976, the contract to design a new village went to Lavalin's recently acquired town planning subsidiary, Daniel Arbour & Associates.

Arbour's Project Manager, Herb Goldman, kicked things off with an exchange: town planners Marie Lessard and François Vézina went to live in Fort George for an entire month, while two of the village's inhabitants took up residence at Lavalin's office in Montreal. Each day, Lessard and Vézina visited several of the small clapboard houses with a translator to learn about the needs and aspirations of their inhabitants. In Montreal, the visitors from Fort George helped decipher the information they sent back by answering questions about Cree traditions.

The arrangement of the houses in the new village turned out to be a key issue for the Cree. During their interviews, Lessard and Vézina learned that the town's layout had long been a source of irritation for its residents. In the Cree culture it was traditional for relatives to live side by side, but in Fort George families were displaced all over the island. The project team subsequently devised a plan for the new site with groups of houses clustered together for each extended family.

With the layout question settled, it was time to choose a location for the new town. Lavalin's team carried out studies throughout the region to find a site that would meet the needs of its future inhabitants. The villagers finally decided on a new location about nine kilometres from Fort George, conveniently wedged between the La Grande River and the new road to LG-2. The Cree named it Chisasibi, "The Great River" in their language.

The big move took place between the summers of 1979 and 1981. Over 300 dwellings, three schools, a hospital, and two general stores were transported to the new site under the leadership of Kai Morawski, Daniel Arbour's project management specialist. Even the village church was loaded onto a ferry and shipped to the mainland. It was a sight that few who were involved in the project would ever forget.

POWERING UP MONTREAL

When Bernard Lamarre approached André Marsan in 1973, the federal-provincial task force Marsan was leading had just completed its mammoth study on the environmental impact of the James Bay project. Balanced and knowledgeable, the 36-year-old engineer seemed an excellent choice to lead Lavalin's first environmental subsidiary.

"We see that the environment is becoming an increasingly important issue," Lamarre had said. "Why don't you join us? We can call the division André Marsan & Associates."

Marsan was skeptical at first. Surely the environmental sector, where revenues were meagre, was no place for a big engineering company with a focus on the bottom line. He wanted Lamarre's assurance that his employees would not be let go if he failed to make a profit one year.

"Don't worry, Mr. Marsan," Lamarre said. "I am aware that environmental subsidiaries make studies, not profits."

One of André Marsan & Associates' first projects was an impact study on hundreds of kilometres of 735-kV transmission lines for James Bay. They would run down through the Laurentian Mountains to Montreal, cutting through swaths of virgin forest, prime agricultural lands, wildlife habitats, Aboriginal territories, and recreational areas. It was up to Marsan's team to strike the best balance between environmental, social, technical, and financial considerations.

As Marsan was finishing his study in 1974, Lavalin formed a partnership with the engineering firm Rousseau Sauvé Warren, called Bureau d'études de lignes de transport (BELT), to go after the next phases. The company immediately picked up contracts to select the precise location of the towers and design their foundations. It was a fine start, but Hydro-Québec refused to give the partnership the most prestigious piece of the pie: the design of the towers themselves. The utility had always used a European firm, and planned to do so again.

The entire town of Fort George, including its church, was relocated to Chisasibi, nine kilometres away.

André Marsan (second from left) surrounded by his team of environmental experts in the mid-1970s.

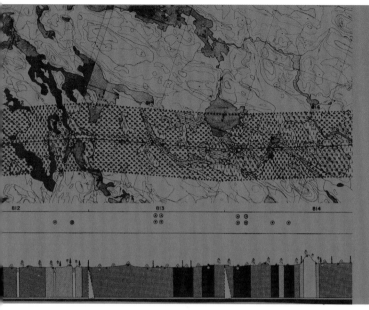

cables and put under increasing tension until they collapsed. Designers had to strike a delicate balance: towers that were too resistant to pressure would be considered to contain excessive steel and be a waste of money; towers that were too weak would be deemed vulnerable to the harsh climate of northern Quebec.

BELT's trump card was Normand Morin. The 36-year-old had been directly recruited by Bernard Lamarre in 1971 from the Université de Sherbrooke in Quebec, where he had been teaching advanced courses in civil engineering. Lamarre wanted him for one reason in particular: Lavalin was launching a computer services division called Cosigma, and Morin had mastered the latest structural design programs while completing his PhD at the Massachusetts Institute of Technology. As BELT's Vice-President, Morin now made use of the same software to design Hydro-Québec's towers.

Representatives from the two companies arrived in Barcelona on a blisteringly hot day in the summer of 1979 to observe the tests. The other competitor's design was up first. Steel cables were attached to its tower and pressure was gradually increased until it began to buckle. The tower collapsed at more than 104 percent of the required strength, which meant it was slightly over-engineered.

BELT finally caught a break in early 1978. Impressed by the quality of its work so far, Hydro-Québec was prepared to give the company the design contract for James Bay's sixth transmission line. It would not be a cakewalk, however. BELT would have to battle it out with the other firm in a head-to-head competition. The companies were instructed to engineer a new family of towers and ship them to a full-scale test site near Barcelona, Spain. They would be strung up with steel

MIT-educated Normand Morin was Lavalin's secret weapon in the design of transmission towers for James Bay.

BELT's model was next. As the steel cables put increasing strain on its tower, its engineers could not help but anxiously reflect on the months of work to get the formula of metal and math just right. Had they forgotten something? Did they overdo it? As the pressure reached 100 percent, they were glad to see their tower begin to fold. It collapsed at just under 102 percent, which was about as close to perfect as you could get.

When the official results were announced, there were congratulations all around. BELT had shown it could stand toe-to-toe with the most capable and experienced transmission line design company in the world.

CHAPTER 13

A NEW IMAGE, NEW EXPERTISE

SNC is stunned by its failure to win James Bay. The loss leads CEO Camille Dagenais to begin to look for ways to raise the company's profile. In 1974, he hires a public relations specialist named Jacques Lefebvre to bring the company into the public eye. Lefebvre urges Dagenais to publish SNC's annual report, and the company logo is revamped. Meanwhile, Jean-Paul Gourdeau is tapped as a potential successor to Dagenais when he is named President. By the end of the decade, SNC has broken into the petrochemical sector thanks to expertise from recent hires like Tony Rustin, Taro Alepian, and Krish Krishnamoorthy.

The Sun Oil project in Sarnia, Ontario.

As Lavalin celebrated its win of the project of the century in September of 1972, SNC's Executive Committee was deep in thought. They had believed SNC was a shoo-in for James Bay. After all, the company had the spectacular Manic-5 dam under its belt, and the Idukki project in India was going well, despite delays caused by civil unrest. It was a devastating blow when they had come up short.

For Camille Dagenais, who had eagerly awaited the next stage in Quebec's expansion of its hydropower capability, the failure to win the contract was difficult to take. He had learned of the decision when he saw an article in *Le Devoir* announcing that Bechtel and Lavalin had been awarded the management of James Bay. What the journalist did not say, but what Dagenais knew only too well, was that SNC was a casualty of the battle between Roland Giroux and Pierre Nadeau.

While he believed the SEBJ had made the wrong choice in going with Bechtel, he could not deny that the firm was a remarkable engineering and construction machine. Even those outside the engineering world had heard of them and knew what they had accomplished: the Hoover Dam, Churchill Falls, the Oakland Bay Bridge, among others. By comparison, SNC was operating in the shadows. Who knew that SNC had designed Manic-5, the largest multiple-arch dam in the world?

Now it hit him: if more people knew what SNC had done, it would not be so easy to write the company off next time. Engineers had a tendency to dismiss the importance of marketing, believing that hard facts and concrete accomplishments would eventually win out. Dagenais now saw that those hard facts had to reach the right people at the right time.

But what did SNC know about corporate branding? The company had mastered engineering and construction. It had elaborated a sophisticated corporate development strategy, but public relations had never been a priority. Dagenais now set about finding someone who could help SNC build a public image.

Jacques Lefebvre was working for Quebec-based snowmobile and train manufacturer Bombardier in late 1973 when

he was contacted by a headhunter and offered the position of Vice-President of Public Affairs at SNC. A talented marketing strategist with a larger-than-life personality and build, Lefebvre seemed like just the man to haul SNC out of the shadows.

The first hurdle Lefebvre saw in the way of SNC's marketing efforts was its logo. The insignia—a large geometrical S cradling an N and a C—had first seen the light of day on SNC's intermural hockey team jerseys in the early 1960s. Gradually, it had made its way onto project reports and other documents. But Lefebvre was not interested in where it came from. He said he thought it was dull and wanted to scrap it. Dagenais, who had been involved in its creation as the hockey team's coach, rose to its defence.

"What's wrong with it?" he asked.

"You need something more aggressive and jazzy," Lefebvre said. "Something daring and modern."

Dagenais was intrigued and wanted to see what Lefebvre could come up with. When the new logo was unveiled a year later, he had to admit that it was a marked improvement. Now the letters SNC stood out in thick red characters. Beneath the company acronym sat a solid black line to underscore the reliability and Cartesian logic on which it prided itself.

Lefebvre next took aim at the company's annual report. Dagenais had decided to publish it, but Lefebvre strongly advised revamping it before doing so. Since 1967, SNC had distributed a spiral bound, typewritten report to its employee shareholders. The text was generally uninspiring, and there were no photos to accompany the brief descriptions of projects. A souped-up version appeared in 1974, with a picture of the Idukki arch dam splashed across its cover. Inside, colour photos, dynamic graphs, and a lively text brought SNC's projects and prospects to life.

The image presented in the report was one of a company in steep ascent, reaching into new markets with confidence while growing existing ones. "During the last ten years, the SNC Group multiplied its revenues by a factor of ten, its personnel grew from 200 to 1,700, and its geographic coverage expanded to include the whole of Canada and some 20 countries on five continents," Dagenais wrote in his President's Message.

In some ways, the report's financial section was more impressive. SNC was not a public company, but here it was, openly divulging its most private financial information: everything

from the value of its investments and accounts receivable to its long-term debt and the overall remuneration of its directors and top management.

That spring, 50,000 copies were printed and distributed to large corporations, government bodies, and financial institutions. There was no turning back now. SNC had thrown open its books to the world, but only time would tell if the world took notice.

SNC's first logo had been created for its hockey team, but Jacques Lefebvre (left) revamped it under Camille Dagenais' guidance.

Absolutely nothing to hide: Jean-Paul Gourdeau (left) and Camille Dagenais peruse the 1973 annual report.

CHANGES AT THE TOP

Dagenais had always planned to sell his interest in the company in accordance with the rules of share ownership set out in his SNC Bible. By early 1974, he was quickly approaching 55, the age when he would have to divest the first third of his shares. With 10 years remaining before he had to sell the rest, he felt the time had come to begin grooming a successor.

He reserved the position for Jean-Paul Gourdeau, the company's Vice-President of Operations. He was a solid administrator, who had always shown integrity and total dedication. The board approved Gourdeau as the group's new President and Chief Operating Officer in the spring of 1975. In addition to his role as CEO, Dagenais now became Chairman of the Board. He would keep his hand firmly on the steering wheel until he felt his protégé was ready to lead the company.

Gourdeau's first decision as President was a difficult one. He needed someone for the top job of Vice-President of Products, and there were a few candidates who deserved serious consideration.

Alex Taylor, the President of Canatom, was one. The gruff and ambitious Scotsman was a brilliant

problem solver and a dedicated company man. Under his leadership, Canatom had won a contract for a second nuclear plant at Gentilly and was getting close to reeling in another in South Korea. Pierre Fortier, the Vice-President of Corporate Affairs, was a second possibility. He was bombastic and smart, with excellent political instincts. He had given everything he had to try to win the James Bay project management contract for Camille Dagenais. Thanks in part to his dogged determination, SNC had at least managed to secure an engineering and construction supervision contract for the LG-3 dam. The other potential candidate was Jacques Laflamme, the Vice-President of Engineering. Ever since his arrival in 1965, Laflamme had endeared himself to his peers with his extreme competence and gentle but direct manner.

Ultimately, Gourdeau had to make his decision based on who would complement him best. He wanted someone with a softer touch who could help deal with the fallout of difficult decisions. That man was Jacques Laflamme.

There were other changes at the top that year. One of them, the departure of Jack Hahn, came as a shock to Dagenais. Hahn had devoted his life to SNC and was one of the architects of its stunning expansion. Now he wanted to take a one- or two-year sabbatical to visit Israel.

"Jack, you can't do that," Dagenais protested. "You can't just leave without some kind of advance warning. We need you for the expansion."

"I'm not leaving without warning," Hahn said. "Don't you remember? During the T-Group discussions, I said that I would leave when I reached 55."

"You're kidding! You said it offhand. We said all kinds of things during those sessions. I never thought you'd be crazy enough to do it."

Jean-Paul Gourdeau

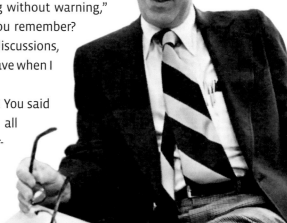

Jack Hahn

"You know, Camille, there is one thing I grasped at that time. For me, there is more to life than work. Of course, I'll keep an eye out for possible contracts in the region while I'm there."

Dagenais tried again to convince him to stay on, but Hahn's mind was made up. Fortunately, Lionel Cook, the President of SNC International, was waiting in the wings to take his place. Cook had helped open doors to new markets around the world, so Dagenais had no doubt that SNC's growth ambitions would be in good hands.

A NEW DIVISION

Since coming to SNC from Brown & Root in 1966, where he had overseen major projects for the likes of Shell, Union Carbide, and Monsanto, Dick Balfour had dreamed of opening a petrochemicals department at SNC. In 1972, he finally got his chance. That year, Hercules Canada hired the company to engineer and manage the construction of a polypropylene plant in Varennes, Quebec.

The euphoria of winning a major project in a new sector soon gave way to consternation, however. The engineering proved more complex than anticipated. The difficulty was the multitude of twists and turns in the facility's maze of piping. Pipe isometrics, the most challenging aspect of refinery design, was a new field for SNC.

The situation improved with the arrival of Tony Rustin, who held a PhD in Chemical Engineering and had worked for Shawinigan Chemicals and Gulf Oil Canada. In August of 1973, Balfour made him the department's Head Chemical Engineer and assigned him to the Hercules project. Rustin's piping expertise was a godsend for the beleaguered project team. More importantly, with his experience at Gulf and Shawinigan, he knew how to speak the client's language.

TRAINING FOR TOMORROW

IN THE EARLY 1970s, SNC EMPLOYEES AT ALL LEVELS BEGAN ATTENDING TRAINING SESSIONS WITH THE AMERICAN MANAGEMENT ASSOCIATION. CAMILLE DAGENAIS FELT SNC'S ENGINEERS NEEDED TO DEVELOP A GREATER BUSINESS SENSE AND BE MORE OUTWARD LOOKING, IN THE TRADITION OF ARTHUR SURVEYER. THE FUTURE GROWTH OF THE COMPANY DEPENDED ON IT.

Vice-presidents and managers from SNC offices in Quebec, Ontario, and Alberta gathered at Mont Gabriel in the Laurentians for an American Management Association seminar in September 1976.

Tony Rustin
Krish Krishnamoorthy
Taro Alepian

had no problem coming up with names. One of the first was Krish Krishnamoorthy. Rustin had seen his work up close when they shared an office together.

Not surprisingly, Rustin's high opinion of Krish was shared by Gulf's Vice-President, Bob Beal. When Beal learned that one of his best young process engineers was defecting to SNC, he immediately called Rustin to complain.

"Tony, this is Bob."

"Hi Bob, what can I do for you?"

"Well, I'm not happy. You're headhunting some of my top guys. I can't afford to lose people like Krishnamoorthy."

"I'm sorry Bob," Rustin said. "You should think of it as a compliment to the quality of the people you have."

From there, he went shopping for someone to head up marketing for the new department. His search led him to Taro Alepian, a process engineer at Shell. Alepian had oil and gas in the blood and could talk about the industry in terms that made it sound exciting. It was the kind of talk that won contracts.

By the new year, Balfour had put Rustin in charge of the entire department, with orders to build it up quickly. The previous fall, the Arab oil embargo had sent the price of a barrel of crude through the roof. If SNC was ever going to make a real breakthrough into the chemicals and petroleum sector, the time was now.

Rustin knew the first step was to assemble a solid team. During his five years at Gulf Oil Canada, he had rubbed shoulders with some of the best engineers in the business, so he

Krishnamoorthy and Alepian immediately teamed up to prepare a submission for a Sun Oil refinery in Sarnia, Ontario. For the first time, SNC had the expertise to go after the front-end work, which meant designing the processes. Process design was not especially lucrative, but it was prestigious and the key to winning larger engineering and construction jobs down the line.

With the guidance of SNC's leading computer expert, Walter Stensch, Krishnamoorthy modified a software program to allow it to optimize the processes for Sun Oil's proposed facility. When the results were demonstrated for its executives, they were dazzled. But mostly, they were amazed that a Canadian engineering company had the expertise to develop such a program.

By early 1974, Krishnamoorthy and Alepian were in Philadelphia working with Sun Oil's own process engineers. The company had taken a minor leap of faith in awarding SNC the work and wanted to keep an eye on their progress. Rustin did not mind. It was all part of paying your dues in a new sector.

BORDER-TOWN REFINERY

BY 1980, DOORS WERE FINALLY SWINGING OPEN IN THE WEST FOR SNC. ONE OF ITS FIRST MAJOR PETROCHEMICAL PROJECTS IN THE REGION WAS FOR HUSKY OIL'S REFINERY IN LLOYDMINSTER. THE COMPANY PROVIDED PROCESS DESIGN, DETAILED ENGINEERING, AND PROCUREMENT SERVICES FOR THE CUTTING-EDGE FACILITY. HUSKY OIL WOULD GO ON TO BECOME A KEY PLAYER IN ALBERTA'S OIL SANDS, AND AN IMPORTANT CLIENT FOR SNC.

AN INVALUABLE PARTNERSHIP

As the Marketing Manager for the Chemicals and Petroleum (C&P) Division, Taro Alepian was asked to focus most of his attention on the booming Alberta oil market. But by mid-1975, after a year of pounding the pavement and knocking on doors, he had made little progress in Calgary. SNC's greatest selling point was the highly publicized success of its Sun Oil project, now months ahead of schedule. But with a total value of only $26 million, it paled in comparison to the multi-billion-dollar megaprojects then being planned in Alberta's oil patch.

"They're saying they're impressed with the job we're doing in Sarnia," Alepian reported to Rustin, "but they don't think we have the size or depth for their projects."

Rustin was coming to an unpleasant conclusion. It looked like SNC would have to swallow its pride and form a long-term joint venture with a more established name in the U.S. The good news was that it would have its pick of suitors. Foreign companies were beginning to run up against new protectionist hurdles in Canada. Without meaningful local content on their project teams, their chances of winning contracts dwindled.

SNC eventually settled on petrochemical engineering giant Foster Wheeler. In the spring of 1977, a formal partnership called SNC/FW was formed to carry out C&P projects in Canada, with Rustin as Vice-President and Alepian as Director of Marketing. Backed by the expertise of the Americans, SNC was soon winning much larger jobs. One of the biggest was a follow-up contract for Sun Oil in 1979, another refinery in Sarnia's Industrial Valley. This time it was 10 times bigger than the last. It was, in fact, the largest single project investment in Sun Oil's history.

Hank Fielding of Foster Wheeler (left) and SNC's Tony Rustin congratulate each other on the new joint venture, SNC/FW.

SNC's first Sun Oil job in Sarnia, Ontario.

Japan Steel Works, which had manufactured the world's largest gun barrel for the battleship Yamato during World War II. The company had assured him that they could make the two 700-tonne behemoths by the deadline of March 1, 1983.

Fabricating the gigantic reactors was one thing, but getting them to Sarnia was another matter altogether. The job was finally given to West India Line, which called itself an "unconventional carrier of unconventional cargo."

In April of 1983, the SNC/FW project team was treated to a rare sight. The cargo ship made its way up the St. Clair River with the enormous reactors sitting on its deck. Overhead, storm clouds unleashed a steady downpour as SNC's Construction Manager, Don Colman, ordered his team into action. They had been preparing for months to execute the two biggest lifts ever on a Canadian project.

At first, the operation went remarkably smoothly, despite the rain. The giants from Japan were hauled to the site on equally massive crawlers. Rain continued to pour down as they were carefully unloaded and attached to the powerful pulley system that would lift them, centimetre by difficult centimetre, into position.

Things got dicey only when it came time to lift the second of the two reactors. At one point, the rain caused the rollers to balk under the enormous burden. The incident was an important test for the worker incentive program SNC/FW had devised to encourage initiative and quick thinking. The erection crew made steel jigs on the spot to brace the load, while riggers sprang into action, making adjustments to the elaborate pulley system. Within a few hours, the operation was completed, and in half the originally estimated time.

Month after month, the team continued to meet its objectives. One year later, SNC/FW turned the plant over to Sun Oil on time, within budget, and with an accident rate that was well under the industry average. It was a great triumph for a division that, only a decade earlier, had barely had enough expertise to complete its first project.

In 1983, SNC oversaw the two biggest lifts ever in the Canadian construction industry for its second Sun Oil project in Sarnia, Ontario.

Construction Manager Don Colman (left) gives CEO Jean-Paul Gourdeau a tour as the project is wrapping up in 1985.

THE GIANTS FROM JAPAN

The price tag was not the only thing that was enormous about the new Sun Oil job. In early 1980, SNC's Procurement Manager, Hart Schubert, hunted high and low for a company that could produce the project's gigantic steel reactors. After an exhaustive search in Canada, Schubert finally turned to

CHAPTER 14

A PAIR OF ENGINEERING MONUMENTS

The mid- to late 1970s are a time of great challenges for Lavalin. The company has mobilized thousands of employees for the James Bay project and a strong balance sheet allows it to diversify across Canada, particularly in the chemicals and petroleum sector. Meanwhile the firm tackles two daring structures. Co-ordinated by Jacques Lamarre, the futuristic Olympic Stadium project in Montreal is finished just in the nick of time, while the Martyr's Arch in Algeria, engineered by Normand Morin and Pierre Lamarre and managed by Pierre Ranger, requires the use of revolutionary construction techniques to meet its deadline.

The Martyr's Arch in Algeria.

From left to right:
Marcel Dufour; Ronald
Collie, the President of
Pipe Line Technologists;
and Bernard Lamarre.

A Pipe Line Technologists
project in Waterton
Lakes, Alberta, and the
construction of the
Charles-J.-Des Baillets
water filtration plant in
LaSalle, Quebec.

By early 1974, Lavalin was feeling the full effect of the James Bay project. Working alongside Bechtel, the company was receiving an accelerated education in the finer points of megaproject management. Employees from both companies rubbed elbows and sweated over the same problems, exchanged ideas, and developed solutions. James Bay was bringing Lavalin much more than world-leading expertise, however. Revenues from the project had put the company comfortably in the black.

At board meetings that year, much of the discussion revolved around how to allocate the influx of capital. It was the sort of problem that managers dream of having. But if the possibility of dividing up the profits was floated, it was not entertained for very long. Prospects were opening up across the country that would finally allow Lavalin to become the company Bernard Lamarre had long envisioned. The time had come to conquer the Canadian market.

That year, Lamarre dispatched Marcel Dufour to look into acquiring a petrochemical company in Alberta, where high oil prices had triggered a new black gold rush. A consultant soon led him to Pipe Line Technologists, a subsidiary of the American company Kaneb Limited. As interest in Alberta's oil grew, new cross-country pipelines were being planned to bring it from the west to the east. The consultant assured Dufour that the acquisition of Pipe Line Technologists would give Lavalin a good chance of participating in those projects.

Lavalin immediately acquired a 70-percent stake in Pipe Line Technologists and renamed it Petrotech. With little petrochemical expertise of its own, Lavalin thought it best to negotiate a 10-year agreement for technical support with Kaneb. The initial success of Petrotech (contracts for a methanol plant in Kitimat, British Columbia, and a primary treatment plant in Norman Wells in the Northwest Territories) encouraged Lavalin to purchase the remaining 30 percent the following year.

Meanwhile, the company had moved to acquire the Canadian interests of Houston-based Parsons in Calgary, which had natural gas and bitumen treatment expertise. Partec Lavalin, as the subsidiary would now be known, soon won a contract to expand an oil refinery in Prince George, British Columbia.

One of the largest acquisitions of this time came by way of Lavalin's work on the Charles-J.-Des Baillets water filtration plant in LaSalle, Quebec. Lavalin had been hired to engineer and manage construction of the state-of-the-art facility in 1972. By February 1975, Janin Construction, the project's largest contractor, had been brought to the verge of financial collapse. Expensive oil had caused the price of steel to double overnight. Janin, which was building the plant for a fixed price, could no longer afford to complete the contract.

When Lavalin's Project Manager, André Fédorowicz, sounded the alarm, Bernard Lamarre called a meeting with the Mayor of Montreal, Jean Drapeau, and the Director of Public Works for the city, Charles-Antoine Boileau. "I am here to tell you that Janin is a victim of economic circumstances," he said. "It makes absolutely no sense to let them declare bankruptcy because of this contract. It will cost us a lot more to finish the job if we hire someone else."

Drapeau had to admit that Lamarre was right. The contract was subsequently modified to take into account the increase in the price of steel, but Janin's problems were not over. The banks still felt the company had to clean up its financials. They insisted that Janin part with Fenco, the pick of its subsidiaries. It had offices in six provinces and a client list that included Algoma Steel, CIP, and Johns Manville, among others. When Fenco went up for sale, Lamarre moved quickly to acquire it. Armand Couture could vouch for its expertise, having worked for the company earlier in his career.

The arrival of Fenco instantly transformed Lavalin from an infrastructure specialist into one of Canada's leading industrial engineering companies. The combined expertise of Partec and Fenco helped Lavalin win an engineering, procurement and construction management (EPCM) contract for its first aluminum smelter located in Grande Baie, Quebec, in August 1977. Like James Bay, it was a major coup. No one had expected the company to be a serious contender, least of all SNC, its main competition for the contract. Gradually, the doubters were learning not to underestimate Lavalin.

THE OLYMPIC STADIUM SAGA

In May of 1970, the International Olympic Committee awarded Montreal the 1976 Games. Mayor Jean Drapeau felt like a long distance runner who had at last crossed the finish line. He had bid hard for the 1972 Olympics only to lose out to Munich. He had won this time by promising a series of ambitious infrastructure projects to support the games.

At the centre of it all would be an audacious, multipurpose sports stadium designed by experimental French architect Roger Taillibert. The stadium's walls would curve in dramatically like an enormous concrete ribcage. The roof would be fully retractable, gathered up by steel cables from a steeply inclined tower. It would be like something out of science fiction.

The city's contractors started excavation work in the spring of 1973, but signs of trouble appeared almost immediately. Before long, the stadium was being compared to a modern day Tower of Babel. Taillibert's visionary designs

Lavalin would never be underestimated again: the company's Grande Baie aluminum smelter project in Quebec.

The Montreal Star

Entertainments

General

Section Four

TUESDAY, MAY 12, 1970

· · · · PAGES 57-72

Marathon effort pays off for Drapeau

Long Olympic run over—Montreal gets Games

■ la météo

LE DEVOIR

Fais ce que dois

Montréal, mercredi 13 mai 1970 10 CENTS

VOL. XLI · NO 111

Un nouveau défi pour l'équipe D-S

Montréal obtient les Jeux d'été

AMSTERDAM (d'après l'AFP, PA, CP) – Montréal organisera les Jeux olympiques d'été 1976. Les membres du Comité olympique international en ont décidé ainsi hier à Amsterdam au deuxième tour de scrutin, qui a donné 41 voix à Montréal, 28 à Moscou et un bulletin blanc.

Jean Drapeau: les Canadiens apprendront l'esprit olympique.

One of Lavalin's "firemen," Jacques Lamarre at work on the Olympic Stadium project.

were difficult to translate into reality, and everyone seemed to be trying to squeeze the city for as much money as they could. By the following year, Gérard Niding, the President of the Executive Council of Montreal, could no longer contain his panic and candidly admitted to the media the project was out of control.

At Lavalin, Bernard Lamarre was becoming increasingly interested in the unfolding debacle. He had always liked mandates whose engineering presented perplexing puzzles, projects that required a steady hand to drive them through to completion. This job had all of the above and then some. He called Mayor Drapeau in July of 1974, offering to fix what many believed was beyond repair. Lavalin, he said, would manage the site, broker peace among the many stakeholders, and co-ordinate the work. At his wit's end, Drapeau gladly lobbed the hot potato into Lamarre's hands.

It was not long before Lavalin's President began to regret his offer. Even his resourceful brother Jacques, who chaired the project's Management Committee, was unable to make much progress. Taillibert was now making regular changes to his already elaborate designs. The architect had been granted carte blanche by the Mayor, so Jacques was powerless to override him. For the younger Lamarre, who insisted on order and accountability, it was the worst kind of nightmare.

By the summer of 1975, Jacques was ready for drastic measures. "It will be impossible to complete the project on time at this rate," he told his brother. "The city has run out of money to pay the contractors, and Taillibert is hardly ever available. When he is around, he makes changes to his plans whether we agree or not. We need to take back control now before it's too late."

"There is an option I've been considering," Bernard said ruefully. "The city will not like it very much, but I don't think we have a choice."

On a dank and dreary day that November, the Lamarre brothers drove to Quebec City to save the project from itself. When they arrived they met up with Guy Coulombe, the Secretary General of the Executive Council of Quebec, and

Claude Rouleau, the province's Deputy Minister of Transportation. The plan was to convince Quebec Premier Robert Bourassa to create an independent body to oversee the project, headed up by the tough-as-nails and streetwise Rouleau.

Cutting the city out of the equation was controversial, but Bourassa soon saw that it was also the only solution. The law creating the Olympic Installations Board (OIB) was drafted that very night and passed at the National Assembly by the week's end. As agreed, Rouleau was installed as President. With one unquestioned captain at the helm, Jacques Lamarre's project team, which included engineers like Paul Roberge, Michel Branchaud, Marius Lavoie, and Maurice Joubert, was finally able to make progress.

Even with Taillibert on the sidelines, however, it was a momentous logistical and technical task. The stadium was a puzzle of 12,000 unique geometrical concrete sections, some heavier than 100 tonnes. It was not possible to complete one section of the curving wall at a time. The stadium's shell had to go up simultaneously from all sides so as not to become unstable during construction. At one point, there were as many as 80 cranes operating on-site and 75 inspectors supervising the work.

The stadium was completed in the summer of 1976 with absolutely no time to spare. Only one blemish marred the project: the tower had been abandoned for lack of time, and now stood at only half its planned height. The failure to complete the tower turned out to be a lucky break when, three years later, local engineering firm Asselin, Benoît, Boucher, Ducharme, Lapointe (ABBDL) realized it could have crumbled under its own weight if built entirely out of concrete the way Taillibert had envisioned.

Perhaps, in time, someone would figure out how to finish the architect's sci-fi masterpiece, but for now, the saga of the Olympic Stadium continued.

The Montreal Olympic Stadium was called both the future of stadium design and a modern-day Tower of Babel.

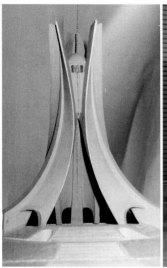

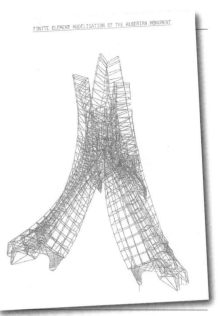

The original plaster model of the Martyr's Arch in Algeria.

The massive ball bearings used during the monument's construction.

A three-dimensional model of the structure generated by Nastran, a sophisticated design program developed by NASA.

ADVENTURES IN ALGERIA

Marcel Dufour had taken over Lavalin International (formerly Lamarre Valois International) in 1979. It had always been his dream to work for a large corporation, and he was determined to use his international marketing network to make Lavalin one of the biggest.

Lavalin had already completed over 300 projects in 60 different countries. Yet, somehow, the Algerian market remained elusive. Out of the last 15 projects it had bid on, Lavalin had managed to pick up only two. What was needed was a presence on the ground in Algeria, someone who could learn the ropes in North Africa the way Yves Beauregard had gotten to know the western part of the continent. As always, Bernard Lamarre had someone in mind. That person was Marie Choquette, the persuasive and intelligent former head of the Arabic Chamber of Commerce of Canada.

It was not long before Choquette brought home the goods. In May of 1981, she called Bernard Lamarre in Montreal and asked him to quickly send over a small team of project engineers. The Algerians had just held a design contest for a monument to commemorate the 20th anniversary of their independence, to be called the Martyr's Arch. Now they needed good structural specialists to tell them if the winner could be built. Lamarre dispatched his brother Pierre, the Head of Lavalin's Structures and Public Works Department, and Claude Naud, one of the company's experts in construction methods.

The Algerians had opted for an 82-metre structure with three massive concrete palm fronds, representing the industrial, agricultural, and cultural revolutions the country had undergone. Pierre Lamarre and Naud grew increasingly concerned as they examined the plaster model created by the winning architect. July of 1982 seemed like an impossibly tight deadline given the monument's size and experimental shape.

It was only when the men were at their hotel that evening that they came up with a solution: what if the lower portions of the three fronds were poured simultaneously and vertically? When concreting reached the point where they began curving away from each other, they could be tilted forward. Concreting could then continue on a vertical axis. It would allow Lavalin to slash as much as 30 weeks from the schedule.

Tilting concrete fronds weighing thousands of tonnes was no simple matter, but the men had a radical solution for that as well: each would rest on two massive lubricated steel hemispheric bearings. When the time was right, the mechanism would allow them to be tipped forward with the help of powerful hydraulic jacks. It sounded crazy, but they were sure it could be done.

Just as Lavalin's team began to believe they could meet the schedule, they were thrown a curveball. Barely two weeks after the contract was signed in October, Commandant Benkortebi of the Algerian Army arrived in Montreal with the tiny plaster model of the monument. He said the government had decided that the structure looked too squat and undignified with its current dimensions. The monument absolutely had to be elongated another 10 metres. It was a matter of national pride.

Lavalin's project team was lost for words. The monument was difficult enough to build with the fronds at 82 metres. Adding another 10 metres would complicate an already titanic task of design and planning. An emergency meeting of Lavalin's Technical Committee was called to evaluate the new proposal. After a three-hour debate, a decision was reached: Lavalin would proceed, but Benkortebi had to agree to help its team navigate some of the difficulties that were bound to arise. There was now absolutely no buffer in the schedule.

Pierre Lamarre immediately got to work on the preliminary engineering of the Martyr's Arch. Normand Morin's team, which included talented young structural engineers like Bernard Breault, used NASA's sophisticated design program, Nastran, to carry out a detailed structural analysis of the monument. Over 2,500 points in the palms were evaluated under 18 different stress conditions. Lavalin's mainframe churned out an enormous pile of paper filled end-to-end with elaborate equations. It took days to comb through all the data, but it would have taken months if they had tried to do the same work manually.

Sheer audacity: Lavalin set a new standard for innovative construction techniques with the Martyr's Arch in Algeria.

When Project Manager Pierre Ranger gave the signal, the jacks began pulling on each leg with the force of 590 tonnes, rocking them gently forward. The entire site held its breath as the centre of gravity of the massive fronds shifted, and the jacks began to restrain them from falling forward.

Centimetre by centimetre, day by day, the jacks drew the monsters closer together. All the while, Construction Manager Richard Limoges sent hourly faxes back to head office in Montreal, where the company's executives were anxiously monitoring the progress. Everyone breathed a sigh of relief when the operation was completed in mid-May. It was not yet time to celebrate, however: the team had less than a month to finish concreting the upper portions.

The Martyr's Arch was completed in the early hours of the morning of its inauguration on July 5, barely nine months after the contract had been awarded. There had not been even a single day to spare in the schedule. Pierre Ranger and his Technical Coordinator, Camille Gallizioli, spent the final hours on their hands and knees, polishing the monument's marble plaza for the elaborate ceremony set to begin just after noon.

The project remained the talk of the engineering world for some time. In August, it earned the cover of the *Engineering News-Record*. The question was beginning to be asked: what could Lavalin not do? The Olympic Stadium, and now the Martyr's Arch: each had been written off as a pipe dream or a disaster waiting to happen. Lavalin had taken on both projects and completed them against all odds.

Camille Gallizioli (left) and Pierre Ranger celebrate after finishing the monument in the nick of time.

The project made the cover of the *Engineering News-Record*.

RACE AGAINST TIME

By the early spring of 1982, the concreting of the three palm fronds reached 50 metres into the air. The time had come to attempt the impossible: the three 4,500-tonne monoliths would now be tilted forward to form a gigantic tripod. An elaborate system of horizontal trusses and powerful hydraulic jacks had been devised to move them into position.

COMPLETING THE TOWER

IN 1984, LAVALIN WAS RETAINED BY THE OLYMPIC INSTALLATIONS BOARD TO COMPLETE THE OLYMPIC STADIUM'S LEANING TOWER AND ITS FUTURISTIC RETRACTABLE ROOF. THE PROJECT HAD TO COMPLY WITH THE ORIGINAL DESIGN AND ARCHITECTURE OF THE STADIUM, BUT THE TOWER COULD NOT BE COMPLETED USING CONCRETE DUE TO A STRUCTURAL PROBLEM AT ITS BASE. A TEAM LED BY NORMAND MORIN, WHICH INCLUDED ENGINEERS CHARLES CHEBL, LUC LAINEY, BERNARD BREAULT, AND YVON LABRECQUE, RESOLVED THE PROBLEM BY REDUCING THE TOWER'S WEIGHT, USING STEEL INSTEAD OF CONCRETE.

CHAPTER 15 | A RISKIER WORLD

The engineering and construction world is changing. SNC is being asked to take on more risk as part of its projects. A case in point is the Sonacome iron foundry in Algeria that SNC wins in 1976. It is by far the company's largest fixed-price engineering, procurement and construction management contract. Camille Dagenais contends that if more such projects await SNC in the future, the time has come to strengthen the company's risk management practices. He begins by inviting four leaders from the larger business community onto SNC's board.

The Sidi Saad dam and spillway in Tunisia.

At the beginning of 1976, the Canadian engineering market was still languishing. But while the percentage of SNC's revenues from domestic operations had dropped in recent years, the contribution from international revenues had been rising.

The message was clear: the company would have to keep winning international contracts to continue to grow. The good news was that there were plenty of large projects going forward on the international scene to feed that growth. The drawback was the additional risk: major engineering, procurement and construction management projects in unfamiliar political, economic, and regulatory environments were not for the faint of heart.

That was certainly true of Sonacome, an iron foundry in Rouiba, Algeria. In the summer of 1976, Gaétan Lavallée and SNC's foundry specialist, Raymond Martel, were locked in tense negotiations with the client. Much was at stake: SNC would be providing the engineering, project management, *and* equipment for one lump sum. Estimating man-hours was easy enough, but with tens of millions of dollars worth of furnaces, moulding equipment, and handling systems, even a slight miscalculation would result in a major loss.

The project would be the validation of SNC's international ambitions, but it would also be the ultimate test of its ability to control costs. Camille Dagenais knew SNC's estimating department, led by Ted Papucciyan, was one of the best in the business, but was it that good? He wanted to find out before committing to the project. As SNC was preparing to present its estimate for the equipment to the client, he called Papucciyan up to his office to review the figures.

SNC signed on the dotted line in September 1976, but it had been a nerve-wracking couple of months. If projects like Sonacome were going to become the norm, Dagenais realized, SNC was now in an entirely new league, one where great rewards had to be weighed against equally enormous risks. Given the new reality, he thought it wise to enlist minds that could bring a broader perspective to the company's internal debates. The time had come to invite outsiders from the larger business community onto SNC's board.

In February 1977, SNC's employee shareholders elected the new directors. Dagenais had hand-picked each of them for their business sense and integrity. There was Guy Godbout, the President and CEO of Valcartier Industries, a munitions manufacturer; Frederick Jones, a financial

The Vice-President of Project Services, Pierre Lamontagne (left), reviews a report with the Vice-President of Project Management Services, Ted Papucciyan.

The Sonacome iron foundry in Algeria was SNC's largest lump-sum contract at the time.

consultant; Frederick Peacock, the President of Peacock Holding Company, a Calgary real estate firm; and Stephen Jarislowsky, President of the investment firm Jarislowsky, Fraser & Company.

Dagenais knew that some private companies had public boards, but that very few had genuine power. To ensure that SNC would be an exception, he asked 10 of the company's 14 employee board members to step down. Only John Turcke, Jack Hahn, Jean-Paul Gourdeau, and he would remain.

THE 1,000-YEAR FLOOD

SNC knew its reputation abroad would be built successful project by successful project, satisfied client by satisfied client. There was no magic formula that would suddenly give the company prominence on the international scene. Sometimes, however, a project like the Sidi Saad dam in Tunisia would catch the eye of the world and instantly raise its profile.

In 1969, the worst floods on record had devastated Tunisia's holy city of Kairouan. From 1972 to 1975, a team led by SNC hydraulic engineer Jean-Pierre Mourez studied the possibility of building two dams to protect against future deluges while irrigating nearby agricultural land. Mourez earned the Tunisians' trust, and SNC was awarded the project for Sidi Saad, the largest of the dams, in early 1976.

The company had designed far larger earthfill dams than Sidi Saad, including LG-3 for James Bay, but this project was by no means run-of-the-mill. The tricky aspect in this case was the spillway that would slice through a limestone mountain on the right bank at a depth of 80 metres. Only such a deep channel

Jean-Pierre Mourez

In 1977, SNC's employee shareholders' board was cut back, and four new directors from the larger business community were welcomed. Clockwise: Guy Godbout, Stephen Jarislowsky, Frederick Peacock, and Frederick Jones.

The Canal of Corinth in Greece (top left) reassured SNC geologist Rock Poulin that his specifications for Sidi Saad's spillway were good.

a reference. After some reflection, he realized that there *was* a precedent for Sidi Saad, although it was not a spillway. The 60-metre deep Canal of Corinth in Greece cut through faulted sedimentary rock in an active seismic zone, and it had held for 100 years.

Poulin boarded a plane and flew to Greece. He spent days at the Canal, examining the rock and making calculations. Within a week, any doubts he had were gone. If the Canal of Corinth had not caved in, neither would Sidi Saad's spillway. He would not take any chances, however. Geophones would be installed throughout the site to detect any movement of the mountain as they blasted down. SNC would also bolt each exposed section of rock in place before proceeding deeper.

With the spillway successfully excavated at the end of the summer, it was up to one of SNC's concrete specialists, Ramy Louis, and a team at the company's subsidiary Terratech to find a concrete mix for the spillway that would withstand a flow of water equal to 7,000 cubic metres per second (the same amount that flows under the Jacques-Cartier Bridge in Montreal). There was only one other spillway in the world designed to handle that quantity of water, and its concrete had been washed out several times.

Louis soon found himself face to face with an enigma. SNC's tests on the concrete made with a nearby aggregate were showing wild variations in its strength. SNC needed a resistance of 30 megapascals, but the test results were all over the map. It was only after an extensive investigation that the mystery was solved: SNC found microscopic amounts of marl in the aggregate, a rock that is severely fissured when dry and highly expansive when moist. It did not take the team long to locate another, marl-free, quarry.

Sidi Saad's spillway was put to the test sooner than anyone anticipated. Another flash flood hit the region in late 1982, as the dam was nearing completion. Over 50 centimetres of rain poured down in a single day—as much as the region usually saw during its entire rainy season. The dam and spillway, soon to be renamed after the country's President, Habib Bourguiba, performed exactly as planned.

would be able to handle the water the dam would need to unleash in a flash flood.

SNC's Chief Geologist, Rock Poulin, and Sidi Saad's Resident Geologist, Richard Simard, had carried out extensive calculations and estimations to ensure it would hold. Nevertheless, in early 1979, as the excavation work was set to begin, Poulin had an uncharacteristic moment of self-doubt. He wanted to be 110 percent sure that he was not leading the company, or the people of the region, into disaster.

If only there were an existing spillway built in similar geological conditions. He would have been able to use it as

THE CITY OF LIGHT

In November 1977, just as the project team on Sidi Saad was getting to work in Tunisia, Marcel Sicard, now the Vice-President of Energy, returned from Saudi Arabia with a contract to electrify the province of Qaseem. SNC would be designing and building 650 kilometres of transmission lines, power plants, and a central energy control system. It was the largest contract of its kind ever awarded in the country.

A new village was soon being built for the 60 families of SNC employees who would spend the next two years there working on the project. Shankar Mantha, the on-site Procurement Manager, went to great lengths to ensure that SNC's team would be comfortable. Each family would have its own three-bedroom villa outfitted with everything from air-conditioning to garlic crushers. There would be a large pool, a recreation centre, a school staffed by Canadian teachers, and a clinic with a Canadian doctor.

Yet, while the majority of families living in the so-called "City of Light" were happy with the accommodations, some had trouble making the adjustment to life in a remote region of an unfamiliar country. Before long, reports of culture shock, heated disagreements, and low morale began filtering back to Montreal.

The news that things were turning sour in Saudi Arabia could not have come at a worse time. The country was

HEELEY OF ARABIA

IN EARLY 1978, SNC ENGINEERING MANAGER STAN HEELEY LED A TASK FORCE WITH A VERY UNUSUAL MISSION. QASEEM WAS APPROXIMATELY THE SIZE OF AUSTRIA AND, FOR THE MOST PART, STILL UNCHARTED. BEFORE THE PROJECT TO ELECTRIFY THE REGION COULD BEGIN, HE HAD TO FIND OUT WHERE THE PEOPLE WERE.

THE KINGDOM DID NOT HAVE UP-TO-DATE MAPS, BUT HEELEY KNEW QASEEM HAD UNDERGROUND AQUIFERS, AND THE PEOPLE OF THE REGION TENDED TO CONGREGATE AROUND THEM TO ACCESS THEIR WATER. WITH THE HELP OF A MAP THAT IDENTIFIED THE AQUIFERS, HIS TEAM DISCOVERED OVER 300 VILLAGES AND AN ESTIMATED POPULATION OF 350,000.

in the middle of an industrial boom, and SNC's scope of work on Qaseem was growing exponentially. The project's 360-megawatt power station had nearly doubled to 600 megawatts. It would now have 20 substations instead of 15. Suddenly, what had begun as a $300-million project, had grown to $1 billion. SNC needed everyone rowing hard in the same direction.

In the summer of 1979, Dagenais and Sicard travelled to the town to deal with the problem head on. Dagenais stood in front of the crowd at a general assembly and listened patiently to the grievances of a handful of the expatriates. Most

The City of Light, where 60 SNC families were housed during the Qaseem project in the early 1980s.

SNC's Executive Committee in 1977. From left to right: Jean-Yves Côté, Vice-President, Subsidiaries; Alex Taylor, President and CEO of SNC/GECO; Richard Balfour, Vice-President, Marketing; Louis Grenier, Vice-President, Personnel; Jacques Laflamme, Vice-President, Products; Pierre Lamontagne, Vice-President, Project Services; Jean-Paul Gourdeau, President and Chief Operating Officer.

were minor, but he tried to reserve judgment. He knew these people were under a lot of stress.

"I know it's not always easy to adapt to an unfamiliar country," he told one villager. "You have to be open and willing to see the world from a new perspective. Look at this as an adventure, and know that we are there to support you. But if you feel you cannot make that adjustment, then we'll move you to another project."

Dagenais' candid talk helped. Some of the disgruntled residents were impressed that the CEO of the company had taken the time to come out there and hear what they had to say. Others chose to accept his offer to be relocated, realizing that the job was not what they had expected.

Qaseem was successfully completed in 1985, but SNC's management was left wondering how its recruitment process could be improved. Clearly, new measures were needed to ensure a similar situation did not repeat itself. As the project was wrapping up, Tom Ross, SNC's Director of International Personnel, retained a psychologist to interview anyone SNC wanted to send overseas. Now, for the first time, as much consideration would be given to the families of employees as to the employees themselves.

SNC would soon get better at vetting its people for sensitive international assignments. But for the time being, it would just have to endure the growing pains that were a natural part of becoming an international company.

PART 5 | SNC-LAVALIN

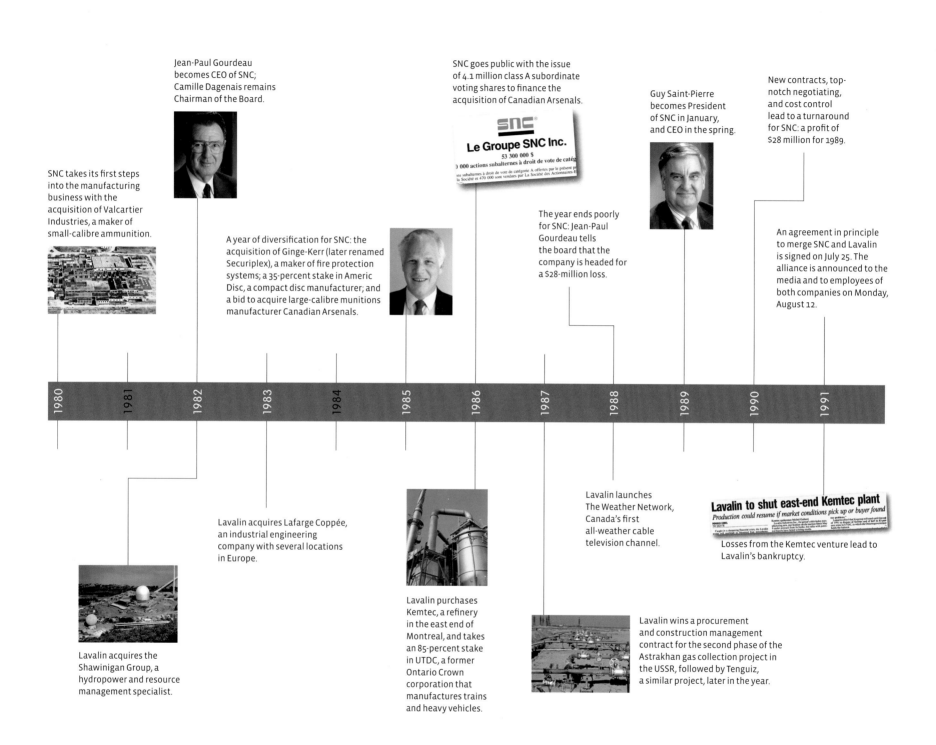

SNC takes its first steps into the manufacturing business with the acquisition of Valcartier Industries, a maker of small-calibre ammunition.

Jean-Paul Gourdeau becomes CEO of SNC; Camille Dagenais remains Chairman of the Board.

A year of diversification for SNC: the acquisition of Ginge-Kerr (later renamed Securiplex), a maker of fire protection systems; a 35-percent stake in Americ Disc, a compact disc manufacturer; and a bid to acquire large-calibre munitions manufacturer Canadian Arsenals.

SNC goes public with the issue of 4.1 million class A subordinate voting shares to finance the acquisition of Canadian Arsenals.

SNC
Le Groupe SNC Inc.
53 300 000 $
000 actions subalternes à droit de vote de catég
us subalternes à droit de vote de catégorie A offertes par le présent p
la Société et 470 000 sont vendues par La Société des Actionnaires-E

The year ends poorly for SNC: Jean-Paul Gourdeau tells the board that the company is headed for a $28-million loss.

Guy Saint-Pierre becomes President of SNC in January, and CEO in the spring.

New contracts, top-notch negotiating, and cost control lead to a turnaround for SNC: a profit of $28 million for 1989.

An agreement in principle to merge SNC and Lavalin is signed on July 25. The alliance is announced to the media and to employees of both companies on Monday, August 12.

1980 1981 1982 1983 1984 1985 1986 1987 1988 1989 1990 1991

Lavalin acquires the Shawinigan Group, a hydropower and resource management specialist.

Lavalin acquires Lafarge Coppée, an industrial engineering company with several locations in Europe.

Lavalin purchases Kemtec, a refinery in the east end of Montreal, and takes an 85-percent stake in UTDC, a former Ontario Crown corporation that manufactures trains and heavy vehicles.

Lavalin launches The Weather Network, Canada's first all-weather cable television channel.

Lavalin wins a procurement and construction management contract for the second phase of the Astrakhan gas collection project in the USSR, followed by Tenguiz, a similar project, later in the year.

Lavalin to shut east-end Kemtec plant
Production could resume if market conditions pick up or buyer found

Losses from the Kemtec venture lead to Lavalin's bankruptcy.

PREVIOUS PAGE
The alliance between SNC and Lavalin was one of the most talked about business stories of the year in Canada.

CHAPTER 16

SNC ON THE TICKER

Ambitions ride high at SNC in the 1980s. In an attempt to protect the company from the swings inherent in the engineering sector, new CEO Jean-Paul Gourdeau and the Vice-President of Finance, Michael Pick, begin acquiring companies in the manufacturing sector. Valcartier Industries and Canadian Arsenals, two Canadian munitions manufacturers, are purchased. To secure the capital for the latter, SNC goes public in 1986. The feeling of euphoria is soon washed away when Canadian Arsenals runs into difficulty, resulting in a $32-million loss in 1988. The decade ends with Guy Saint-Pierre taking the reins of the company and refocusing it on its core business.

Jean-Paul Gourdeau (left) and Michael Pick watch as SNC stock makes its appearance on the Montréal Exchange in June of 1986.

SNC moved into Complexe Desjardins in Montreal in May of 1976. The building was designed by its competitor, Lavalin.

SNC's foray into manufacturing began with the signing of the contract to acquire Valcartier Industries in September of 1980. From left to right: Jean-Paul Gourdeau, Guy Godbout, and Michael Pick.

By 1980, Michael Pick had been SNC's Vice-President of Finance and Development for almost two years. Boisterous, with a reddish complexion and a corona of white hair, Pick sometimes seemed to literally be burning up with new ideas. Where others saw only risk, Pick occasionally saw phenomenal hidden opportunities.

He generated his best ideas while walking, so it was not unusual to see him pacing the corridors of the executive floor of the Complexe Desjardins building, lost in thought. Occasionally he would stop, eyes suddenly ablaze with excitement, and rush into Jean-Paul Gourdeau's office with a brainwave. But, while Pick acted on inspiration, he was guided by careful financial reasoning.

These were qualities that Gourdeau felt made him the ideal man to engineer SNC's diversification. The regular boom and bust cycles in the engineering sector had always been an albatross around the company's neck. With Pick's guidance, Gourdeau hoped to enter new sectors that would provide a cushion against the downturns. The ideal acquisitions would offer economic stability and solid growth while spinning off new technologies applicable to SNC's other activities.

A first candidate came along in April of 1980. One of SNC's most senior board members, Guy Godbout, approached Gourdeau about buying his company, Valcartier Industries (IVI), a manufacturer of small-calibre ammunition for military, law enforcement, and sporting use located just outside Quebec City. Following some disagreements over management style, Godbout had bought out his partners. Now that he was at the helm, however, he realized that running a company of 1,000 with a partly unionized staff was more than he could handle on his own.

The numbers excited Pick, and he strongly urged Gourdeau to move on the offer. It was perfect, he told him. With the Department of National Defence (DND) as a customer, the acquisition would help provide some of the stability they were looking for.

SNC's board of directors scrutinized Pick's acquisition proposal at a meeting on May 1, 1980. Godbout left the room for the discussion and waited outside impatiently. When he was called back in, SNC offered him two options: either $7 million right away, or three times the after-tax profits from the next three years of sales, up to $9 million. Godbout chose the latter, and by September, SNC had closed the deal and taken its first step into the manufacturing business.

THE BAD NEWS...

At the 1982 Annual Meeting of Shareholders, Camille Dagenais officially relinquished the position of CEO to Gourdeau, although he would remain Chairman of the Board for a little while yet. It was time; he had recently turned 61. Still, it had not been an easy decision. He knew he was turning over control to his protégé in some of the most miserable economic conditions in Canadian history.

The root of the problem lay in the skyrocketing cost of oil, which greatly accelerated the pace of inflation. The Canadian government had reacted by raising interest rates, but the tactic had completely frozen the flow of capital. Economists had to come up with a new term to describe the phenomenon: "stagflation," a hybrid of *stagnation* and *inflation*.

For SNC, stagflation meant the cancellation of projects large and small. The biggest setback was in Alberta, where the difficult economic situation was only aggravated by the Canadian government's National Energy Policy. The previous summer, Imperial Oil had announced that its Cold Lake oil sands megaproject, on which SNC/FW was working, would be suspended until the federal and provincial governments could stop bickering and agree on a single energy policy.

"Jean-Paul, we both know what's coming down the pipe," Dagenais had said before handing over the position of CEO. "Maybe I should stay on for another year to make the cuts and bear the brunt of the criticism."

"Thank you, Camille, but that's always been my role," Gourdeau replied with characteristic stoicism. "I'll clean up this time, too." Indeed, Gourdeau had been the axe man in 1967, and then again in 1976. It had been hard on him. He cared about his employees, but SNC absolutely had to come first. His father, an orphan at the age of nine, had taught him that you do what you need to do to carry on, no matter how difficult.

Besides, Dagenais had done more than enough for the firm during his long career. SNC had grown from a company of 650 employees with revenues of $7.4 million in 1967 when he took the reins, to one with 4,600 employees and revenues totalling $231 million in 1982. It had been an amazing journey,

and Gourdeau was determined that it should continue. He just had to get SNC through what was shaping up to be one of the toughest periods in its history.

...THE GOOD NEWS

It was not all doom and gloom. As Pick and Gourdeau had hoped, IVI provided a modest but crucial revenue stream during 1982.

SNC also received a sizable contribution to its bottom line from Canatom, of which it was still a one-third owner. The nuclear services provider was currently working on power plant projects in South Korea and New Brunswick. Both facilities were at the absolute forefront of safety design. The core meltdown of the Three Mile Island nuclear station in Pennsylvania had occurred when the projects were still at the design phase. Canatom had subsequently worked with Atomic Energy of Canada Limited (AECL) to dramatically raise the safety standards of the plants to meet new, more stringent international requirements. SNC also had help at home from the Canadian International Development Agency (CIDA) and

A 'DAM' GOOD ENGINEERING FIRM

IN APRIL 1982, CAMILLE DAGENAIS WAS UNANIMOUSLY ELECTED PRESIDENT OF THE INTERNATIONAL COMMISSION ON LARGE DAMS (ICOLD) AT THE ORGANIZATION'S ANNUAL CONGRESS IN RIO DE JANEIRO. IT WAS THE REALIZATION OF A LIFELONG AMBITION AND RECOGNITION THAT SNC'S DAM ENGINEERING EXPERTISE HAD REACHED THE ABSOLUTE CUTTING EDGE. SNC'S KNOW-HOW WOULD BE CONFIRMED AGAIN THE NEXT YEAR WHEN THE COMPANY WAS AWARDED THE FIRST PHASE OF THE CHAMERA HYDROELECTRIC DEVELOPMENT IN INDIA. THE PROJECT HAD MANY CHALLENGES, NOT THE LEAST OF WHICH WAS ITS LOCATION IN AN ACTIVE SEISMIC ZONE IN THE HIMALAYAS.

Henno Lattik (left) and Bob Minto inspecting a model of Tintaya. The copper mine and concentrator, SNC's first major contract in South America, was built at an altitude of over 4,000 metres in the Peruvian Andes.

The Wolsong 1 nuclear power plant in South Korea.

Export Development Canada (EDC). CIDA funded its expansion of the Idukki hydroelectric development in India, while EDC financed close to $100 million worth of equipment and materials from Canadian suppliers for the Tintaya copper concentrator project in Peru. SNC had completed a couple of projects in the country, but this was by far the largest. It helped that SNC had top copper expertise in its new Vice-President of Mining and Metallurgy, Bob Minto, and an experienced project manager in Henno Lattik, but there was no doubt that EDC financing had made SNC's submission more attractive.

THE LURE OF MANUFACTURING

By the end of 1984, Michael Pick and Bill Pearson, the Vice-President of Power, were exploring the concessions market with investments in mini-hydro plants in the United States. The company was buying small facilities in the northeast of the country, refurbishing them, and putting them up for sale a couple of years later. The projects were bringing in more than badly needed revenues. They were also providing work for SNC's top engineers during a time when man-hours were scarce.

For now, however, the main focus of the diversification remained manufacturing. Just prior to the Annual Meeting in March 1985, SNC had finalized the purchase of the Canadian operations of Ginge-Kerr (later renamed Securiplex), a maker of fire protection systems. Another move into manufacturing was being made even as Gourdeau spoke to shareholders. SNC had recently signed on to design and build a compact disc factory in Quebec for the French company Moulage Plastique. There was a catch, however. Jittery about expanding its activities, the company wanted SNC to take a 35-percent stake in the venture, to be called Americ Disc. Pick, who was enamoured with the technology, had urged SNC to snap up the deal.

The third manufacturing acquisition that year would give SNC a monopoly in the Canadian munitions market. On May 23, 1985, Canadian Arsenals went up for sale. The Conservative government of Brian Mulroney was in the process of privatizing certain Crown corporations, and Canadian Arsenals was the latest. The company was Canada's main provider of large-calibre munitions, with some 850 employees at plants in Le Gardeur and Saint-Augustin, Quebec.

When the sale was announced, Gourdeau called a special board meeting to request permission to make an offer. The first move into munitions had provided an essential cushion during a tough year, allowing SNC to make a modest profit. Canadian Arsenals, Gourdeau and Pick believed, would finally give SNC real protection from the fluctuating demand in the engineering market.

The success of IVI tipped the scales in Gourdeau's favour, and the board gave him the go-ahead to make a $59.6-million offer. SNC was confident its figure would put it ahead of the other bidders, but on November 14, the government upped the ante. All interested parties received a surprising telex: "The Government arranged for an independent valuation of Canadian Arsenals Limited as an ongoing business by a recognized consulting firm," it read. "This valuation indicates a value range of $80 to $98 million dollars…"

It was an enormous amount of money for SNC at a time when a sluggish economy made for few opportunities. It looked like the company would barely generate $224 million in revenues for the year, but the assessment suggested the acquisition would quickly pay for itself. The numbers had to be correct since the seller was also the only client. SNC decided to bid at the high end, and offered $92.5 million. It could not afford to lowball since it was known that engineering rival Lavalin was gunning hard for Canadian Arsenals as well.

Michael Pick, Senior Vice-President, Finance and Development (left), and Michel Villemaire, who played a leading role in the new compact disc company, examine their product.

In a November 1987 profile of Jean-Paul Gourdeau in the Montreal daily *Le Devoir*, the CEO of SNC outlined his rational for investing in the defence sector.

Jean-Paul Gourdeau
Voulant la paix, SNC prépare la guerre
PORTRAIT

CLAUDE TURCOTTE

Encore cinq ans et le Groupe SNC aura un chiffre d'affaires de $ 1 milliard M Jean-Paul Gourdeau avance ce pronostic sur le ton banal d'une conversation de routine. Pourtant cette entreprise, dont il est président du conseil depuis l'an dernier et chef de la direction depuis 1982, se relève à peine de la récession de 1982 et pour donner raison à M. Gourdeau elle devra doubler au moins le chiffre d'affaires de $ 450 millions qui devrait être le sien cette année.

Le ton du président s'explique de deux façons. D'une part, la rhétorique et la communication ne sont pas ses points les plus forts; d'autre res de SNC atteignait $ 223 millions et l'an passé il effleurait $ 350 millions.

Le Groupe SNC, reconnu comme l'une des principales sociétés d'ingénieur-conseil au monde, connaît d'ailleurs une évolution marquée depuis 1979, alors qu'il décidait de diversifier ses activités pour compenser l'effritement prévu de ses débouchés traditionnels en ingénierie-construction. Au lieu de toujours construire pour d'autres, pourquoi ne prendrait-on pas nous-mêmes une croissance économique mais surtout parce qu'il nous installe sur le chemin de la haute technologie. Je n'ignore pas que cette industrie n'a pas la cote d'amour de tout le monde mais je dois dire que nous n'avons pas l'intention de nous en cacher explique M. Gourdeau.

En 1981, le Groupe SNC achète donc Industries Valcartier, qui fabrique balles et cartouches de petit calibre. Par la suite, il fait l'acquisition de Sécuriplex de Pointe-Claire, un spécialiste des systèmes électroni-cipal client est le gouvernement canadien pour le moment du moins, car l'entreprise cherche à exporter davantage, ce qu'elle fait déjà un peu dans certains pays de l'OTAN.

Le Groupe s'intéresse en outre à des activités non militaires, en possédant en tout ou en partie des installations diverses, comme des minicentrales hydro-électriques aux USA. On le retrouve dans la fabrication de disques audionumériques à Drummondville. Il est actionnaire aussi de Petro-Sun International, spécialiste du recyclage et de la protection de l'environnement, un domaine qui intéresse beaucoup SNC. Il investit aussi dans l'immobilier dont $ 40 millions dans la construction de la Place Félix-Martin à Montréal, un édifice de 21 étages dans lequel tout le siège social déménagera au début de 1988.

Cette diversification ne pouvait survenir à un moment plus opportun, puisque la récession de 1982 a frappé très durement le Groupe SNC, en lui faisant perdre des contrats d'ingénierie pour des projets de $ 16 milliards, tels ceux de Cold Lake en Alberta et de l'aluminerie de La Terrière. En fait, la récession se termine à peine SNC, puisque son chiffre d'affaires dans les activités de construction dépasse en 1987 de 5 %, seulement celui de 1982. Pour la première fois en trois-quarts de siècle, les revenus manufacturiers dépasseront cette année ceux de l'ingénierie-construction. Le secteur de la défense pour sa part apportera environ 55 % du chiffre d'affaires, soit $ 240 millions, dont 10 % en ventes à l'exportation.

■ « Nous avons identifié la défense comme étant l'industrie la plus stable et qui est du reste un puissant moteur économique dans la plupart des pays. Nous avons choisi ce secteur pour son grand potentiel de croissance économique mais surtout parce qu'il nous installe sur le chemin de la haute technologie. Je n'ignore pas que cette industrie n'a pas la cote d'amour de tout le monde mais je dois dire que nous n'avons pas l'intention de nous en cacher ».

In the end, SNC's figure was just enough to officially make it the highest bidder on December 2. The company's Vice-President of Law, Denis Crevier, immediately began preparing an Initial Public Offering for the SNC Group to raise the massive amount of capital needed to complete the transaction.

At the Annual Meeting on March 19, 1986, shareholders authorized the board of directors to issue a block of shares valued at about $30 million. SNC issued 4.1 million subordinate class A shares, each entitling the holder to one vote. In order to maintain control of the company, employee shareholders retained most of the class A shares and all of the unlisted class B shares, which entitled a holder to 15 votes.

Gourdeau, Pick, Crevier, and Treasurer Gerard Legault were invited to the Montréal Exchange on June 11 to welcome the appearance of SNC on the ticker. The first public issue, which was also offered on the Toronto Stock Exchange, raised $53.3 million, significantly more than anticipated. Two thirds of the fresh capital went to the acquisition of Canadian Arsenals, while the remainder was earmarked for new acquisitions.

At the Annual Meeting in March of 1986, shareholders voted overwhelmingly in favour of a public issue of SNC shares. Denis Crevier was charged with filing the prospectus.

While SNC was finalizing the deal, Dagenais had given up the chairmanship of SNC's board to Gourdeau, who would remain CEO. It seemed fitting that he should depart now that the journey, which had begun with his bible so many years earlier, had been completed. For decades, Dagenais had run SNC like a public company. Now, at long last, it was one.

ANNUS HORRIBILIS

The bad news began in the summer of 1987, when Michael Pick lost his short battle with throat cancer. His death was more than a personal loss for Gourdeau. Only Pick, the guiding light in the transformation of SNC, had been fully aware of all the financial nuances of its recent acquisitions and investments.

Pick had been gone only a few weeks when Americ Disc ran aground. The market, it turned out, was already saturated with major CD manufacturers. The biggest problem with Americ Disc did not have anything to do with external forces, however. The fact was that SNC simply did not know how best to market its product. Its people were engineers and constructors, not CD salesmen. They could carry out projects that were second to none, but they were at a loss when it came to hawking high-tech wares.

Now in 1988 there were more headaches. A strike at IVI began in April. Backed by the Confederation of National Trade Unions, workers were demanding a three- to five-percent raise every year for three years. Gourdeau countered with two percent, a generous offer given SNC's financial situation. The union had so far refused to budge, and orders were backing up.

The final blow came in May, when DND unilaterally cancelled 50 percent of the orders it had promised to Canadian Arsenals. Gourdeau, though bloodied by the string of bad news, was far from beaten. He felt he had grounds for taking the government to court for the shortfall in orders, and enlisted the services of the company's Legal Department in the fight. He had no illusions, however: the dispute would not be resolved quickly. The loss of hundreds of thousands of man-hours at Canadian Arsenals, combined with the problems at IVI made for a worrisome outlook.

This prospectus constitutes a public offering of these securities only in those jurisdictions where they may be lawfully offered for sale and therein only by persons permitted to sell such securities. No securities commission or similar authority in Canada has in any way passed upon the merits of the securities offered hereunder and any representation to the contrary is an offence.

May 22, 1986

Initial Public Offering and Secondary Offering

The SNC Group Inc.

$53,300,000
4,100,000 Class A Subordinate Voting Shares

Of the 4,100,000 Class A Subordinate Voting Shares offered by this prospectus, 3,630,000 are issued and sold by the Corporation and 470,000 are sold by The SNC Employee - Shareholders Corporation Inc. (the "Holding Company").

The price of the Class A Subordinate Voting Shares offered hereby was determined by negotiation between the Corporation and the Underwriters. The price of each Class A Subordinate Voting Share exceeds by $5.36 its pro forma consolidated net tangible book value at December 31, 1985, after giving effect to this offering (see "Dilution").

The Corporation confirms that the 3,630,000 Class A Subordinate Voting Shares issued and sold by the Corporation pursuant to this prospectus will qualify for inclusion in a Quebec stock savings plan entitling an eligible purchaser to _____ _____ 1986 taxation year, 50% of their acquisition cost.

_____ approved the listing of the Class A

That summer, Gourdeau ordered an internal audit to assess the damage. Meanwhile, he took pains to reassure the board that all was not lost. He still believed that Canadian Arsenals could be turned around. Gourdeau was also labouring day and night to reel in some potential contracts in Quebec. SNC was getting tantalizingly close to winning a pair of important aluminum smelter jobs for Pechiney in Bécancour and Reynolds in Baie-Comeau. If they materialized, the company would soon find itself back in the black.

AN ENGINEER, A SOLDIER AND A DIPLOMAT

As Gourdeau was trying to set SNC back on the rails, he was also attending meetings of the board's Human Resources Committee to review possible candidates to replace him when he retired in April 1989 after eight years as CEO. The other committee members were Paul Paré, a former Chairman of Imasco, Robert Vachon, Chairman of the Christie Group, Harry Macdonell of the Toronto law firm McCarthy & McCarthy, and a new board member named Guy Saint-Pierre, a former Provincial Liberal minister of Industry and Commerce and currently the Senior Vice-President of John Labatt.

An excellent candidate emerged in April 1988. During yet another meeting to discuss replacements for Gourdeau, Paul Paré mentioned that his company had hired its new CEO directly from its board. Dagenais, who had been specially invited, had an epiphany as he left the meeting: SNC also had the perfect candidate on its board. He was an engineer, he had been in the military, and he had gained sorely needed

manufacturing experience through his work at Labatt. Clearly, the best man for the job was Guy Saint-Pierre.

The only question was, would he be willing to become the captain of a ship that appeared to be taking on water? Gourdeau, who had known him for many years, asked him.

Saint-Pierre's first reaction was a disbelieving smile. "You're not serious?"

"We're absolutely serious."

"Well, I wasn't thinking of leaving Labatt. I was planning to stay another two or three years before taking early retirement. Let me think it over. If ever I decide to leave, I promise you'll be the first to know."

In 1988, SNC and Lavalin competed for a pair of aluminum smelter projects in Quebec.

A PLACE TO CALL HOME

IN 1986, SNC BEGAN CONSTRUCTION OF ITS OWN HEADQUARTERS IN MONTREAL. THE BUILDING WOULD BE LOCATED ON THE FORMER SITE OF COLLÈGE SAINTE-MARIE, ARTHUR SURVEYER'S ALMA MATER. SNC WOULD CALL IT PLACE FÉLIX-MARTIN IN HONOUR OF THE ARCHITECT, ARTIST, SCHOLAR, HISTORIAN, AND JESUIT TEACHER WHO HAD PLAYED AN IMPORTANT ROLE IN THE CITY'S HISTORY.

snc

NOUVEAU SIÈGE SOCIAL

Dès le 4 janvier 1988,
vous pourrez nous rejoindre au

2, Place Félix-Martin
Montréal (Québec) Canada H2Z 1Z3
Téléphone (514) 866-1000
Télécopieur 866-0795

NEW HEADQUARTERS

From January 4, 1988,
you can reach us at

2, Place Félix-Martin
Montréal, Québec, Canada H2Z 1Z3
Telephone (514) 866-1000
Fax 866-0795

Guy Saint-Pierre

In 1988, Jean-Paul Gourdeau led a tough rationalization program that slashed spending and eliminated unprofitable operations.

It was one of the most difficult decisions of Saint-Pierre's career. Labatt was no longer the same company since its operations had been informally split into two separate units. Saint-Pierre headed up the agrifood side, and had little communication with those who led its beer brewing business. He had begun to feel like he was working in a silo. The top job at SNC, on the other hand, would be complex and demanding, to say the least.

By mid-June, the balance had tipped slightly in favour of SNC. Saint-Pierre called Gourdeau to tell him he was willing to consider the offer. He felt SNC had a remarkable history, talented employees, and, with some hard work, good prospects. Besides, he had never been one to turn down an assignment just because it was challenging.

By early October, Saint-Pierre and SNC had come to an informal agreement. He would become President in January 1989, but would not sign on as CEO until the spring. Gourdeau insisted on remaining at the helm until the Annual Meeting in April to address the Canadian Arsenals problem. Afterwards, he would continue to help Saint-Pierre restructure the company as its Chairman.

Later that month, Gourdeau presented the Assessment Committee's report to the board, along with a recovery program. First came the good news: the company had made some progress in its negotiations with the federal government over the cut to orders for Canadian Arsenals. SNC had managed to claw back half of the promised 700,000 person-hours.

From there he moved on to the bad news. There was no use sugar-coating it. The company, he told them, was headed for a loss of at least $28 million, or $2.61[1] a share. As expected, the poor results were largely due to a downsizing of operations at Canadian Arsenals.

The board members had been anticipating losses in the neighbourhood of $10 or $12 million, but never $28 million.

Saint-Pierre, who had not yet even taken up his new position, began to wonder what he had gotten himself into.

"I know it's enormous," Gourdeau continued, speaking over the reactions of disbelief, "but if we wait any longer, it will be worse. The company is still in good financial health, but we must act immediately."

SNC chairman Jean-Paul Gourdeau stands in front of Place Félix-Martin.

SNC focuses on core businesses after axing unprofitable operations

By ROBERT WINTERS
of The Gazette

Jean-Paul Gourdeau, chairman of SNC Group Inc., said yesterday the company's $4.3-million loss in 1987 should not scare away investors from its stock because the loss represents elimination of money-losing operations.

"It's very much un... the moment," ...e interview ...m the ...me de... ...se to ...7.5

... year for SNC," and predict... ...ng performance in ...tions

fence production includes ammunition and shells.

SNC had profit of $12.1 million in 1985 and $8.7 million in ... company

SNC stocks haven't recovered since crash.

1. Adjusted for future stock splits on May 31, 1996 and March 10, 2006, the amount would be $0.29.

CHAPTER 17

FROM CORPORATION TO CONGLOMERATE

And then there were four. Lavalin's owners in the 1980s. From left to right: Armand Couture, Marcel Dufour, Bernard Lamarre, and Jacques Lamarre.

The 1980s see Lavalin continue with acquisitions. Several new companies are purchased, including Shawinigan, an engineering firm in the power sector. Like its rival SNC, Lavalin then moves into the manufacturing sector. It acquires Kemtec, a refinery in the east end of Montreal, and then Urban Transport Development Corporation (UTDC), a maker of heavy vehicles and trains in Ontario. UTDC fails to meet expectations, and Kemtec turns to disaster when the price of its main feedstock rises above the cost of its principal product. By the end of the decade, Lavalin must face the fact that its long winning streak has come to an end.

The recession of 1982 was the first time since the Second World War that Lavalin had made cuts to its personnel. Bernard Lamarre called all department managers into his office and solemnly told them he needed 10-percent reductions across the board. The managers were then invited to counter and propose lower percentages, some of which were accepted, some of which were not. It was excruciating work. There were real families behind the numbers. Fortunately, the Martyr's Arch project in Algeria and the follow-up contract for an associated cultural centre helped preserve several hundred jobs that would otherwise have been lost.

The devastation caused by the recession only confirmed to Lamarre that his diversification strategy had not been bold enough. Ideally, the more areas you were active in, the less likely you were to be affected by downturns, which tended to hit certain regions or sectors harder than others.

Lavalin proceeded to step up the pace of its Canadian expansion. The early 1980s saw the acquisition of several major companies, including James F. MacLaren, which was active in municipal engineering, water treatment, and industrial and nuclear waste disposal, and had offices in Ontario and Manitoba. Next came King, Murphy & Associates, in Richmond, British Columbia, which operated mainly in the pulp and paper sector. The biggest acquisition of the time was the Shawinigan Group. It was what was left following the nationalization of the Shawinigan Water and Power Company in 1963, but it was by no means a small company. Specializing in hydropower and resource management, it had six main operating units across Canada staffed by over 1,000 employees. Shawinigan was also a one-third partner in Canatom, along with SNC and Monenco, so it had considerable nuclear expertise as well.

With the rapid growth came another reorganization of Lavalin's management. By 1983, Lavalin's top executives numbered only four: Bernard Lamarre, who owned 41.92 percent of the shares, and his brother Jacques, Marcel Dufour, and Armand Couture, who each held 19.36 percent. Bernard Lamarre had less than half the shares, but he maintained control over the direction of the company thanks to an old clause that stipulated that any change to its charter required a 67-percent majority approval.

While there was never any question about who was running the show, Lamarre had come to rely heavily on the

Lavalin's successful completion of the Martyr's Arch in 1982 quickly led to a follow-up contract for an associated cultural centre, a godsend in a tough year.

talents of his associates. Each had carved out a specialty niche within the company. Armand Couture, whose analytical abilities allowed him to cut incisively through the dense legal thickets of even the most complex contract, was responsible for Lavalin's multi-divisional jobs. Marcel Dufour could dial a long distance number to the other side of the world and reach exactly the right contact. He had built up a marketing network that was quite literally the envy of the engineering business. Bernard's younger brother Jacques commanded immediate respect on project sites through a remarkable combination of force of personality and humility. If there was a problem on a project that required special attention, Jacques was often parachuted in to put things back in order.

They made a formidable team, but they would have to redouble their efforts to stay afloat during such trying economic times.

BACK IN THE USSR

Lavalin first made contact with the Soviet Union following the signing of a co-operation agreement with the USSR and Alberta for gas projects. The Soviets had come to the province to have a look at the gas extraction abilities of Partec and had left impressed. The highly corrosive gas in Alberta, which Partec had been extracting for decades, was almost identi-

cal to the gas in the USSR. Partec was also adept at drilling through permafrost, and the Soviet Union had plenty of that.

In 1977, Lavalin was invited to bid on the Astrakhan gas collection project in the Caspian Sea. Negotiations got off to a promising start, but the USSR's invasion of Afghanistan two years later put a halt to Lavalin's dreams of penetrating an unlimited oil and gas market. As a reprisal for the invasion, the Canadian government refused to guarantee financing on the project.

When Astrakhan was resurrected a few years later, Lavalin's hopes ran high once again. Determined to win the

The mid-1980s saw Lavalin break into the Soviet oil and gas sector with Astrakhan and Tenguiz, a pair of high-profile gas extraction projects.

PARTNERS ON THE LOWER CHURCHILL

IN 1979, 12 YEARS BEFORE THE TWO COMPANIES OFFICIALLY MERGED, SNC AND LAVALIN FORMED A JOINT VENTURE TO PURSUE PROJECTS IN NEWFOUNDLAND CALLED SNC-LAVALIN NEWFOUNDLAND. SEVERAL PROJECTS WERE WON, INCLUDING A FEASIBILITY STUDY FOR THE TRANSMISSION AND DISTRIBUTION COMPONENT OF THE LOWER CHURCHILL FALLS HYDROELECTRIC DEVELOPMENT.

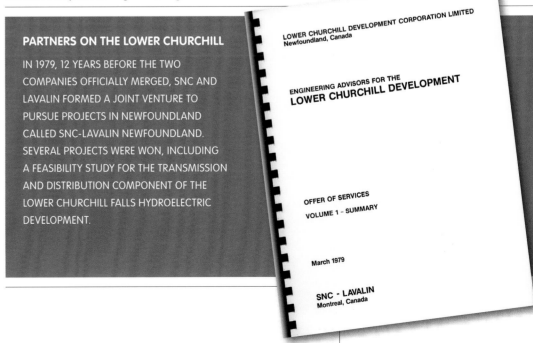

LOWER CHURCHILL DEVELOPMENT CORPORATION LIMITED
Newfoundland, Canada

ENGINEERING ADVISORS FOR THE
LOWER CHURCHILL DEVELOPMENT

OFFER OF SERVICES
VOLUME 1 – SUMMARY

March 1979

SNC - LAVALIN
Montreal, Canada

Rodolphe Chiasson
Marcel Dufour

Lavalin Industries is born with the acquisitions of the Kemtec refinery in the east end of Montreal and UTDC in Ontario.

job this time, Marcel Dufour marshalled the company's full marketing might and millions of dollars to pursue the project. Lavalin then submitted a proposal and waited . . . and waited some more. Four years later, they learned that the contract had gone to a German competitor.

Dufour was deeply discouraged and ready to give up on the USSR, but Rodolphe Chiasson, his Vice-President, urged him to persist. "Marcel, we've paid our entrance fee, and learned a lot about bidding in the Soviet Union as a result. Don't give up now."

"What we've done is waste a lot of money," Dufour countered.

"Yes, but maybe we can be smarter about how we spend money in the future," Chiasson said. "The Soviets have no interest in hiring a Canadian firm because Canada buys little from them. On the other hand, they export a lot of natural gas to France, so they are much more inclined to buy goods and services from them. If we could work through a French company, we would have a better chance."

In December of 1983, Lavalin took Chiasson's advice and acquired Lafarge Coppée, an industrial engineering company with offices in Brussels, Paris, and London. The expertise of Partec, combined with Coppée's presence in France, finally opened the gates. In 1987, state-owned Machinoimport awarded Lavalin a procurement and construction management contract for the second phase of the Astrakhan project. A few months later came Tenguiz, a similar contract for a similar project.

At a time when the Soviet Union was all but closed to Western firms, many industry watchers wondered how the company had pulled off the feat. There seemed no limit to what Lavalin, and its highly entrepreneurial president, could accomplish.

LAVALIN INDUSTRIES INC.

In March of 1986, Lavalin plunged into petrochemicals manufacturing with the purchase of Kemtec, a refinery in the east end of Montreal. The facility, which produced phenol, cumene, acetone, and benzene, among other compounds, had originally belonged to Gulf Canada. The company had sold the refinery to Ultramar, which then turned around and sold it to Lavalin for $6.5 million.

There was only one catch: in order to get the plant's 100 unionized workers on side, Lavalin had to promise to keep the refinery running at a minimum 80 percent of its capacity for at least five years. It was a risk, but Lavalin's management was put at ease by an independent review that extolled the benefits of going ahead with the deal. The company had also received verbal assurance from the provincial government, which desperately wanted Montreal's petrochemical industry to survive. They said Kemtec would have their support if things got tough.

Lavalin would soon conclude another major manufacturing acquisition. That summer, it secured an 85-percent stake, worth $50 million, in the Ontario government's Urban Transport Development Corporation (UTDC). The Crown company had plants in Kingston and Thunder Bay that made

trains and heavy vehicles. It had manufactured the cars for the first phase of the Skytrain in Vancouver, so its expertise was clearly top-notch.

As always, Bernard Lamarre had big plans for his latest acquisition. Intelligence was coming in from Lavalin International about the great potential of the Asian mass transit market. Countries in the region were not rich enough to afford conventional underground subways, but UTDC's ground level and elevated track systems were less expensive. Lavalin International was already canvassing potential clients in Indonesia, Malaysia, China, and India.

Modernizing a refinery and pursuing far-flung mass transit contracts in Asia required significant capital, however. To get it, Lavalin combined UTDC and Kemtec under a single holding company called Lavalin Industries and took it public in April of 1987. It was the company's second subsidiary to be listed on the stock market. Two years earlier, Lavalin had launched an Initial Public Offering for its research and development subsidiary, LavalinTech. In both cases, the company felt it best to retain the majority of the shares for now.

TELEVISION…REAL ESTATE…

In early 1988, Lavalin decided to add paraxylene to Kemtec's list of products. It purchased a plant that produced the compound in Puerto Rico, and began shipping its components to Montreal. Once the facility was reassembled at the Kemtec site, the enhanced capacity would allow Lavalin to capture over two percent of a lucrative market. By the year's end, it also looked like the acquisition of UTDC was about to bear fruit. Lavalin was in negotiations with Turkish officials for a mass transit system in Ankara and was on the shortlist for a similar project in Bangkok, Thailand.

Feeling upbeat about the company's recent acquisitions, Bernard Lamarre continued to seek out other ventures that would expand Lavalin's reach and transform it into the global conglomerate he envisioned. He was prepared now to move even further afield from the engineering and construction market if the numbers made sense.

At the start of the year, the company launched The Weather Network, Canada's first all-weather cable television channel. The idea originated from MacLaren Plansearch's meteorological team in Halifax, Nova Scotia, which provided the station with data. From its first day on the air in September, the network was reaching 5 million households across Canada.

Lamarre also heard the real estate sector beckon. Back in 1958, when he had visited New York City for the first time, he had been profoundly impressed by the towering skyscrapers that formed its skyline. Gazing up at the Rockefeller Center and the Chrysler Building had been an awe-inspiring experience. During that visit, the dream of building a skyscraper in Montreal was born. It was finally realized in 1989 when ground was broken for Le 1000 De la Gauchetière. Lamarre went to the renowned architect Dimitri Dimakopoulos, who had designed Lavalin's headquarters at 1100 René-Lévesque boulevard several years earlier.

Lamarre had wanted to build a structure that would tower majestically above the city's skyline, but had to settle for one that would barely peak above it. A municipal by-law stipulated that no building could obscure the view of Mount Royal, limiting its height to 232.5 metres. That would still make it the tallest building in the city, however, and among the 10 tallest in the country. It would have other distinguishing features, including a full-sized indoor skating rink and a major bus terminal in its basement. Lavalin would own 35 percent of the building and move its head office into the first 15 floors when it was completed in 1992.

In the late 1980s, Lavalin was getting close to securing a major mass transit contract in Bangkok, Thailand.

The realization of a dream: Le 1000 De la Gauchetière under construction in the early 1990s.

The outbreak of war in the Persian Gulf marked the beginning of the end for Kemtec.

Lavalin prepares for a long legal battle: the company was sued for $200 million by the bank that lent it the capital to purchase the planes it intended to sell to Aeroflot.

HARD DECISIONS

In January of 1991, mere weeks after Kemtec began producing paraxylene, American fighter planes were flying missions over Iraq, fuelled by the plant's main feedstock, naphtha. Naphtha became so expensive that it soon cost more to produce paraxylene than Kemtec could ever hope to sell it for. Contractually obliged to maintain production, Lavalin was soon funnelling over $5 million a month into the facility.

The Gulf War did more than sink Kemtec deeper into debt. By destabilizing the entire region, it also hurled an enormous wrench into Lavalin's negotiations for the Ankara transit project in Turkey. Contract talks in Thailand would suffer an unforeseen setback that year as well when a bloodless military coup ousted the country's government. The ruling junta immediately began reviewing all contracts approved by the previous regime. It was terrible news to say the least. Lamarre had been counting on the transit projects to shore up Lavalin's finances.

All was not yet lost, however. There was still hope that a recent venture would help Lavalin bounce back. The deal had been in the making since late 1989, when Lavalin had learned that Aeroflot, the Russian airline, wanted to buy 10 Airbus A-310 planes from PWZ Corporation in Calgary. Due to the longstanding Western embargo, the Soviet company needed an intermediary. Lavalin had moved quickly and set up a deal to broker the planes in January 1990, buying two of the jets, and committing to purchase eight others.

Now, one year later, Lavalin was still waiting for Aeroflot to complete the transaction. As the weeks passed, Lamarre grew increasingly concerned. His fears were finally confirmed in February, when Aeroflot announced it was pulling out of the deal. Mikhail Gorbachev's ambitious economic reforms had led to a serious downturn in the Soviet economy, and Aeroflot was no longer able to honour its commitment. Lavalin had to give up its $52-million deposit when it reneged on the purchase of the remaining Airbus planes. Paris-based Caisse Nationale de Crédit Agricole, which had financed the deal, immediately sued the company for $200 million, alleging breach of contract.

It was incredible: it seemed as if the fates were conspiring against Lavalin to thwart its recovery. Under increasing strain, the company's management was realizing that, this time, they were in an unwinnable situation. Now even the National Bank, the only financial institution that it had done business with for most of its existence, was marshalling its lawyers. The unavoidable reality was that Lavalin simply had no cash. All of its profits had been sunk into an ambitious expansion program since the early 1970s. The cupboard was, as the expression goes, totally bare.

PHOENIX FROM THE FLAMES

Lavalin's debts lead to its bankruptcy and bring it face to face with SNC to negotiate a merger of the two companies. Discussions begin when Armand Couture approaches Guy Saint-Pierre with an offer in the summer of 1991. After a few weeks of feverish negotiations and a round-the-clock due diligence investigation led by Chief Financial Officer Pierre Robitaille, SNC acquires Lavalin's engineering assets. The result is the largest Canadian engineering company, and a major player on the world scene. CEO Guy Saint-Pierre must now manage the integration of the two companies with the same care he displayed during the negotiations.

Guy Saint-Pierre addresses the assembly of Lavalin and SNC employees.

The numbers looked so good to SNC's new President and Chief Operating Officer, Guy Saint-Pierre, that he hesitated to believe them at first. It was February 22, 1989, and he had put together a budget forecast that he knew would dumbfound SNC's top management when he presented it to them in two days' time. It said the company would make a profit of $13.3 million for the year on revenues of $385.6 million. After the difficulties of 1988, it was an unbelievable turnaround.

Tony Rustin, SNC's Senior Vice-President of Operations, warned him that his figures would be greeted with scepticism. Saint-Pierre trusted Rustin's judgment, but he also believed in his numbers. They had come directly from his vice-presidents, division managers, and presidents of subsidiaries. There was also solid evidence to suggest they would hold up.

First, there were major new contracts. SNC had landed the Pechiney and Reynolds aluminum smelter expansions just before Saint-Pierre's appointment. Both projects were in Quebec and valued at well over $500 million. Second, Jean-Paul Gourdeau had aggressively cleaned house, slashing overhead, closing offices, and leaving Saint-Pierre with a scaled-down but more efficient organization. Third, SNC was getting closer to resolving the Canadian Arsenals problem. The company's new Vice-President of Law, Michael Novak, was focusing on the fact that Public Works and Government Services Canada (PWGSC) was both the seller and only client of Canadian Arsenals. That had made the original valuation assessment, based entirely on PWGSC's future munitions orders, all the more reliable. In a normal situation it was buyer-beware when it came to revenue projections, but this was clearly a special case. It now looked like the government was ready to award SNC a $29-million settlement, including $15 million in cash, and the remainder from future sales of surplus munitions to approved international markets.

For all of these reasons, Saint-Pierre decided to go ahead and present the numbers to his top managers—which included Frank Bury, the head of Defence Products, Taro Alepian, who oversaw Process Plants, André Gagnon, from Power and Heavy Civil Works, Gordon Gerry, who looked after western Canada, and Bill Pearson, in charge of the U.S. The meeting

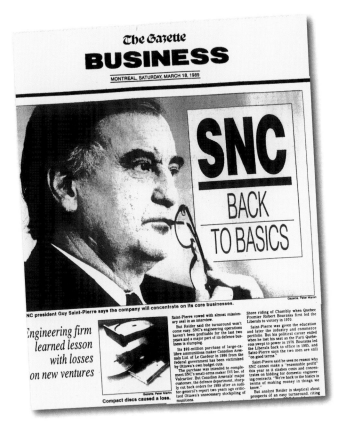

The Gazette

BUSINESS

MONTREAL, SATURDAY, MARCH 18, 1989

SNC BACK TO BASICS

SNC president Guy Saint-Pierre says the company will concentrate on its core businesses.

Engineering firm learned lesson with losses on new ventures

Compact discs caused a loss.

took place in the third-floor conference room of Place Félix-Martin, the company's new headquarters.

"As you can see," Saint-Pierre said after listing off the projections for each division, "that brings us to a total of $13 million for the year." As Rustin had warned they were less than enthusiastic.

"Look, I know you don't believe me," Saint-Pierre said. "Let's go over the figures line by line, and each of you can ask questions about whatever bothers you."

The managers scrutinized Saint-Pierre. Some of them were still deciding what to make of their new President. He was tall and broad shouldered with the poised air of a veteran diplomat. There was definitely something about him that inspired confidence, an unshakable level-headedness. Maybe it was true and SNC was indeed on the road to recovery.

They agreed to go ahead and take a hard look at the numbers. It was no-holds barred, brutal honesty all the way. "You say that you'll make $200,000 this year even though you lost $200,000 last year," Saint-Pierre said to the first manager. "What have you done to turn things around?"

"Well, we won an important contract, and we put in a lot of effort to make sure it was well negotiated," he answered. "We didn't make the same mistake as last year."

Gradually, as manager after manager justified his figures, the atmosphere in the group shifted to one of cautious optimism. For his part, Saint-Pierre was now certain SNC was going to hit its target. What the managers did not know was that the original forecast had actually indicated a profit of $20 million. Saint-Pierre knew the figure would have been ridiculed as pure fantasy, so he had trimmed it by $7 million. His six-year career in provincial politics had taught him many things, including the importance of caution when it came to projections.

BREAKFASTS WITH THE PRESIDENT

When Saint-Pierre used to tour Labatt's various manufacturing sites, managers often wanted to show him the equipment the moment he arrived, vaunting its amazing output and efficiency. But Saint-Pierre would always stop them, saying that he first wanted to talk to workers on the factory floor.

Employees were the real value of the company, he would remind the managers. It was this fundamental belief that led Saint-Pierre to launch the Breakfasts with the President program.

In the spring of 1989, when Saint-Pierre officially replaced Gourdeau as CEO, he began holding early morning meetings with employees from all levels. As many as 24 attended the breakfasts each week. By summer, the tour had taken him to every office and allowed him to meet over 600 employees. The CEO was always careful to note what he learned from them, but, he too had a message to convey: "We have to quickly become profitable," he said. "But if I'm here and you're here, it's because we believe we can make it."

The mission that year was to target the Canadian market, rebuild relationships with clients, and focus on SNC's core strengths: aluminum, chemicals and petroleum, and power. The strategy quickly paid off. By mid-year, there were contracts for a polypropylene plant in Quebec, the second phase of the James Bay project, and Husky Oil's upgrader on the Alberta-Saskatchewan border. Of course, all the new work

A PAIR OF BREAKTHROUGHS

IN 1990, AFTER A SIX-YEAR EFFORT, TARO ALEPIAN BROUGHT HOME A BREAKTHROUGH CONTRACT TO DESIGN AND BUILD SNC'S FIRST PROJECT IN THE SECTOR, THE HIBERNIA OFFSHORE PLATFORM ON THE GRAND BANKS OF NEWFOUNDLAND AND LABRADOR. THE SHALLOW-WATER PLATFORM INCLUDED A CONCRETE GRAVITY BASE STRUCTURE WITH A CRUDE OIL LOADING SYSTEM, SUBSEA INSTALLATIONS, AND TOPSIDES FOR THE DRILLING, PRODUCTION, PROCESSING, AND SHIPMENT OF 110,000 BARRELS A DAY OF CRUDE.

THAT SAME YEAR, SNC WAS AWARDED A CONTRACT TO ADD A THIRD POTLINE TO THE TOMAGO ALUMINUM SMELTER IN AUSTRALIA, A COUNTRY WHERE IT HAD NEVER WORKED BEFORE. THE 140,000-TONNE-PER-YEAR EXPANSION, LED BY TOP PROJECT MANAGER PIERRE LAMONTAGNE, WOULD BE COMPLETED AHEAD OF SCHEDULE, BELOW BUDGET, AND WITH AN EXCELLENT SAFETY RECORD.

snc

horizon

ASSEMBLÉE ANNUELLE

La meilleure année de notre histoire

«À l'assemblée annuelle de l'an dernier, nous avons dû donner les résultats de la pire année de l'histoire de l'entreprise. Aujourd'hui, nous sommes… vélés avisés et nous en recueillons les fruits aujourd'hui. Je songe particulièrement aux entreprises qui sont devenues fructueuses en 1989 grâce, en des divisions des Produits de défense SNC : IVI, Sécuriplex… tré une reprise à la fin de 1988 et connu une année des plus partie, à la construction de deux importantes installations d'usines d'Électa… *Nous pouvons maintenant considérer que 1988 a fait partie des revers qui marquent l'évolution et la croissance de toute entreprise».*

ANNUAL MEETING

Spectacular turnaround no miracle, says president

"If you were with us here last year, you may have been septi-cal about our chances of suc-… struction contributed $168.9 million; $180.6 million came from defence. *From a net loss of $32.9 million in 1988, or $3.14 a share, the company jumped in one year to a net income… 1989 revenues rose* million from $86 million last year. The total split into $45.6 million from engineering-construction and $50.7 million from defence.

In 1989, the best results in SNC's history were "no miracle."

would mean little if the contracts were not well negotiated. Tony Rustin had been working to reinvigorate SNC's Proposal and Contract Review Committee.

Quarter after quarter, Saint-Pierre's projections held up. Soon, the $7-million buffer began to look like excessive caution. By the annual meeting in April 1990, SNC's CEO was grinning ear to ear as he announced not only a spectacular turnaround, but the best results in the company's history. Net income had rocketed to $20.3 million in 1989, and that was without counting $7.8 million generated mainly from the sale of Sandwell Swan Wooster in Vancouver. It was almost a mirror image of the previous year, when SNC had recorded a loss of over $32 million.

"No miracle came to our aid," he said. "The patience of our shareholders, the confidence of our clients, and the loyalty, competence, and team spirit of all our employees were the sole ingredients that brought about this spectacular turnaround."

Saint-Pierre was pleased to remind shareholders of the stunning performance of SNC's stock price. Its dramatic rise from $4[2] in January 1989, to over $11[3] by early 1990, had earned it first place in terms of growth on the Montréal Exchange, and third on the Toronto Stock Exchange. It was still undervalued, he felt, but it was once again headed in the right direction.

DÉNOUEMENT

By the start of 1991, Bernard Lamarre was distracted by a million preoccupations. His year-long battle to save his empire from the flames of bankruptcy had taken a heavy toll on him.

Now it would extract the ultimate concession: In January, the consortium of banks to which Lavalin owed over $120 million handed immediate control of the company's finances to accounting firm Raymond Chabot Martin Paré et associés. Lavalin would need to ask the firm's permission every time it wanted to make a financial transaction—no matter how small.

Each of the eight banks in the consortium had its own interests, but they agreed on one thing: Lavalin had to cut its expenses drastically to reduce its debts, or they would never be repaid. They asked the company to produce an in-depth report on its finances, and come up with a strict cost-cutting program.

Lavalin's accountants did not need to look very deep to see that, aside from its profitable engineering business, not much was going well. The biggest culprits were Kemtec and UTDC. In May, the company began shopping around the troubled subsidiaries, but there was little interest in either. UTDC received a few light nibbles, but Kemtec, which had lost $21 million in the last nine months, sent potential buyers running.

In early June, with Lavalin's $135-million line of credit almost exhausted, the consortium issued a final ultimatum: either sell UTDC and Kemtec soon to start repaying your debts, or we will cut off your supply of money. The Quebec government, which had been nervously eyeing Lavalin's collapse, now felt compelled to act. On June 14, it issued a $10-million loan guarantee for Lavalin through the Société

2. Adjusted for future stock splits on May 31, 1996 and March 10, 2006, the price would be $0.44.

3. Adjusted for future stock splits on May 31, 1996 and March 10, 2006, the price would be $1.22.

de développement industriel (SDI). It was the only way that the banks would agree to raise Lavalin's line of credit to $145 million.

Lavalin appreciated the loan, but there was a general feeling among its executives that it was too little, too late. The company had ventured into the Kemtec deal with verbal assurances from the government that it would support them if things got tough. When the price of naphtha went through the roof in January of 1990, destroying Kemtec's business model, the government had not been there.

Nevertheless, the loan bought the company a little more time to find buyers for Kemtec and UTDC. The banks were now also pressuring Lavalin to unload some of its profitable interests like The Weather Network. Clearly there was no way Lavalin would be able to repay its creditors by selling only money-losing ventures. Most painful of all for Bernard Lamarre, the company had to give up its 35-percent stake in the remarkable Le 1000 De la Gauchetière.

Through all this, Bernard Lamarre's chief concern was the jobs. Lavalin had been many things to him, but it had always been first and foremost an employer of people. The thought that all those jobs might suddenly disappear was a horrifying proposition that kept him up late into the night.

Lavalin's associates were not faring much better. Bernard's younger brother Jacques had his own regrets. He took responsibility for his role in the mess but was grateful for the valuable lessons he had learned in the process. He would never forget the horror of being under the thumb of the banks nor the risks inherent in being dependent on the government for aid.

Armand Couture was shaken, but he remained composed and tactical in his thinking. He investigated the possibility of merging with other companies on behalf of the four owners. He was also working hard to keep Lavalin's executives together while the headhunters circled the camp. As a united front they would have far more bargaining power with potential partners and the banks.

Marcel Dufour, meanwhile, concentrated on maintaining Lavalin's enormous backlog of international projects worth hundreds of millions of dollars. Clients were beginning to learn of Lavalin's difficulties, and they were getting nervous. He spent much of his time reassuring them that a solution would soon be found, and that their projects would go forward. The daily speculation in the press about Lavalin's financial woes was making that increasingly difficult, however.

©1991 The Globe and Mail ■ Canada's Business Newspaper Saturday, June 8, 1991

Lavalin empire showing stress

Lamarre may no longer be running conglomerate

©1991 The Globe and Mail ■ Canada's Business Newspaper Friday, June 14, 1991

Lavalin seeks loan guarantee worth 'tens of millions'

Cash-strapped engineering empire wants provincial help

Lavalin to shut east-end Kemtec plant

Production could resume if market conditions pick up or buyer found

RONALD LEBEL
THE GAZETTE

Caught in a deepening financial crisis, the Lavalin group will mothball its Montreal East petrochemicals complex in the next two weeks and lay off most of the 300 employees.

Kemtec Petrochemical Corp., in which Lavalin has invested over $150 million in the past three years, said yesterday its 230 production workers will be let go by Aug. 9 as chemical departments shut down one by one.

Company president Damien de Gheldere said he remains confident that manufacturing will resume once conditions improve in the plastics and polyester industries, Kemtec's main markets.

Sales and plant-maintenance operations will continue, but head-office layoffs were not ruled out. "After Aug. 9, we'll see which measures must be taken," said

Kemtec spokesman Michel Guitard.

Lavalin Industries Inc., the group's debt-laden manufacturing arm, put Kemtec on the auction block May 9 under pressure from its banks, but talks with potential buyers have failed to bring results.

De Gheldere said he is "on the lookout for new investors," suggesting that Lavalin now wants to retain a stake in the unit instead of selling it outright.

In a terse statement, he blamed the temporary shutdown on "the combined impact of the corporate financial situation and the depressed state of world markets for its products."

Lavalin chairman Bernard Lamarre complained last month that the group's bankers were pressing for rapid disposal of affiliates like Kemtec and UTDC, the Toronto-based transit-system builder.

"If we sell quickly in the current economic climate, the sale will bring nothing much," he told La Presse. "And if we don't get anything much, that won't solve

our problems."

Lamarre added that his group will need until the end of 1991 to dispose of Kemtec and of half its 85-percent stake in UTDC, in which the Ontario government holds the balance.

Lavalin Industries, which consists largely of the Kemtec and UTDC operations, has piled up a debt load of $230 million since it went public just before the 1987 stock-market crash. The company lost about $4 million last year on sales of $548 million. First-half results have not been issued.

Officials have said the modernization of the Kemtec complex cost much more than expected because of an explosion, a fire and other mishaps that sharply curtailed output for 15 months ending last January.

The old Gulf Oil refinery was overhauled and enlarged with equipment imported from Puerto Rico to produce a wide range of petrochemicals. Lavalin bills the paraxylene plant as the 14th-largest in the world.

As Lavalin's financial woes deepened, the attention from the media grew more intense.

Lavalin's Airbus transaction dealt the company a final blow.

OPERATION PHOENIX

By early 1991, few in the engineering world did not know Lavalin was in financial difficulty—least of all its main competition in Canada, SNC. Guy Saint-Pierre had been following the evolving story in the press, but was by no means savouring Lavalin's misfortune. Admittedly, the two companies had long been fierce competitors, but they had also worked together successfully on many joint ventures, and there was much mutual respect between their engineers.

What bothered Saint-Pierre most about Lavalin's predicament was the possibility that a major foreign competitor might sweep in to gobble up the company, sparking a battle for the Canadian engineering market.

"I don't know exactly what Lavalin's situation is," Saint-Pierre warned Quebec's Industry Minister, Gérald Tremblay, in January, "but like everyone else, I know things are not going well. That makes them tempting prey, as we ourselves were not so long ago, for large European and American firms. If Bechtel buys Lavalin and Fluor comes after us," he continued, "they may very well have the support of the American

government. Canada would then lose its two largest engineering firms, along with know-how painstakingly built up over decades."

By March, Saint-Pierre had asked SNC's new President of Operations for Engineering and Construction, Alain Perez, to head up "Operation Phoenix." As the name suggested, the goal was to figure out how Lavalin might rise from the ashes through an association of some kind with SNC.

"Come up with a few scenarios," Saint-Pierre told him. "Obviously we don't want to buy everything, but there are excellent parts, like the engineering arm, that we should be looking at. Figure out a few ways this could happen."

FIRST CONTACT

Guy Saint-Pierre had just begun his vacation on the morning of June 5, when his secretary, Nicole Girard, called his country home on Lake Memphremagog. She hesitated to disturb him, but she suspected he would want to take this call.

"I have Armand Couture on the line," she said. "He says it's urgent." Saint-Pierre knew Couture was Lavalin's resident diplomat and deal-maker. Given the circumstances, there could be only one reason why he was calling.

"It's no secret that we're having difficulties," Couture began cautiously. "We're looking at several restructuring scenarios. Some options might be better than others, and one of them might concern you."

Saint-Pierre drove back to Montreal that afternoon and went straight up to the main conference room on the 21st floor of SNC's headquarters, where he found Couture waiting. The Lavalin executive drew a one-page handwritten proposal out of his briefcase.

"The situation has reached a point where we must separate the engineering business from the Lavalin Group, which will very likely go into bankruptcy," he said, handing the sheet to Saint-Pierre. "So what we are discussing now is really just the engineering and construction business."

Couture explained that the firm's 14 top executives wanted to incorporate a new company to take over Lavalin's engineering operations. A symbolic investment of one dollar plus goodwill, evaluated at $33 million, would give Lavalin's executives a 33-percent stake. SNC was being asked to put up $20 million for 20 percent of the company. The remaining 47 percent, equal to an investment of $47 million, would temporarily belong to the banks. A merger of SNC's engineering arm and the new joint company would take place two years later, after which SNC would hold more than 50 percent of the shares.

There were a few things that Saint-Pierre did not like about the deal. For one thing, the value of Lavalin's goodwill, its intangible assets, was based on a combination of its technical reputation and its estimated backlog, which could not be assessed without delving into the company's books. Couture said Lavalin was unwilling to open them until they had an agreement in principle. There was also the fact that Couture's deal would preserve Lavalin's current salary structure. Saint-Pierre did not like the idea of having two sets of executives under two different remuneration systems.

Still, it was a real first offer and a major gesture from Lavalin. Saint-Pierre proposed that they have a second meeting the following Monday. It would give him time to review the offer with his Chief Financial Officer, Pierre Robitaille.

Robitaille was more than a brilliant number cruncher. As Ernst & Whinney's Managing Partner for Quebec, he had led several corporate financial restructuring programs, which put

him in an ideal position to dissect Couture's proposal. Within a few days, he had put together a counteroffer that he felt would give SNC a better guarantee for its investment, while ensuring a more rapid integration of Lavalin's personnel.

"Your proposal is too rich, Armand," Robitaille began. "We would like to pay for the goodwill on the basis of actual results instead of projections." Robitaille then laid out SNC's counteroffer. A new company would be created for a nominal sum of $1. A full 55 percent of the shares would be held by Lavalin's 14 top executives, and 45 percent by SNC. The shares would be worth nothing at first, but their value would grow

Armand Couture

Pierre Robitaille

THE GAZETTE   WEDNESDAY, AUGUST 7, 1991

FOCUS

Engineering a rescue?

2½ years ago SNC Group was losing money now it's seen as possible savior of rival Lavalin

SHIRLEY WON
THE GAZETTE

When Guy Saint-Pierre took over the reins at SNC Group Inc. 2½ years ago, the engineering and defence-products manufacturing firm was losing money. And its stock had plummeted to as low as $3.25 a share.

With a backlog of orders and a combination of business and political savvy, Saint-Pierre, 57, has managed to turn the Montreal company into a profitable enterprise. SNC stock closed yesterday at $16.625.

Now, SNC Group is being hailed as a potential savior of its financially-strapped arch-rival Lavalin group of Montreal through some kind of a merger between their engineering divisions.

PLEASE SEE **SNC**, PAGE C2

Analysts say an engineering alliance would produce a powerful Quebec-based giant that could compete more effectively for projects on the world stage.

"It would make sense," Jon Reider, a Montreal-based analyst with stockbroker Richardson Greenshields of Canada Ltd., said yesterday.

"They are the two largest engineering companies in Canada, both based in Montreal, very reputable on the international stage and known for expertise in hydro-electric power. There are a lot of synergies between the two."

SNC has confirmed it is holding intensive talks with Lavalin, which has been under pressure by the Quebec gov-

$ Closing stock price on TSE

Source: Infomart   The Gazette

Stock generally up since 1989.

La Presse
LE PLUS GRAND QUOTIDIEN FRANÇAIS D'AMÉRIQUE

DÉTAILS CAHIER SPORTS   ● MONTRÉAL, MARDI 6 AOÛT 1991   107ᵉ ANNÉE Nº 282   58 PAGES, 4 CAHIERS

La fusion de Lavalin et SNC se négocie activement

VALÉRIE BEAUREGARD

a fusion de Lavalin et SNC est imminente et pourrait intervenir d'ici à une se... ine.

...e ministre de l'Industrie, du ...merce et de la Technologie ...ld Tremblay a « bon espoir » ...les problèmes de Lavalin se ...ront « avant la fin de la se... ...ine », selon son attaché de presse Jean-Luc Trahan. Le minis-

tre estime qu'il est « important d'avoir un secteur de génie-conseil d'envergure mondiale » dans un contexte de globalisation des échanges commerciaux.

Lavalin et SNC, toutes les deux de Montréal, figurent respectivement au premier et au deuxième rang des sociétés de génie-conseil canadiennes.

Des sources proches du dossier indiquent que la fusion des deux compagnies se négocie activement.

M. Trahan dit que les partenaires sont en place, que les discussions ont lieu et que la volonté est la. Il qualifie de « très bonnes » les chances de succès des négociations sans vouloir toutefois préciser l'identité des intervenants. Cependant, tout porte à croire que la société d'ingénierie SNC est le candidat idéal pour former un tandem de cette envergure.

De plus, le gouvernement a déjà clairement indiqué qu'il s'av-

surera que le contrôle de Lavalin puisse demeurer québécois.

Le président de l'Ordre des ingénieurs du Québec, M. Jean-Pierre Brunet, donne son appui au projet de fusion entre Lavalin et SNC. Il estime qu'une société de cette taille pourra décrocher des contrats qui n'étaient pas accessibles autrement. « Une fusion

VOIR LAVALIN EN A 2

with time as contracts materialized. "When the shares appreciate, you will be in a position to accumulate new assets," Robitaille said.

Couture was not enthusiastic. SNC was proposing an asset sale: a deal in which it would take on the contracts and employees of Lavalin's Engineering Division, but not buy its debt-laden subsidiaries. Without the subsidiaries, Couture argued, the contracts would be in jeopardy. SNC countered that most clients would agree to re-sign with the new company, but Couture was not convinced—particularly when it came to international contracts, where bidding procedures were more formal.

Talks between SNC and Lavalin continued over the next week with a third meeting. There were now more players at the table, which suggested both growing seriousness and caution. Lavalin had hired Serge Saucier of the accounting firm Raymond Chabot Martin Paré et associés to counsel its executives. Yves Bérubé, Lavalin's new President, was now also attending the negotiations. On the SNC side, there was André Gagnon, SNC's Senior Group Vice-President of Power, and a former Lavalin associate who had maintained relations with many of his erstwhile colleagues. Saint-Pierre and Robitaille were, of course, there as well.

Despite the talent at the table—or perhaps because of it—little progress was made. After a fourth meeting on July 17 ended in a stalemate, Couture felt the need to hint that SNC was not Lavalin's only option. He did not name names, but if SNC really wanted to make the deal happen, he suggested, they had better be quick.

THE LEAK

On Friday, July 19, Alain Perez received a phone call from a reporter at the *Financial Times*. The journalist had some questions about an RBC Dominion Securities publication in which SNC was mentioned. Saint-Pierre and Robitaille could not be reached, so he asked if Perez would comment.

During the interview, the subject of Lavalin inevitably came up. There had been a directive not to discuss a potential

FINANCIAL TIMES

JULY 22-28, 1991   FINANCIAL TIMES OF CANADA

SNC pushes a Lavalin merger

An alliance of the top Quebec engineering companies would create a world-class Canadian competitor

By Robert Melnbardis
Montreal Bureau Chief

SNC GROUP Inc., now Canada's second-largest engineering firm, is pushing to become the country's largest in a merger with its bigger, but ailing, long-standing rival, Lavalin Group Ltd. An alliance between the two,

Lavalin's engineering businesses intact, rather than sell them piecemeal. Quebec, always a staunch supporter of its engineering firms, considers the prospect of a foreign player like Bechtel scooping up Lavalin to be even more unsavory.

Although a merger between SNC and a restructured Lavalin would produce annual sales of about $1

merger, so Perez at first hesitated to comment, but the reporter was insistent. He returned to the issue repeatedly, until Perez finally broke down and gave him something he could work with.

"It would be in everybody's interest, including Quebec's, to have a very large firm that has the size and the talent to compete with those big guys," conceded Perez.

On Monday July 22, an article appeared on the first page of the *Financial Times* with the dramatic headline, "SNC pushes a Lavalin merger." Perez had not been able to warn Saint-Pierre about the interview in time, so the CEO of SNC learned of it when he picked up a copy of the newspaper.

"Who spoke to the journalist?" Saint-Pierre asked in a meeting of the company's top executives that morning.

"I'm sorry to say that I was the source," Perez said.

"Alain, we agreed we were not going to talk about it. Now that it's in the public domain it's going to make things much more difficult."

Perez said he had only given a hint that SNC was interested in a merger, and he was just as surprised as Saint-Pierre to read the headline in the press. He had not expected the reporter to make so much of his statement.

Saint-Pierre expected a call from Lavalin at any time, but the first reaction came from the Toronto Stock Exchange. At 4:00 p.m., Michael Novak received a call from the market supervisor. "The article has created some excitement about SNC's stock," he said. "We need a press release confirming or denying the rumour of a merger, and we need it before trading starts tomorrow."

Saint-Pierre immediately got to work drafting a press release with the help of Mary Hall of Public Affairs. Meanwhile, SNC tried numerous avenues throughout the evening to reach someone at Lavalin, but their calls were not returned. They did not know that Lavalin's top executives were locked in their 10th-floor conference room examining an offer from the Quebec construction firm Sofati.

The press release was sent out the following day at 9:30 a.m., and a courtesy copy was faxed over to Lavalin's headquarters a half hour later. It quoted Saint-Pierre as saying that rumours of a merger between the two companies were premature, although he noted that a solution needed to be found to protect the engineering expertise of Canada and Quebec.

Hours passed with still no reaction from Lavalin. Finally, having still not heard from anyone at the company by the afternoon, Saint-Pierre called Serge Saucier.

"What's the matter with you people?" Saucier said. "Your press release dropped like a bomb at Lavalin. If they had rocket launchers, they'd be firing at you through the windows."

"Serge, it came out in an article in the *Financial Times* yesterday, so we had to…"

"Article? What article?" Saucier asked, cutting him off. Neither he, nor anyone at Lavalin had seen the piece in the *Times*.

"Listen, an article has appeared about a potential merger between SNC and Lavalin. The stock exchange forced us to issue a press release since we are a public company. We tried to reach you all evening…"

Over the next few days, André Gagnon would play an invaluable role in calming the furies of Lavalin's executives. When he explained that the press release had been forced on SNC by the Toronto Stock Exchange, and that the original leak had not been a shrewdly calculated ploy to put pressure on Lavalin, they began to calm down. Of course, it also did not hurt that SNC said it was now prepared to modify its offer.

Lavalin's executives agreed to hold off signing the Sofati agreement long enough to have a final meeting with SNC. That night, Bérubé invited Perez and Gagnon to his house to see if they could restart negotiations. Armand Couture was there as well. The talk had a tone of seriousness that the previous negotiations had lacked. This was real, and both sides were committed to going as far as they could towards reaching a deal.

SNC issued a news release suggesting the rumour of an imminent merger was an exaggeration. More articles followed confirming that the reports were premature.

SNC PRESS

For immediate release

SNC RESPONDS TO RUMOURS OF MERGER WITH LAVALIN

Montréal, July 23, 1991 - "Through media coverage and ongoing normal professional relationships, we are all aware that Lavalin is currently facing serious difficulties, SNC Group president and chief executive officer Guy Saint-Pierre said today. "We regret to see such an important Québec-based firm in this situation."

"Given the great economic benefits that engineering has brought to Québec and Canada over the years, it is clear to many interested parties that a solution must be found, and Québec's and Canada's engineering capabilities maintained. Whether or not SNC might be part of such a solution, it is far too early to tell," he continued. "Meanwhile we continue to work in joint ventures with Lavalin, as we have done for many years. But the question of any merger being imminent is premature and speculative."

The SNC Group is a Canadian company with operations in engineering-construction and manufacturing. It is listed on Montréal and Toronto stock exchanges.

- 30 -

Contact: Robert Racine
Director, Public Affairs

REPORT ON BUSINESS   The Globe and Mail, Wednesday, July 24, 1991

Lavalin engineering rival denies reports of merger

'Too early' to talk of marriage, SNC president says

BY BARRIE McKENNA
Quebec Bureau

MONTREAL — The president of engineering firm SNC Group Inc. is eager to see the financial woes plaguing Groupe Lavalin Ltée solved, but says talk of a merger with its rival across town is premature.

In a statement yesterday, Guy Saint-Pierre said it was "too early to tell" whether SNC might be interested in helping out Groupe Lavalin and its subsidiary Lavalin Inc., Canada's largest consulting engineering

Given the great economic benefits that engineering has brought to Quebec and Canada over the years, it is clear to many interested parties that a solution must be found, and that Quebec's and Canada's engineering capabilities are maintained," Mr. Saint-Pierre said.

He added that SNC, Canada's No. 2 engineering firm, regrets that "such an important Quebec-based firm" is facing serious difficulties.

But he described as "premature and speculative" reports of an imminent merger between Lavalin and SNC, both based in Montreal.

SNC would get involved only "if we were asked and if we felt it was critical," Pierre Robitaille, executive vice-president of finance, added in an interview.

He said SNC, a partner of Lavalin in several joint ventures, can't be indifferent to its competitor's plight. In engineering, competitors must often work as partners, he said.

"If one partner can't meet its obligations, then the other partners must take responsibility," Mr. Robitaille said.

Analysts say that a marriage of Canada's engineering majors makes sense and could save a troubled Lavalin from being swallowed by an outside giant, such as Bechtel Group Inc. of San Francisco.

"A merger could happen eventually, but there are still a lot of impediments," said a Montreal-based financial analyst. He said Lavalin first must get rid of its non-engineering operations.

Lavalin vice-president Clément Richard could not be reached for comment.

SNC shares were among the most actively traded on the Montreal Exchange yesterday, rising 12 cents to close at $14.87.

Lavalin had sales of $1.2-billion and about 7,000 employees in 1990. SNC had revenue of $447-million and 3,400 employees.

In May, the Quebec government bailed out Lavalin with a $10-million loan guarantee that was not disclosed until the next month. That gave Lavalin's banks the guarantees

they wanted to boost the company's already-stretched line of credit to $145-million from $125-million.

Lavalin said the aid package will allow it to conduct an orderly selloff of a number of businesses. Now on the block are most of the assets of its key public subsidiary, Lavalin Industries Inc.: half its 85-per-cent stake in transportation equipment maker UTDC Inc. and all of Kemtec Petrochemical Corp. of Montreal. Also for sale are a 35-per-cent stake in a 55-storey office development in downtown Montreal that was to have been Lavalin's new head office and **Météomédia Inc.**, a television weather service.

Other investments have simply been written off, including International Aeroplane Co., a failed jet-leasing venture.

SNC and Lavalin have been bitter rivals since the early 1970s, when Lavalin chairman Bernard Lamarre outmanoeuvred SNC for a piece of a lucrative contract to build the James Bay hydroelectric development.

Shut out last time around, SNC now is jockeying for a share of the $12.6-billion Great Whale project, the next phase of James Bay.

Lavalin's troubles stem from heavy losses at Kemtec, its Ontario engineering unit and jet leasing as well as from delayed subway ventures in Thailand and Turkey.

« Les rumeurs de fusion entre SNC et Lavalin sont prématurées »

— Guy Saint-Pierre

La question qu'une fusion entre SNC et Lavalin soit sur le point de se concrétiser est prématurée et spéculative », dit Guy Saint-Pierre, patron de

Par suite des problèmes de Lavalin, le bruit court que les deux sociétés d'ingénierie fusionnent, plaçant ainsi SNC dans le rang des géants mondiaux avec les Californiens Bechtel et Fluor.

Richard Johnson

chiffre d'affaires combiné des sociétés montréalaises serait à plus d'un milliard de dollars, et la compagnie compterait 8 000 employés.

Ces affaires vont tellement mal pour Lavalin que la société a même sollicité l'aide de Québec pour s'en sortir. Lavalin a demandé à Québec de garantir un prêt d'une dizaine de millions de dollars.

« Nous sommes conscients des problèmes de Lavalin, dit Guy Saint-Pierre, président de SNC, et nous regrettons de voir une société québécoise aussi importante dans une telle

« Il est clair qu'une solution doit être envisagée pour protéger les capacités en ingénierie au Canada et au Québec, mais à savoir si SNC pourrait faire partie ou non de la solution, il est beaucoup trop tôt pour se prononcer.

« Entre-temps, nous continuons de travailler en coentreprise dans bien des cas avec Lavalin, comme nous l'avons fait pendant des années. Cependant, la question qu'une fusion soit sur le point de se concrétiser est prématurée et spéculative. »

L'an dernier, SNC a réalisé un profit de 23 millions sur des ventes de 447 millions de dollars, et les analystes prévoient de très bons résultats pour 1991.

Avec la mondialisation des affaires, la fusion des deux groupes serait une doute une excellente chose parce que la nouvelle société aurait énormément de ressources.

Une partie des problèmes de Lavalin proviennent de sa filiale Lavalin Industries, qui a perdu 4 millions de dollars en 1990 contre un profit de 1,4 million l'année précédente.

Le nouveau président de Lavalin, Yves Bérubé, a le mandat de vendre certains éléments non productifs tels Kemtec et UTDC de Toronto.

Photo Pablo DURANT

Guy Saint-Pierre

The Ritz-Carlton hotel in Montreal.

Lavalin's headquarters on René-Lévesque Boulevard in Montreal.

From seven in the evening until two in the morning, the two parties pushed and pulled, gradually coming to agreements on various issues: compensation for Lavalin's executives so that they could finance their participation in SNC, the preservation of Lavalin's identity in some form, the importance of maintaining certain subsidiaries and as many jobs as possible. By the time the meeting broke up, it was clear that there had been a breakthrough.

The parties met again the next night, this time at the residence of Alain Perez. Marcel Côté, a consultant from Secor SNC had hired for strategic planning, was also now taking part in the discussions. Couture had just finished meeting with Lavalin's executives, and had secured their permission to continue ironing out a deal with SNC.

The next day, Guy Saint-Pierre was in a meeting of Suncor's board in Fort McMurray in northern Alberta, when he received an urgent phone call from Perez. "Guy, things have moved much quicker than expected," he said. "We've come to an agreement in principle with Lavalin. We're supposed to sign a deal tonight at the Ritz-Carlton."

Saint-Pierre was amazed: he would certainly have skipped the meeting if he had thought a deal would have been reached so rapidly. Now he had perhaps five hours to get to Montreal. Luckily, a colleague on Suncor's board was on his way back to the U.S. and offered to fly Saint-Pierre to Toronto in his private jet. From there he would be able to hop on a flight to Montreal.

It was past nine when Saint-Pierre arrived at the Ritz. Lavalin's executives had just signed the agreement in principle when he walked into the small conference room. The atmosphere was heavy with emotion. These were proud men who hoped their accomplishments and talents would be evaluated fairly by SNC. Well into their 40s and 50s, they did not relish the idea of starting back at square one in a new company.

Marcel Côté immediately took Saint-Pierre aside and briefed him on what he had missed. "Guy, they've all signed, and now they're waiting for you to say a few words," he told him. "There are a lot of mixed emotions."

Saint-Pierre had not prepared a speech, but he knew exactly what he wanted to tell them. "I have tremendous respect for all of you," he began, "and I know that we can accomplish great things together. You know, they say that in order for a marriage to be successful, both parties have to do more than their share. If each only gives 50 percent, the marriage is not sure to be a success. If, on the other hand, both give 60 percent, they will be assured a happy union."

Saint-Pierre knew that was far easier said than done, of course. Especially when the two companies that were getting married had been competitors for so long. It would be crucial to ensure that both sides felt appreciated and that mutual understanding was fostered regularly. He would start by telling his staff that it was of the utmost importance that the deal be positioned as a merger and not an acquisition. Yes, they were coming to Lavalin's aid, but Lavalin was bringing a great addition of talent and projects to SNC. The new company would be far greater than the sum of its parts.

OPERATION X-RAY

The next day, July 26, the most challenging part of the process began. SNC had only 48 hours to come up with a solid first assessment of the state of Lavalin's finances. On the basis of their report, Saint-Pierre would decide to proceed with or call off the deal.

Pierre Robitaille assembled a small army of accountants and lawyers to examine Lavalin's books. One of the first people he chose was Gilles Laramée, the company's Treasurer. Gilles was young at 30, but his ability to juggle an array of

financial details in his head would make him invaluable. Yves Laverdière, the company's fiercely loyal Corporate Secretary, would be charged with dealing with the inevitable claims from Lavalin's service and equipment providers once the alliance was made public. Tony Rustin, who had overall responsibility for project management and quality at SNC, would be scrutinizing contracts from an operational perspective. Robert Racine, a public relations expert, would handle the delicate job of drafting a communications plan. The team also included a pair of talented hired guns: Michel Goudreau, a top lawyer from Lavery O'Brien, and David Azoulay, Robitaille's former partner at Ernst & Whinney and one of the best negotiators in the business. Michael Novak, SNC's Vice-President of Law, would soon join them as well, cutting short his vacation to help investigate Lavalin's legal structure for weak spots and pitfalls.

The "Deal Team" set up shop in a conference room on the 10th floor of the Lavalin building. Its walls were covered in whiteboards, so it was ideal for sketching out the multifarious legal connections between Lavalin's subsidiaries and its contracts. Robitaille immediately nicknamed it the War Room, because it looked like the sort of place where an epic battle might be planned. But if this was war, SNC's team would not be alone in the struggle. Couture, who had an elephant-like memory, provided details about many of the legal and commercial agreements the company had signed. Lavalin's counsel,

Ginette Pérusse, and one of its accountants, Mario Martel, also proved invaluable in facilitating access to information.

By the evening of Sunday, July 28, the team had enough of an idea of the state of Lavalin's books to be able to present a report to Guy Saint-Pierre and Alain Perez. Lavalin had an incredibly complex structure, with dense legal and administrative thickets, but they had managed to come up with a good first appraisal. The bad news was that Lavalin was $140 million in debt, about $20 million more than previously estimated. The good news was that, along with the company, would come about $200 million worth of international contracts and another $500 million in Canadian jobs.

Saint-Pierre had a moment of hesitation. He was concerned that other debts might emerge down the line, but Robitaille assured him that his team would be able to avoid most, if not all, of them. SNC's bargaining position was incredibly strong, since the banks needed an engineering firm to collect the company's accounts receivable and finish its ongoing contracts. If they were not completed, the banks stood to lose close to $100 million in guarantees they had issued to Lavalin's clients, in addition to the $140 million they were already owed.

"Okay, Pierre, keep going," Saint-Pierre said, "but if at any moment you feel like this deal is no longer in the best interests of SNC or its shareholders, I give you the authority to stop the process."

Gilles Laramée

Yves Laverdière

Tony Rustin

Robert Racine

Michael Novak

The Deal Team had provided a first snapshot of Lavalin, but now an in-depth audit of every contract and subsidiary needed to follow, and follow fast. The banks had repeatedly moved Lavalin's deadline and were willing to provide only one more extension. Everything had to be finalized by August 9.

The next morning, Robitaille gathered his troops together once again in the War Room. In keeping with the military theme, he had drawn an enormous hill across several of the whiteboards—it was the symbolic hill they had to take at all costs, no matter how impossible that seemed.

"First, within a period of two weeks, we must conclude a complex transaction that would normally take three months," Robitaille said. "This is no place for ego trips. Every minute counts. We must operate like a well-oiled machine. Second, I want everyone to be clear on this: if in fact this is an acquisition, in spirit it is a merger. We must never lose sight of that."

SHOWDOWN WITH THE BANKS

The first substantive meeting with the consortium of eight banks took place on Tuesday morning, July 30. SNC's Deal Team had come up with a solution to the problem that had been raised by Couture during the first round of talks: namely, how to secure the contracts of Lavalin's subsidiaries without also taking on their liabilities.

SNC would use some legal sleight of hand and create a series of mirror companies. The new entities would have the same names as the subsidiaries, with the exception of a little

A page from Pierre Robitaille's notes during Operation Phoenix. The priorities for the week of August 5 were to close all transactions and prepare SNC-Lavalin to absorb the activities of Lavalin.

"(1991)" at the end. The addition would signify they were not the companies that were indebted to the banks, but were otherwise identical, especially when it came to their ability to carry out contracts. That meant the only real money the banks would see would come from Lavalin's accounts receivable, which SNC would endeavour to collect for a 20-percent fee.

The banks agreed to let SNC have Lavalin's healthiest assets, while leaving aside its debt, but they were sure a portion of the accounts receivable would never be collected. A representative of one of the banks in the consortium gave SNC their terms.

"We agree with your proposal *in principle*," he said, "but you must realize that we could lose a great deal of money. We feel that we should receive part of the shares of the new company. What we want is between 15 and 25 percent of the SNC Group."

Robitaille was flabbergasted. "Your proposal would put the partnership's capital structure at risk," he said. "In any event, you are asking far too much." He decided that a bit of theatricality might help him drive the point home. He stood up and gave the signal to leave. "Clearly, with such a gap, we will never come to an agreement, particularly when we have so little time. We'll go and calm down, and on your side, please think it over. We'll return in 15 minutes and if you haven't modified your position, there simply won't be a transaction."

Outside the conference room, SNC's negotiation team met up with Serge Saucier, who had just left the meeting to make a phone call. When they told him what had happened, he could not believe his ears. Saucier, who had good credibility with the banks, went back into the conference room to talk to them. A few minutes later, he emerged with the news that they were ready to revise their position. Apparently, the National Bank, the leader in the consortium, had been as surprised as SNC by the other bank's demand.

The banks had not quite finished with their attempt to get a more advantageous deal, however. Towards the end of the meeting, they pulled Armand Couture and Yves Bérubé aside and tried to persuade them to convince Lavalin's other

Banks take over Lavalin assets as talks continue

LYNN MOORE and RON LEBEL
THE GAZETTE

pers assigning "debts, accounts and

...a and Industry ...blay

Lavalin official Clément Richard refused to comment yesterday ...

THE GAZETTE   SATURDAY, AUGUST 10, 1991

IN BRIEF

SNC Group directors meet

Directors of SNC Group Inc. held an unusual day-long session yesterday without making any announcement on a proposed alliance with the debt-laden Lavalin group. SNC is expected to make public its financial results for the second quarter on Monday. The rival engineering groups maintained a news blackout on their negotiations, which also involve several banks and government agencies.

Presse
LE PLUS GRAND QUOTIDIEN FRANÇAIS D'AMÉRIQUE

DÉTAILS CAHIER SPORTS   ● MONTREAL, LUNDI 12 AOÛT 1991   107ᵉ ANNÉE Nº 288   54 PAGES, 4 CAHIERS   Îles de La Madeleine : 1.00   50¢ Taxes en sus

Saisie de 35 filiales de Lavalin

executives to take over the firm themselves. The banks would own the company, and gradually sell it back to the executives once all debts had been paid off.

Couture and Bérubé were not swayed. After nearly two years of living under the thumb of the banking consortium, they did not relish the idea of doing it for another decade or more. More importantly, they knew that by merging with SNC, most of Lavalin's jobs would be preserved, and its engineering core would continue to thrive.

"I'm sorry, but we've already made up our minds about how we want to move forward," Couture said.

With their last-ditch attempt having failed, the banks got serious about SNC's offer. They would not be pushovers, however. If SNC wanted to pick and choose from among Lavalin's spoils, then they would have to justify each decision. With just over a week left to go, the hard work was only just beginning. Robitaille's team would now have to double their productivity. Some 35 subsidiaries, each with its own list of detailed contracts, would have to be given an in-depth legal and financial probing.

SPRINT TO THE FINISH LINE

Saint-Pierre had been keeping board members apprised of developments throughout the negotiation process. On Friday August 9, Robitaille and Perez joined him for a final meeting before the deal was concluded. SNC's board had a well-earned reputation for thoroughness, so they knew they were in for a long and tough meeting.

The deal they presented would see SNC choose from among Lavalin's engineering assets. SNC would create a new company made up of those assets called SNC-Lavalin. The new entity would, at first, be a wholly owned subsidiary, but would eventually be merged with the SNC Group.

The banking consortium would now have the participation they wanted in SNC, but it would be in the form of stock warrants, not a flat percentage of the company. They would have an option to purchase 265,000 class A shares at a price of $16.88[4] for two years. If SNC's stock rose after the merger as anticipated, they stood to make quite a bit of money.

The total cost of the acquisition was $67 million, which included initial reorganization expenses and costs related to the accrued rights and incentives of about 4,000 Lavalin employees. The financing would come from a long-term bank loan of $20 million, and the issue of $30 million in debentures to the Société de développement industriel du Québec (SDI) and to Export Development Canada (EDC). These

4. Adjusted for future stock splits on May 31, 1996 and March 10, 2006, the price would be $1.88.

Bernard Lamarre's last
message to his employees
was reprinted in *Le Devoir*
on August 13, 1991.

organizations would also receive stock warrants: 175,000 for SDI and 35,000 for EDC.

This was real money, and the board wanted to make sure that absolutely nothing had been overlooked. At the end of the three-hour meeting, it was evident that the team had done a phenomenal job in reaching an agreement that had advantages for all.

The board ratified the agreement, but by then the stock exchanges had closed, so SNC postponed the announcement to Monday. It was not quite time to break out the champagne, however. At the offices of Lavery O'Brien, the Deal Team was in the process of finalizing the acquisition. Everyone was exhausted, but there would be no time to rest until all the parties had put pen to paper.

A LAST MESSAGE FROM THE CHAIRMAN

On August 12, Bernard Lamarre, who had been kept abreast of developments through nightly meetings with Couture, sent a last letter to his employees. He had spent weeks crafting it, agonizing over it. He wanted to convey the immense gratitude he felt for having worked with so many remarkable men and women. More than that, he wanted to reassure his employees that their futures were bright as employees of SNC-Lavalin.

"Today, a merger agreement between Lavalin and SNC will be made public," he began. "This means that a major firm called SNC-Lavalin will unite the engineering, procurement, and construction activities of the two groups. Sometimes hardship is a good thing," he mused. "Over the course of long months we have endured fear and uncertainty in order for the great alliance between Lavalin and SNC to take place.

"Of course, I would have preferred this event, in itself desirable, to have occurred under less trying circumstances. But destiny, it seems, uses curious means to reach its ends.

"I know that hardship, agonies, and letdowns have been your daily lot during the months that preceded this event. The great solidarity and determination that you have always

Bernard Lamarre

Bernard Lamarre à ses employés

Bernard Lamarre

Voici le texte intégral de la lettre que Bernard Lamarre a fait parvenir hier matin (12 août) à tous ses employés et dont LE DEVOIR a obtenu copie

AUJOURD'HUI même sera rendu public un accord de regroupement entre Lavalin inc et SNC inc. Cela signifie que d'ores et déjà une grande firme qui porte le nom de SNC-LAVALIN INC. rassemble les éléments d'ingénierie-approvisionnement-construction des deux groupes.

• À quelque chose malheur est bon •, dit-on. Ainsi, aura-t-il fallu, durant de longs mois, vivre de bien pénibles secousses et les affres de l'incertitude pour que se réalise la Grande Alliance de Lavalin et de SNC.

Bien sûr, j'aurais préféré que cet événement, en soi souhaitable, survienne dans un contexte moins tourmenté. Mais le destin, semble-t-il, emprunte parfois de bien curieuses voies pour s'imposer.

Je sais les difficultés, les angoisses et les déceptions qui ont été votre lot quotidien depuis les quelques mois qui ont précédé le dénouement d'aujourd'hui. Aussi, l'émouvante solidarité et l'inébranlable détermination que vous avez toujours manifestées, même aux heures les plus désespérantes, ont été pour moi source d'émerveillement et de grand réconfort.

C'est cette équipe d'hommes et de femmes d'une rare qualité que je veux saluer et remercier. Par vos accomplissements et aussi, à l'occasion, par vos prouesses, vous avez porté Lavalin au firmament des entreprises d'ingénierie. Vous lui avez en outre donné ses lettres de créances pour exporter le savoir-faire d'ici à travers le monde. Pour cela, ma reconnaissance, ma loyauté et mon admiration vous sont à jamais acquises.

Aux cadres et à mes collaborateurs immédiats, à qui je dois tant, je veux adresser des remerciements particulièrement chaleureux. Et, on ne me tiendra pas rigueur, j'en suis certain, de mentionner ici mes trois associés, Marcel Dufour, Armand Couture et Jacques Lamarre, à qui je veux témoigner du bonheur et de la satisfaction que j'ai toujours éprouvés à travailler à leurs côtés. Leur compétence, leur dévouement, leur solidarité et leur leadership exemplaires auront puissamment contribué à façonner l'entreprise et à y rassembler autant de talents.

Ni regret du passé, ni surtout peur de l'avenir. Conjuguées, les forces de SNC et celles de Lavalin constitueront un formidable gage de fécondité. Vraisemblablement, la fusion instantanée des deux cultures d'entreprise provoquera quelques chocs, mais ils porteront bien peu à conséquence par rapport aux immenses avantages que vous saurez, à n'en point douter, en tirer. Vous êtes de la race des conquérants et vous voilà mieux armés encore pour livrer bataille à la concurrence internationale. Le défi devient de plus en plus exaltant. Et, j'ai la conviction que, sous la gouverne adroite et éclairée de MM. Guy Saint-Pierre et Alain Perez, SNC-LAVALIN INC. est vouée à un brillant avenir.

Quant à moi, le temps est opportun pour prendre quelques distances avec mes tâches habituelles. Le rôle de conseiller que j'assumerai au sein de SNC-LAVALIN INC. me permettra cependant de continuer de vous côtoyer et d'être témoin de vos succès. J'envisage cela avec plaisir et sérénité.

Je vous remercie tous et toutes. Mes meilleurs voeux vous accompagnent.

demonstrated, even in the most desperate hours, have for me been a source of wonderment and great comfort.

"It is this remarkable group of men and women that I would like to salute and thank. Through your accomplishments, and sometimes your courage, you have brought Lavalin to the very top of engineering firms. You have, among other things, allowed the company to export local know-how around the world. For that, my acknowledgement, my loyalty, and my admiration are forever yours."

Lamarre spent the last part of the letter looking to the future, and, with SNC and Lavalin working together as one, he felt there was much to be optimistic about.

"Do not regret the past nor fear the future. Together, the strengths of SNC and Lavalin will be a fertile reservoir of skill and knowledge. Undoubtedly, the instant merger of two corporate cultures will create some turmoil, but that will be nothing next to the great advantages that will result."

ONE PLUS ONE EQUALS FOUR

Just after 5:00 p.m. on Monday, August 12, 1,500 employees of SNC and Lavalin gathered at the Hilton Montreal Bonaventure hotel ballroom to hear an announcement they all knew would change their careers, although they were not sure in what way. Some wondered if their jobs would be safe. Others imagined how formidable a united SNC and Lavalin would be. Still others questioned how the two dramatically different corporate cultures would blend. Lavalin had always been more entrepreneurial in its pursuit of new markets. SNC, on the other hand, had been a pioneer of corporate transparency within Canada. It had elaborate risk evaluation procedures, a well-respected board, and generally thought twice, and even thrice, before plunging into new projects.

One thing was certain: the companies fit together like two pieces of a puzzle when it came to their expertise and geographical presence. SNC had made great inroads into India, for example, while Lavalin did much of its international

business in Russia. Lavalin was slightly more present in Quebec, but SNC was a little stronger in the rest of Canada. Even in countries where both were highly active, their experience was mostly complementary. In Algeria, SNC had carried out major industrial projects like Meftah and Sonacome, while Lavalin had built world-class structures such as the Martyr's Arch and its associated cultural centre.

It was against this backdrop that Guy Saint-Pierre took the stage. At a long table next to the podium, were seated Perez, Couture, and Bérubé. "As you can see," he began, "one plus one equals four!" The four heads of the two companies side by side on the stage was the first concrete evidence of the merger.

Clockwise:

From left to right: Armand Couture, Guy Saint-Pierre, Alain Perez, Yves Berubé, and Pierre Robitaille at the merger announcement.

Lavalin and SNC employees listening to news that would change their careers.

Armand Couture speaking with the press on the day of the announcement.

Un géant de l'ingénierie naît de l'union SNC-Lavalin

Une des cinq plus grandes firmes d'ingénieurs au monde

Claude Turcotte

LES DÉBOIRES financiers de Lavalin ont en quelque sorte précipité l'évolution de l'industrie du génie-conseil québécois en forçant deux compagnies rivales très fières et dynamiques à fusionner leurs activités. SNC-Lavalin, une filiale du Groupe SNC dont la création a été annoncée hier, regroupera bientôt quelque 6000 ingénieurs et employés; elle aura l'an prochain un chiffre d'affaires d'au moins 800 millions $, son carnet de commandes de 5000 projets représente une valeur de 1 milliard $. Bref, SNC-Lavalin se situe parmi les cinq plus grandes firmes d'ingénierie au monde.

« Notre marché sera la planète toute entière », a lancé M. Guy Saint-Pierre, président et chef de la direction du Groupe SNC, au moment où il confirmait officiellement cette transaction de 90 millions $, en ajoutant diplomatiquement que « les circonstances veulent que cela se fassent sous l'égide de SNC ». M. Yves Bérubé, qui devient vice-président exécutif dans la nouvelle structure de SNC-Lavalin, mentionnait pour sa part que ce mariage est « le fruit d'une longue maturation que la conjoncture a permis d'accélérer ». Il a aussi souligné que Lavalin aurait pu accepter un financement étranger ou se replier ici en s'associant avec une société moins importante, ce qui aurait été aller à contre-courant. « Une alliance des deux plus grands était la solution la plus difficile, mais la plus porteuse pour l'avenir. Nous avons privilégié l'offensive », a conclu celui qui était p-d g. de Lavalin Inc., il y a encore deux jours.

Toutefois, la construction de ce géant ne se fait pas sans frais. La Banque Nationale en tête et les autres institutions financières qui participaient au financement du Groupe Lavalin, ne retrouveront jamais tout l'argent prêté. Il en va sans doute de même pour le gouvernement québécois qui a donné des garanties de prêts dépassant les 40 millions $. M. Saint-Pierre se dit incapable de préciser le montant exact de ces pertes, qui ne portent d'ailleurs pas nécessairement toutes sur les activités de génie-conseil, bien que les banques aient saisi dans un premier temps les 34 filiales québécoises de Lavalin dans le génie-conseil.

Ce sont ces 34 filiales dont SNC se porte acquéreur. Il s'agit d'une transaction de l'ordre de 90 millions $, selon les chiffres fournis par M. Saint-Pierre. Ce montant se décompose en 20 millions $ payés comptant par SNC, 25 millions $ en prêt de la part de la Société de développement industriel (SDI) sous forme de débentures subordonnées à un taux d'intérêt de 10 ¾ %, un autre montant de

Voir page 4: Un géant

Guy Saint-Pierre, président et chef de la direction du Groupe SNC voit cette fusion comme une étape décisive vers la mondialisation du génie-conseil québécois et canadien.

PHOTO JACQUES GRENIER

"The engineering alliance that we are celebrating tonight is the point of departure in a great adventure," he said. "There are no losers in this alliance. SNC and Lavalin have voluntarily chosen to pool their resources. Now, we have the opportunity to take part in creating a major worldwide engineering force." The crowd applauded. The apprehension in the room was gradually being dispelled. It was hitting home now: they belonged to one of the largest and most skilled engineering companies in the world. "I welcome and salute all employees of the new company, SNC-Lavalin, an emerging global powerhouse, a powerhouse that exists as of today," he concluded.

The buzz in the press continued for weeks after the merger. There was great anticipation about what the new Canadian engineering titan could accomplish. It would have assets of more than $600 million, with equivalent revenues and close to 7,000 employees. It would have 16 offices in Canada and 14 abroad, and top expertise right across the spectrum of engineering services.

But for now, much work still needed to be done. Bringing the two companies together in such a short time had been a herculean task, but integrating them into a unified organization that was greater than the sum of its parts would bring a whole new set of challenges.

THE GLOBE AND MAIL
REPORT ON BUSINESS.

©1991 The Globe and Mail · Canada's Business Newspaper · Tuesday, August 13, 1991

SNC buys Lavalin's prized engineering firm

$90-million deal marks end of months of speculation

BY BARRIE McKENNA
Quebec Bureau

MONTREAL — Entrepreneur Bernard Lamarre and three close associates surrendered control of their prized Lavalin Inc. engineering firm yesterday, giving it up to smaller rival SNC Group Inc.

In a $90-million deal, SNC bought the assets and contracts of Lavalin Inc., Canada's largest engineering firm with nearly 4,000 employees and sales of $413-million. Both firms are based in Montreal.

The deal was a dramatic denouement to months of speculation and culminated intense negotiations between Lavalin's senior partners, an eight-member banking consortium, SNC and the Quebec government.

SNC president Guy Saint-Pierre said the merged company, to be named SNC-Lavalin Inc., would count $650-million in revenue and 6,000 employees, ranking it fifth internationally behind such U.S. engineering giants as Fluor Corp., Bechtel Group Inc. and M. W. Kellogg Co.

"Today we're witnessing a great day in Canadian engineering history," Mr. Saint-Pierre, a former Quebec cabinet minister, told a packed Montreal news conference.

"It's the beginning of a great alliance and the birth of an engineering firm that I'm convinced will be crowned in success."

SNC president Guy Saint-Pierre, left, said the acquisition creates the world's fifth-largest engineering company. Alain Perez, centre, is the president of the new firm, and Yves Bérubé, right, is vice-president. *(Canadian Press)*

GLOBAL REACH

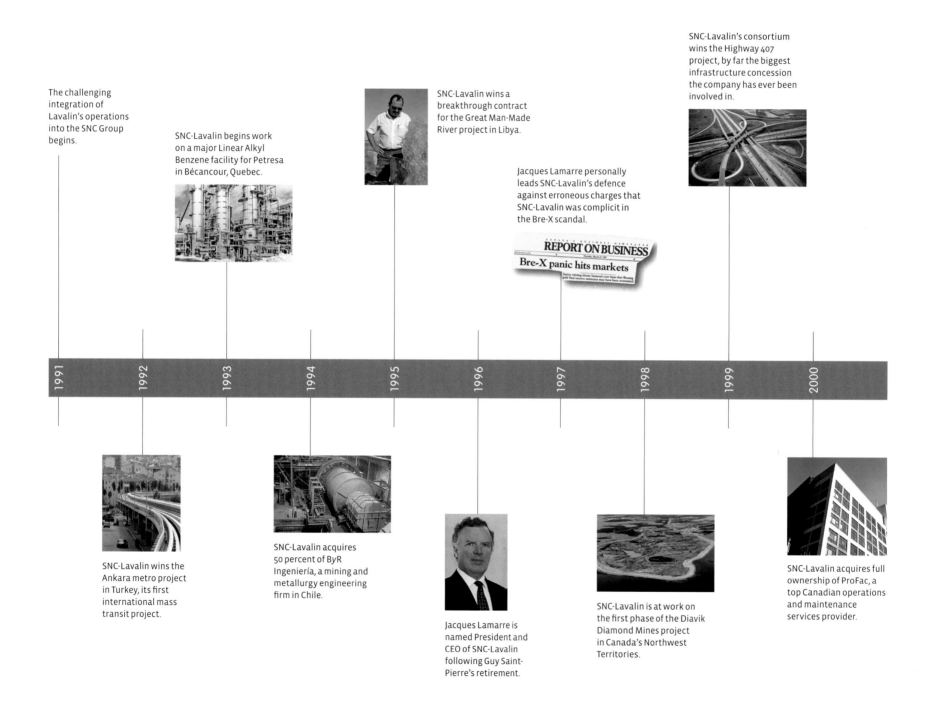

The challenging integration of Lavalin's operations into the SNC Group begins.

SNC-Lavalin begins work on a major Linear Alkyl Benzene facility for Petresa in Bécancour, Quebec.

SNC-Lavalin wins a breakthrough contract for the Great Man-Made River project in Libya.

SNC-Lavalin's consortium wins the Highway 407 project, by far the biggest infrastructure concession the company has ever been involved in.

Jacques Lamarre personally leads SNC-Lavalin's defence against erroneous charges that SNC-Lavalin was complicit in the Bre-X scandal.

REPORT ON BUSINESS
Bre-X panic hits markets

1991　1992　1993　1994　1995　1996　1997　1998　1999　2000

SNC-Lavalin wins the Ankara metro project in Turkey, its first international mass transit project.

SNC-Lavalin acquires 50 percent of ByR Ingeniería, a mining and metallurgy engineering firm in Chile.

Jacques Lamarre is named President and CEO of SNC-Lavalin following Guy Saint-Pierre's retirement.

SNC-Lavalin is at work on the first phase of the Diavik Diamond Mines project in Canada's Northwest Territories.

SNC-Lavalin acquires full ownership of ProFac, a top Canadian operations and maintenance services provider.

PREVIOUS PAGE
An outline view of the stern of a Maritime Coastal Defence Vessel.

CHAPTER 19

INTEGRATION

It is hard to imagine that SNC and Lavalin were brought together in a matter mere of weeks, but the task of integrating them into a unified company will be an even greater challenge. Guy Saint-Pierre knows that SNC-Lavalin must begin winning major international jobs if it is to be successful. The projects come quickly. In the early 1990s, Jacques Lamarre heads up the Ankara metro project in Turkey, and Pierre Lamontagne leads the Richards Bay aluminum smelter project in South Africa. These projects demonstrate what SNC and Lavalin can accomplish together. An operations office is acquired in Chile in 1994, kicking off a new expansion program.

The Ankara metro project in Turkey.

On the morning of Tuesday, August 13, 1991, Guy Saint-Pierre flipped through the press kit prepared for him by Public Affairs. The alliance of SNC and Lavalin was the business story of the year, but while many articles discussed the challenge of bringing two old rivals together, few speculated about what it would take to make the partnership succeed.

That was all Saint-Pierre was thinking about. He knew that, like the negotiations, the integration of the two companies would need to be handled with consummate care. A limited organizational chart had been drawn up before the merger, with a mix of top personnel from both companies, but operations, systems, and cultures would now have to be blended as well. Fairness and transparency would be essential. If there was a perception that one side was being favoured, there could be an exodus.

The delicate job of managing the integration went to Tony Rustin, an English gentleman who knew how to get results without needlessly ruffling feathers. Rustin accepted the job eagerly, but had no illusions. Divisions that had competed tooth and nail for the same contracts would suddenly have to become seamless, well-oiled units. Legendary Shawinigan Lavalin would be merged with SNC's own storied Energy Division. Fenco Lavalin would have to tie the knot with SNC's industrial activities. Partec Lavalin would be melded into SNC's chemicals and petroleum (C&P) activities in western Canada. In each case, there was top talent, great pride, and a particular way of doing things.

ALLIANCE
VOL. 1 Nº. 1 SNC · LAVALIN AUGUST 19, 1991

ENGINEERING AN ALLIANCE OF STRENGTHS
for better and for better

By engineering an alliance of the strengths of two of Canada's largest engineering firms, Lavalin Inc. and SNC Inc., a major corporation is born: SNC-LAVALIN Inc. By the mere size of our team, a little over 6,000 strong, we are a corporation that matches the American and European giants of the engineering-construction industry. What now remains is the successful engineering of our alliance so that we can compete in terms of the quality of our services.

In the beginning, of course, it will not always be easy but we will learn about ourselves and discover our respective strengths. We have among us all the numbers and the diversity of talents that a large corporation could need. If we give the best of ourselves, especially during this transition period, our success is assured.

Good luck to all of us,

Guy Saint-Pierre
President and Chief Executive Officer
The SNC Group

Saint-Pierre knew the mandate would be a great drain on Rustin's time, so he retained Marcel Côté of Secor to give him a hand. Together, they devised a way forward that was painstakingly impartial: 11 committees would be created, one for each sector of activity, service, or key region. The leadership would be distributed fairly between the highest-ranking SNC and Lavalin people. If one side did not have the chairmanship of a particular group, it would at least have the vice-chairmanship.

Each committee had the same mandate: carry out an analysis and figure out how to merge the elements of each group into a productive new unit. Rustin encouraged them to hash out their differences, but he held all to the deadline of January 1992.

Discussions occasionally became heated, but an atmosphere of goodwill generally prevailed. Every so often, there were impressive displays of what could be accomplished when the two sides dropped their guard and made a concerted effort to work things out. Such was the case in Calgary, where Partec Lavalin and SNC's C&P activities came together to form SNC Partec in a matter of mere weeks.

Another immediate priority was the rapid integration of the two treasuries. SNC's Treasurer, Gilles Laramée, a member of the original Deal Team, spent long hours at Lavalin's offices while Assistant Treasurer Alain Lemay held the fort at Place Félix-Martin. There were new bank accounts to open and new treasury policies to draft.

It seemed endless, but he was not alone. Lavalin International's Vice-President of Administration, Georges Boutary, helped to transfer the company's extensive and well-structured bank guarantees over to the newly combined treasury. Helen Bock, Lavalin's billing department head, helped Laramée decide which of Lavalin's many suppliers should be paid and which of its contracts should go forward, while SNC's Corporate Secretary, Yves Laverdière, had the job of breaking the good, or bad, news to many of them.

A CHANGING WORLD

Saint-Pierre was first and foremost the CEO of SNC-Lavalin, but the aspects of his character that had drawn him into politics back in 1970 had not diminished with time: he was still a big-picture thinker; he liked to speculate about the future and, above all, prepare for it.

"It's human to look back with wisdom and hindsight, but that is not very useful," he was fond of saying. "The real trick is to be able to look ahead, and to foresee the effects of present trends."

In the early 1990s, there were two trends that Saint-Pierre felt SNC-Lavalin urgently needed to address.

One was the increasingly rapid pace of globalization. More countries were adopting free-market economic systems, and barriers to commerce were crumbling. With the larger playing field came new opportunities, but also increased competition. Yes, there were now more projects to go after, but there were also new players from Asia and Latin America with which to contend.

At the same time, developing countries were becoming more assertive and confident. In the 1960s and 1970s, it had not been uncommon for SNC or Lavalin to arrive in a developing country with a few hundred Canadian workers in tow. Today, those same nations were insisting that foreign engineering companies employ local firms. They expected them to make a contribution by transferring know-how and technology.

Saint-Pierre saw that SNC-Lavalin could respond to both trends by establishing permanent operating offices in eight or

Guy Saint-Pierre among the Asian Tigers: the CEO of SNC-Lavalin took multiple trips to Asian countries in the early to mid-1990s as the region was undergoing the biggest economic boom in its history.

The Globe and Mail, Monday, October 31, 1994

ON BUSINESS

SNC-Lavalin plugs in to Asia

GOING GLOBAL

The news that SNC and Lavalin had merged sent ripples through the Canadian business world. In Toronto, Larry Stevenson of the consulting firm Bain & Company saw the alliance as a chance to participate in the birth of a new world-class company. In October 1991, he cold-called Saint-Pierre and offered his services.

"Mr. Saint-Pierre, we've done work with other major engineering firms in the U.S. and helped them structure a game plan for the international market. We know that you've just gone through a dramatic transformation, and we think we can help you set a course for the new company."

Saint-Pierre had his own ideas about what SNC-Lavalin needed to do to grow internationally, but he always welcomed other opinions, even dissenting ones. "Yes," Saint-Pierre said. "It might do us some good to get an outsider's viewpoint."

Stevenson's team moved in a few weeks later and began compiling detailed information about SNC-Lavalin's current strategies. They conducted regular interviews with Saint-Pierre, Alain Perez, Pierre Robitaille, and the company's new group vice-presidents: Taro Alepian, Normand Morin, Tony Rustin, André Gagnon, and Pierre Dufour. They also spoke to SNC-Lavalin's clients to find out what they thought of the company. What were SNC-Lavalin's strong points, and in what sectors was the company a true market leader?

Seven months later, in April 1992, Stevenson was ready to deliver his report to SNC-Lavalin's board. As always, he offered to let the CEO see it beforehand. It was standard practice, so Stevenson was surprised when Saint-Pierre declined the offer.

"No, that's fine," Saint-Pierre said. "The reason I hired your firm was to get objective input. I want our board to see it as is. We'll have a discussion about it during the meeting."

The consultant spoke for two full hours. The overall message was that SNC-Lavalin's existing plan to establish operations centres abroad was the right one. Having a permanent local presence was increasingly important to clients, and it would provide better access to international financing. But

Larry Stevenson and his colleagues at Bain & Company presented SNC-Lavalin's board with an analysis of its market share position across various sectors of expertise.

nine regions. The new units would both provide the essential local element countries were demanding and give SNC-Lavalin an edge over the increasingly intense global competition.

The question remained, however: which countries and which sectors? Every division head seemed to have different answers. What the company needed was someone who could assemble all the various strategies into one cohesive plan for the international market.

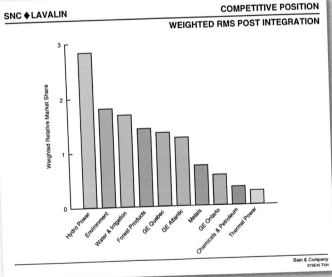

Stevenson stressed that the company should limit its focus to sectors where clients recognized SNC-Lavalin's expertise as world-class, such as aluminum, water, power, and infrastructure. The countries it should target were ones where there was an existing affinity, or, at least, less competition from major American firms.

"In summing up," Stevenson said, "our message is *go global*, but go global in markets where you can be a major player."

Many within SNC-Lavalin found the exercise useful. Even those who disagreed with some of Bain & Company's findings were glad that a first step had been taken to formalize a strategy for the new, integrated company.

SNC-LAVALIN: SHIP BUILDERS

Fenco was one of Lavalin's subsidiaries that Armand Couture had insisted SNC preserve to maintain its contracts. Just prior to the acquisition, a team led by former military man Bob Mustard had managed to be selected by the Department of National Defence (DND) as its preferred bidder to design, build, and deliver 12 Maritime Coastal Defence Vessels (MCDVs).

60,000 MAILBOXES

IN 1992, SNC-LAVALIN FORMED A JOINT VENTURE WITH CLIENTECH, A DIVISION OF BRACKNELL CORPORATION, TO CARRY OUT A COMMUNITY MAILBOX PROGRAM FOR CANADA POST. THE FIVE-YEAR CONTRACT INCLUDED THE ENGINEERING, INSTALLATION, MAINTENANCE, AND SNOW CLEARANCE OF 60,000 MAILBOXES ACROSS THE COUNTRY. THE JOINT VENTURE WOULD SOON EVOLVE INTO PROFAC, A 50/50 PARTNERSHIP BETWEEN SNC-LAVALIN AND BRACKNELL.

Couture said that if SNC simply acquired Fenco's assets, it stood a good chance of losing the job.

Keeping Fenco proved a smart move. In June of 1992, the subsidiary signed the contract as expected. The award was a first for both SNC-Lavalin and the government. It was the largest lump-sum contract in the company's history, and it was the first time that DND had gone to the private sector for the total execution of a major ship project on a fixed-price basis.

The move was partly out of necessity: in the past, major projects managed by DND had been publicly criticized for cost overruns. The culprit was generally "scope creep," additions

Bob Mustard (right) shakes hands with Commodore Ray Zuliani, Commander of the Naval Reserve.

Charlie Rate hard at work in his office.

Ron Rhodenizer, a key member of the MCDV project team.

the sum of money indicated in the contract. So my hidden agenda is to protect you from yourselves, while protecting our reputation."

Rustin gave the same speech to SNC-Lavalin's four principal sub-contractors. The project was going to be carried out within budget, he said. No one was going to make any more money than indicated in the contracts, and if they didn't like it, they could walk away.

If DND or the contractors believed that Rustin had just been making a sales pitch, they soon found out that he was deadly serious. The change orders came, but each time SNC-Lavalin saw costs escalating significantly, high-level meetings were held with the Crown to find ways of bringing the project back within the budget. The additional costs were generally compensated for by the withdrawal of some other element or design flourish. It was not easy. A delicate mix of flexibility and firmness was required, but Rustin knew it would all pay off in the end.

"They'll thank us when it's all over," he told his team.

FROM SOUTH AFRICA...

In November of 1992, the Vice-President of SNC-Lavalin's Aluminum Division, John Barter, signed a contract to design and build a 466,000-tonne-per-year aluminum smelter for Alusaf in Richards Bay, South Africa. The company had no experience in the country, but it had technical expertise in spades. Together, SNC and Lavalin had worked on five of the world's six largest aluminum smelters built in the last decade using the Pechiney process that Alusaf wanted for Richards Bay.

As a result, Barter had been able to field a team that was, without exaggeration, the very best the industry could offer. It would be led by SNC's expert Project Manager, Pierre Lamontagne. The Construction Manager would be Don Colman, another old-time SNC luminary. The area managers would be Pierre Dubuc and George Filacouridis from Lavalin, and Pierre Lacaille and Gerry Gray from SNC. It was this all-star team that had finally sealed the deal.

and modifications while the project was under way that bumped up the final bill.

Tony Rustin and his team, which included Project Manager Bob Mustard, the Director of Engineering and Construction, Charlie Rate, and the Manager of Systems Integration, Ron Rhodenizer, were highly conscious of the importance of the contract for both the government and SNC-Lavalin. If it went poorly, DND would be criticized for delegating the management of the job to the private sector, while SNC-Lavalin would be accused of squandering public money.

Before signing the contract, Rustin laid out his intentions in a meeting with top DND personnel. "Gentlemen, I have a hidden agenda on this contract, but I am going to tell you what it is. I want SNC-Lavalin to complete this project for

LE MONDE

AFRIQUE DU SUD

Mandela salue la victoire de l'ANC

Tous les Sud-Africains sont désormais libres, dit De Klerk

Johannesburg (AFP) — Nelson Mandela a salué hier soir la victoire de son mouvement, l'ANC (Congrès National Africain), aux premières élections démocratiques d'Afrique du Sud en affirmant que les Sud-africains pouvaient désormais se proclamer: «Libres enfin».

«C'est l'un des moments les plus importants dans la vie de notre pays...

manière équilibrée qui donnera l'assurance qu'il a à coeur les intérêts de toutes les comm...

Late Edition

New York: **Today,** sunny, pleasant. High 66. **Tonight,** becoming cloudy. Low 49. **Tomorrow,** cloudy, chilly, a few showers. High 58. **Yesterday,** high 65, low 44. Details, page B7.

The New York Times

NEW YORK, TUESDAY, MAY 3, 1994   75 cents beyond the greater New York metropolitan area.   **50 CENTS**

MANDELA PROCLAIMS A VICTORY: SOUTH AFRICA IS 'FREE AT LAST!'

DE KLERK CONCEDES

Victors Get Big Margin in Vote — Leaders Vow to Cooperate

By BILL KELLER
Special to The New York Times

JOHANNESBURG, May 2 — With a dignity that owed nothing to defeat, Frederik Willem de Klerk...

The contract was a great morale booster, but Saint-Pierre hoped it would do more than generate badly needed revenues during a recession year. Richards Bay would be the first time that former SNC and Lavalin personnel would be working together on a project from start to finish. If it was successful, it would be a dramatic demonstration of what two old rivals could accomplish together.

Lamontagne understood what was at stake as well as anyone. On the first day of the project, he assembled the area managers together for a pep talk.

"You guys are the future of this company, and I expect nothing less than perfection," he said. "This project is one of the most important we've ever carried out, but with the talent on this team, I'm sure we'll deliver it on time and on budget."

At a time when the country was undergoing great political change, Pierre Lamontagne, one of SNC-Lavalin's most seasoned project managers, was assigned to build an aluminum smelter for Alusaf in Richards Bay, South Africa.

...TO TURKEY

Before the merger, Lavalin had been in hot pursuit of a metro contract in Ankara, Turkey. The company had come tantalizingly close to winning it before the Gulf War had sidelined the project. Now, in early 1992, it looked like the city of Ankara was ready to proceed, but was SNC-Lavalin? The project was a massive fixed-price lump-sum job in a region that still appeared to be unstable.

With Pierre Lamontagne occupied in South Africa, Armand Couture, the Senior Vice-President of Major Projects, felt there was only one person who could pull it off: Jacques Lamarre. He had not even appeared in the first organizational chart, but Couture knew what he was capable of when his back was against the wall—which it certainly was now.

The final decision belonged to Saint-Pierre, who had so far only had one brief exchange with Lamarre during a recent Breakfasts with the President meeting. The former Lavalin executive had expressed frustration about the difficulties he was having getting his phone calls returned within the new company. Now here he was again, this time being presented as a candidate to lead one of the biggest and most patently risky projects to have crossed the path of either company.

Saint-Pierre did not know him well, but he trusted Couture's judgment implicitly. Within a week, Lamarre was given a million dollars to go after Ankara, a major gesture in a year when SNC-Lavalin's net income looked unspectacular.

Lamarre and Project Manager Mario Laudadio had a problem to resolve right away. In the old contract, the rolling stock provider was Lavalin's former subsidiary, UTDC, but the train manufacturer had since been sold to Bombardier, and its President, Laurent Beaudoin, had serious reservations about the project.

For one, it unnerved him that Bombardier would be "joint and several" with SNC-Lavalin, meaning that if one of the parties went into receivership, the other would have to complete the job at its own cost. Lavalin had recently been through financial difficulties. What insurance was there that the merged company would not get into trouble, too?

Lamarre understood that the way to bring Beaudoin on side was risk mitigation. He developed a strategy with the

An unbeatable team: Jacques Lamarre, Mario Laudadio, and Raymond Favreau.

support of several old-time SNC hands, including counsel Raymond Favreau, the company's maestro of turnkey contract writing. He also worked extensively with Tony Rustin and Krish Krishnamoorthy, SNC's senior risk experts, and Jim Burgess, its leading project controls man.

In the end, SNC-Lavalin was able to put together an effective risk mitigation mechanism that calmed Beaudoin's fears. When the contract was formally announced in December 1992, its value broke the record for fixed-price jobs, set by the MCDV project only months earlier.

Now, of course, the question was: would Lamarre live up to his reputation?

THE EXPANSION BEGINS

The company was on its way to meeting another of the objectives Saint-Pierre had set for it: the plan to install eight or nine operating offices throughout Asia, South America, and Europe was moving ahead.

In 1993, Taro Alepian had given a special task to Pierre Duhaime, the Director of Technology of the Industrial Division. Before joining Lavalin's subsidiary Fenco in 1989 as a project manager, Duhaime had worked for the mining company Noranda, an important client in the industry. Alepian wanted Duhaime to use his insight into the other side of the business to draw up a strategic plan that would make the most of SNC-Lavalin's mining and metallurgy resources.

Duhaime liked the Bain Report's insistence on targeted growth and applied the same principle to his own strategy.

For the time being, he felt the company should focus its development in the sector on only one country and one metal.

The metal was copper, one of the most useful commodities in the world. It was unparalleled as a conductor of electricity and in demand for piping of all kinds. Clearly, with so many countries developing so rapidly, the demand for copper would remain strong for decades. The country he chose was Chile. In the mining world there was an old saying that went: "Only God chooses where to put mines." God, in the case of copper, had situated a large portion of the world's known deposits in South America, particularly in Chile, the heart of the continent's mining industry. Since Alepian was looking

The Ankara project marked a turning point in both SNC-Lavalin's development and Jacques Lamarre's career.

In search of an acquisition: Pierre Duhaime, Bob Minto, and Kam Francis.

to acquire a permanent operating office in South America, Duhaime suggested the office be located there.

At the end of the year, Alepian sent Duhaime, Bob Minto, the Vice-President of Mining and Metallurgy, and Kam Francis, the Vice-President and General Manager of the Industrial Division, down to Chile to scout for a potential acquisition. They spent a couple of weeks speaking with clients to see whom they liked to work with. The country's national copper company, Codelco, soon pointed them in the direction of ByR Ingeniería in Santiago, a firm of 200 that had provided engineering services for many of its projects over the years.

By May 1994, negotiations with the shareholders of ByR were under way. For the time being, Alepian wanted to acquire only 50 percent of the company to maintain the local image that was so important to the Chilean government. He did, however, retain an option to purchase the rest at a later date.

Meanwhile, back in Montreal, Guy Saint-Pierre was trying to pick up a solid working knowledge of Spanish. He wanted to be able to welcome the newest members of the SNC-Lavalin Group in their own language. He also hoped his efforts would serve as an example to his managers and employees. In a globalized economy, you had to learn to operate in more than just two languages to be efficient. Ultimately, however, it was a matter of respect. For Saint-Pierre, becoming a multinational company was about more than simply amassing acquisitions; it also meant genuinely embracing the cultures of the countries where you wanted to do business.

THE HEIRS APPARENT

SNC-Lavalin is doing well. As the recession comes to an end in 1993, the company gets back on track in Quebec with important projects including a Petresa refinery and a gold mine for Metall. To prepare the ground for his eventual retirement, Guy Saint-Pierre forms the Office of the President: Taro Alepian, Pierre Robitaille, Pierre Dufour, and Jacques Lamarre are named executive vice-presidents, and each is considered a candidate to replace Saint-Pierre. Lamarre soon proves his worth once again by reeling in a second major mass transit project in Kuala Lumpur, Malaysia. In 1995, revenues pass the $1 billion mark for the first time on the strength of such new projects.

The Petresa LAB project in Bécancour, Quebec.

In July of 1994, Robert Racine pulled Guy Saint-Pierre out of a strategic planning meeting. "What is it?" the CEO asked when he emerged from the large conference room on the 15th floor of Place Félix-Martin. He knew his Vice-President of Public Affairs would not interrupt a meeting unless something needed urgent attention.

"There are people in your office that have something very important to tell you," answered Racine gravely, trying hard to suppress a smile.

In the seconds that it took Saint-Pierre to walk back to his office, the CEO of SNC-Lavalin imagined the worst: a terrible accident on a project site, a coup in a country where SNC-Lavalin had just signed a major contract ...

What he found were two emissaries from *The Financial Post Magazine*, who had come to tell him that he had been named Canadian CEO of the Year.

In 1990, The Caldwell Partners International, a global recruiting firm, had teamed up with *The Post* to launch a program to recognize outstanding leadership and achievement by a Canadian chief executive officer. Saint-Pierre was the winner in 1993 for two reasons. It was clear now that the alliance of SNC and Lavalin had been a success, and that this achievement was, in large part, thanks to Saint-Pierre's measured approach. The judges also felt he had given the company a new direction in uncertain economic times. SNC-Lavalin's successful pursuit of international markets had allowed it not only to get through the recession but also to thrive. On the strength of new international work, net income had surged 74 percent in 1993.

It was ironic that the award should come now, when Saint-Pierre's thoughts were turning increasingly towards succession. While he did not anticipate taking his retirement anytime soon, he knew that the most important decision a CEO ever makes is choosing whom to recommend as a replacement. Getting a head start would allow him to take his time and choose carefully.

It was now that the idea for an Office of the President came to him. It would not be unlike a caucus or cabinet in the political world, which Saint-Pierre knew so well. Its members would each be given the title of executive vice-president

Guy Saint-Pierre was named CEO of the Year for 1993 by The Caldwell Partners International and *The Financial Post Magazine*.

In January 1995, he created the Office of the President to prepare the ground for his eventual retirement. From left to right: Jacques Lamarre, Taro Alepian, Guy Saint-Pierre, Pierre Robitaille, and Pierre Dufour.

INSIDE: 200 OF CANADA'S MOST POWERFUL CEOs

The Financial Post Magazine

November 1994

Guy Saint-Pierre
CEO of the year

along with the responsibility for a set of products, one or two regions, and particular functions. Those he named to the Office of the President would be getting more than a promotion. They would also be considered as potential successors.

One of the first he chose was Taro Alepian, an SNC veteran who had worked hard to build up the company's oil and gas résumé in the 1970s and 1980s. Alepian would continue to have responsibility for all of the company's Industrial, Mining and Metallurgy, and Oil and Gas divisions. His region would be Latin America, and his functions would be risk and project management.

Pierre Dufour, the son of Lavalin marketing man Marcel Dufour, was another one. Like his father, Pierre possessed an instinct for making a sales pitch and sizing up a market. He would continue to oversee SNC-Lavalin International, and add Hydropower, Transmission and Distribution, and Canatom to his responsibilities. His functions would include Public Affairs, while his region would be Asia.

Pierre Robitaille, the company's Chief Financial Officer, was a candidate as well. He had led the Deal Team that had pulled off the challenging feat of finalizing the merger of SNC and Lavalin in a matter of mere weeks. He would now be responsible for Information Technology, General Engineering, and Securiplex. His regions would be Europe and Africa, and his function would remain everything to do with Finance.

Last but not least was Jacques Lamarre, a pleasant surprise to Saint-Pierre. If the success of Ankara was an indication of his abilities, then he deserved serious consideration. At the outset, the project had appeared to present almost unmanageable risks, but they were being well controlled. He would maintain responsibility for the Transportation Division he had created, and be charged with developing the company's activities in Eurasia and the Middle East. His functions would be Legal Affairs, Human Resources, and the new financing services division, SNC-Lavalin Capital.

The Office of the President would have the additional advantage of providing support to Saint-Pierre at a time when he felt the company's operations were growing too big for any one person to manage alone. SNC-Lavalin was currently

DISTRIBUTING LEADERSHIP

AT THE SAME TIME THAT SAINT-PIERRE SOUGHT APPROVAL FROM THE HUMAN RESOURCES COMMITTEE OF THE BOARD OF DIRECTORS TO CREATE THE OFFICE OF THE PRESIDENT, HE ALSO RECOMMENDED THAT SNC-LAVALIN'S MANAGEMENT COMMITTEE BE EXPANDED FROM 12 MEMBERS TO A MAXIMUM OF 30. THE RECENT GROWTH OF THE COMPANY HAD BROUGHT IN MUCH NEW TALENT, AND SAINT-PIERRE WANTED TO USE IT TO MORE EFFICIENTLY SHAPE SNC-LAVALIN'S GLOBAL STRATEGY.

working on more than 230 projects in some 90 countries. There was simply no way he could monitor all of the group's diverse activities at once.

Given how closely he planned to work with his new "cabinet," Saint-Pierre assigned the four candidates to offices near him on the 21st floor of Place Félix-Martin. When they assumed their new positions on January 1, 1995, he would be watching to see if they could set aside their egos and work as a single decision-making body. Only someone who could put the welfare of the company above their own ambitions would be considered a contender.

QUEBEC REBOUNDS

The Quebec market was hit hard by the recession of the early 1990s. Unemployment rose to near record levels, and investment was down across the board as the government looked to rein in expenses and regain control over its ballooning deficit.

Things had finally started looking up for SNC-Lavalin in 1993. In June, the General Engineering Division had begun work on the highly publicized Molson Centre. The 21,407-seat arena would be the new home of the city's beloved hockey

Georges Rode

team, the Montreal Canadiens, and the main concert venue in town. The project team, led by Luc Lainey, a top structures specialist from the Lavalin side, was designing it in the downtown core on a constrained site, under considerable media scrutiny.

One month later, under Project Manager Krish Krishnamoorthy, the Industrial Division started work on a large lump-sum contract for a Linear Alkyl Benzene (LAB) plant in Bécancour for Petresa. There was growing interest in LAB-based detergents as biodegradable alternatives to those produced with phosphate.

Now, in July 1994, the division scored another victory in Quebec. While not as big as Petresa, or as high-profile as the Molson Centre, Metall Mining Corporation's Troilus gold project in the north of the province was noteworthy for its importance to SNC-Lavalin. It had been years since the company had worked on a significant job in the gold sector, and much longer since it had won one on its home turf.

The project's sponsor, Pierre Duhaime, had secured the job by giving Metall exactly what it wanted: Australian gold processing technology. The Australians were the best in the world at extracting gold from low-yield sources, and the rock at the Troilus site had less than 1.4 grams per tonne, well below the minimum requirement for a viable mining operation. Now that SNC-Lavalin had the contract, however, it had to figure out how to build a large gold concentrator in the subarctic, where long winters compressed the construction season into a few months.

Project Manager Georges Rode and Construction Manager Adrien Goulet came up with a solution. They would arrange to have all the electrical and mechanical systems delivered by the fall. That way the outer shell of the main building could be erected around the equipment before the winter set in. The project team would then be able to complete the foundations and install the equipment in a heated environment.

The weak link in their plan turned out to be the German supplier of the project's massive ball and semi-autogenous grinding (SAG) mills. In the summer of 1995, the manufacturer's

production line broke down, eliminating any possibility of a fall delivery.

The project was suddenly facing a massive delay. There was no way the building could be closed without the two biggest pieces of equipment in place, and no real construction work could be done in -45°C. Rode and Goulet sat down and brainstormed. They looked at every option, including sourcing the mills from another supplier. None of the ideas they came up solved the problem. Then they realized that there was no reason why they had to completely abandon their previous plan. Why not close off everything except for the section at the end of the building where the ball and SAG mills had to go? In the spring, when the mills arrived, they would take down the temporary wall, install them, and complete the building with no time lost.

Metall agreed to the plan and work was able to proceed uninterrupted through the winter. When the mills were delivered in March of 1996, the project had not lost a single day, and the budget was still under control.

Afterwards, Rode could not help trumpeting the talents and dedication of his team. "This entire project has been difficult to manage," he said in the company's internal newsletter that spring, "but thanks to our team's efforts, we are still on schedule."

THE "MALAYSIAN" SKY TRAIN

In early 1993, Robert Adachi, the Senior Vice-President of the Transportation Division, made a presentation to the Malaysian Economic Planning Unit in Kuala Lumpur, Malaysia. The city had recently been awarded the 1998 Commonwealth Games and needed a mass transit system to accommodate the millions of expected visitors. Adachi's biggest selling point was the Vancouver SkyTrain, which Lavalin had worked on from the earliest phases.

When he finished, Adachi was approached by a representative of Putra, a subsidiary of the country's biggest industrial group, Renong. He said he found the presentation fascinating and wanted to know if SNC-Lavalin could build a 30-kilometre system in the city based on SkyTrain's driverless technology.

When Jacques Lamarre learned of Putra's interest, he immediately set about assembling a team that could deliver exactly what they wanted. That summer, he flew out to Vancouver to meet with Robert Tribe, the head of Capital Projects at BC Transit. Tribe had been involved in the management of all three phases of the SkyTrain, so he was an ideal candidate to lead the bid.

Lamarre's timing was excellent: Tribe just happened to be at a crossroads in his career and was looking for other challenges. He agreed to join SNC-Lavalin and, in turn, enlisted two of his consultants: Jen Liew, a specialist in track systems and project management, and Jim Burke, an electro-mechanical systems expert. Lamarre then informed SNC-Lavalin's Assistant Treasurer, Alain Lemay, that

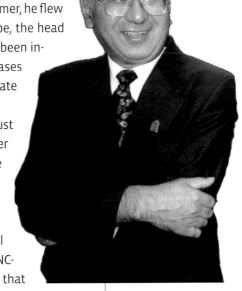

Robert Adachi

The Kuala Lumpur project was put back on the rails by an innovative construction technique.

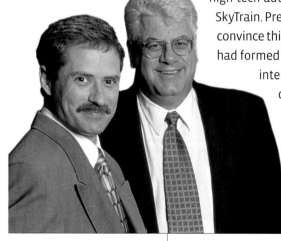

Jim Burke (left) and Robert Tribe during the construction of the Kuala Lumpur mass transit system.

should the company win the contract, he would be sent to Malaysia to head up the financial side of the project.

Meanwhile, Lamarre had invited Bombardier on board as a consortium partner. Its subsidiary, UTDC, had built the high-tech automated trains for the first phases of the SkyTrain. President Laurent Beaudoin was far easier to convince this time: the consortium the two companies had formed for Ankara was fast becoming a model of inter-corporate co-operation. Why not double down and see if they could do it again in Malaysia?

The SNC-Lavalin / Bombardier consortium proved to have the winning combination once again when it was awarded the contract in October 1994. But there was little time for mutual congratulations. The team had just

over three and a half years to build a major transportation system in the heart of one of the most quickly expanding cities in the world.

A NOVEL SOLUTION

SNC-Lavalin moved ahead quickly on its part of the contract. Not all parties made such rapid progress, however. By late 1995, the construction of the guideways and tunnels being carried out by the civil works contractor was nearly a year behind schedule. SNC-Lavalin would not be held responsible for the delay, but Tribe felt duty-bound to find a solution that would allow the system to be delivered in time for the Games.

The original plan had been to pour a second layer of concrete over the guideways to refine their geometry before the track work was installed. It was standard practice in the industry, but SNC-Lavalin now proposed replacing the time-consuming second pour with a layer of precision-engineered, pre-cast track slabs. Surveyors would take measurements of the guideway surface and feed the data to the engineering team. A pre-casting facility would then fashion a series of individually engineered slabs. Each would come complete with the anchors for the electro-mechanical components allowing them to be installed in record time.

Putra at first balked at the idea. It was a new technique that had only been used once before, on a rapid transit project in Europe. SNC-Lavalin was so sure it would work, however, that it proposed building a test section in a local maintenance yard at its own cost. If it was successful, the client would pay for the tests, if it was not, SNC-Lavalin would foot the bill.

After a series of adjustments, the team was able to demonstrate that it was a viable technique. Before long, SNC-Lavalin was laying 200 metres of track per day. By early 1996, all but about a month of the original delay had been erased. Putra was impressed enough to expand SNC-Lavalin's scope of work to include two underground stations and a complex tunnelling operation in the heart of the city.

THE GREAT MAN-MADE RIVER

Riadh Ben Aïssa had come to Lavalin in the mid-1980s, when his firm, which specialized in studies for developing economies, was acquired by the company. Barely two years later, he had gained a reputation as one of Lavalin's "firemen" after successfully extricating the company from a tricky lawsuit in Tunisia. It had all begun with a phone call from Marcel Dufour in 1987.

"I hear that you are a capable Tunisian," the President of Lavalin International had said when he reached Ben Aïssa in Rabat, Morocco, where he was working on a World Bank study.

"Well…I guess I am."

"Listen, we have a big problem in Tunisia that we need your help with. An agriculture project there is in trouble, and the client is taking us to court for $3 million in compensation.

I need you to get over there and sort things out." The relationship between the client and Lavalin had soured to the point where the company's own lawyer had thrown in the towel.

"Okay, give me a week to…"

"We don't have a week," Dufour said, cutting him off. "We go to court in two days."

Ben Aïssa hopped on a plane the next day. He had little time to prepare, but he had always performed best under pressure. With no time to spare, he went straight to see the client. Within a couple of days, he had managed to convince them that it was in their best interests to drop the lawsuit and give Lavalin an extension to finish the work.

Now, in January of 1995, he demonstrated that he could do more than just get the company out of sticky situations. Through sheer persistence, he had secured for SNC-Lavalin a piece of the most ambitious engineering undertaking in recent history, the Great Man-Made River project in Libya.

Its origins extended back to 1953, when an American company had found immense underground aquifers in the southern Libyan desert while prospecting for oil. By the late 1960s, the audacious project had taken shape. The plan was to pump the ancient water to populated coastal areas in the north. To do this, the Libyans planned to drill many hundreds

One of Lavalin's "firemen" from the 1980s, Riadh Ben Aïssa proved his salesmanship credentials with the Great Man-Made River project.

of ultra-deep wells (800 to 1,200 metres) and lay nearly 4,000 kilometres of underground pipe.

The technical difficulties involved in such a project had become clear by the mid-1980s, when many of the first wells drilled in the Sarir region began to be infiltrated by sand. At the time, water wells had to be almost perfectly straight to keep their casings from becoming damaged, but no one had ever tried to drill a flawlessly vertical 1,000-metre well before.

Ten years later, the Libyans were ready to try drilling in Tazerbo, where the wells had to be just as deep. After the difficulties in Sarir, however, the Great Man-Made River Authority had produced specifications that were only just within the limits of possibility. They wanted 117 wells, many of which would descend almost a kilometre into the earth and could not deviate by more than 0.5 percent from a perfectly vertical path.

The design criteria provided the project's Head Engineer, André Béland, with a formidable challenge, but the greatest test turned out to be the U.S.-led embargo against Libya. It prevented SNC-Lavalin from buying top-notch American drilling rigs, and meant everything had to be delivered by land since no planes could fly in Libyan airspace.

By mid-1997, after a rocky start, the project was making good progress. The Libyans were impressed with SNC-Lavalin's tenacity. The project team, which also included Construction Manager Samir Habib and finance man André Dufour (Marcel Dufour's youngest son), seemed to have an inexhaustible supply of solutions. Most importantly, through Ben Aïssa, SNC-Lavalin had maintained open channels of communication with the client. Now that the company had the Libyans' trust, Ben Aïssa was in an excellent position to secure other contracts for the project. The Great Man-Made River was only just beginning to flow.

André Béland, the Great Man-Made River project's Head Engineer, and one of the drills in action.

CHAPTER 21

THE BEST IN THE WORLD

Guy Saint-Pierre decides to retire in late 1995 and recommends that Jacques Lamarre replace him as CEO. Both the Ankara and Kuala Lumpur projects have gone exceptionally well, and the former Lavalin executive's Transportation Division has outperformed all others. Lamarre expands the Office of the President with new members, and tells them to put more emphasis on closely managing their divisions. There are several acquisitions during this time, including Pingat Ingénierie, an agrifood firm in France, and Kilborn, mining and metallurgy process specialists in Canada. Both acquisitions are seen as gateways to sectors where SNC-Lavalin has never had a strong presence.

The Rhourde Nouss gas project in Algeria.

A job well done: Guy Saint-Pierre retired after successfully leading the integration of SNC and Lavalin.

By late 1995, Guy Saint-Pierre had decided the time had come to take his retirement. He had found a worthy successor in Jacques Lamarre.

Within three years, Lamarre's Transportation Division had gone from non-existent to the company's main profit generator. In the process, he had demonstrated drive and determination. The Canadian ambassador to Turkey, where the successful Ankara metro project was now nearing completion, had told Saint-Pierre that Lamarre was like a pit bull. When he wanted something, he latched on and did not let go until he had it.

There was only one problem with his candidacy: Lamarre had not yet fulfilled one of the board's prerequisites for becoming CEO. Stephen Jarislowsky, the company's longest-serving director, had insisted that all four candidates complete a three-month executive management course at Harvard, and Lamarre was still holding out.

He said that he didn't have time to spare with Ankara and Kuala Lumpur both entering delicate phases. He had been heavily involved with the jobs from the very beginning and wanted to stay at the helm until they were complete. "It's much more important for me to do a good job on Ankara and Kuala Lumpur," he said.

Seeing that Lamarre was underestimating the importance of the management course, Saint-Pierre decided to lay all the cards on the table.

"Listen Jacques, Jarislowsky is really pushing for this, and I completely agree with him. I can assure you that you will not become CEO unless you take this course. And it would be a shame because you're a serious candidate."

Lamarre was genuinely surprised. He had suspected that his deep involvement with Lavalin would have placed him out of contention. Now he saw that was not the case. True to his word, Saint-Pierre had made the nomination of a new CEO contingent on performance, not politics. Lamarre decided to go to Harvard and, in the end, was glad he did. He enjoyed the course so much that he called Jarislowsky from Boston to thank him a week later.

"Steve, you were right. I'm meeting all kinds of people here who are in a similar position, from all kinds of corporations all over the world," he said. "It's not so much the classroom, but talking to these people that's been really valuable."

The candidate came back fired up and ready to take on the challenge of leading the company. For their part, Saint-Pierre and Jarislowsky were now sure they had their man.

A MAJOR MILESTONE

IN AUGUST 12, 1995, A MAJOR MILESTONE WAS REACHED ON THE MCDV PROJECT WITH THE LAUNCH OF THE HMCS KINGSTON, THE FIRST OF 12 SHIPS. BY THEN, SNC-LAVALIN HAD ANOTHER OCCASION TO CELEBRATE. DND HAD AWARDED THE COMPANY A FIRST FIVE-YEAR CONTRACT TO MANAGE THE MAINTENANCE AND REPAIR OF THE MCDVS EARLIER THAT YEAR. DND CHOSE A PRIVATE CONTRACTOR FOR IN-SERVICE SUPPORT BECAUSE THE SHIPS WOULD BE STAFFED MAINLY BY RESERVISTS WHO LACKED TRAINING IN ENGINEERING AND MAINTENANCE.

THE SNC-LAVALIN WAY

Jacques Lamarre was officially named President and CEO at the Annual Meeting of Shareholders on May 8, 1996. Saint-Pierre, who would now become Chairman of the Board, in the SNC-Lavalin tradition, reiterated his absolute confidence in Lamarre's ability to lead the organization to new heights.

"By establishing the Transportation Division and giving it international stature in only a few years, he demonstrated the astuteness of his vision and the excellence of his management skills," he said.

For his part, Lamarre decided to pre-empt an obvious question. "For those who are wondering if I will run the company the SNC way or the Lavalin way, I say that there is one way of doing things: the SNC-Lavalin way."

The "SNC-Lavalin way" had thus far proven successful. In 1995, the company had burst through the $1-billion revenue threshold, with profits of $31.3 million and a backlog of $1.8 billion. Surpassing $1 billion in income was a major milestone, but Lamarre was looking to go beyond it now. He wanted to double that figure within five years.

His strategy for growth involved a renewed focus on quality and diversification into new sectors but, conscious of the company's past mistakes, he was not willing to stray too far from the engineering and construction business. At the moment, he was considering purchasing pharmaceutical and telecommunications engineering firms.

Lamarre also wanted to pump new life into the company's existing divisions through acquisitions and internal development. They had done well in recent years, but he still felt that enormous strides could be made in a short period of time.

"Right now, only three or four divisions of our operating sectors could be considered world-class product leaders," he said. "We need to bring more divisions and operating sectors to this level."

In the end, he believed it boiled down to self-esteem. "My message to employees is that we should be ready to forge even further ahead," he said, "and not be afraid to count ourselves among the best in the world."

A HANDS-ON LEADER, A HANDS-ON TEAM

One of the first decisions Lamarre faced as CEO was what to do with the Office of the President. He saw no reason to disband it now that a successor had been chosen. On the contrary, he wanted to expand it: as the company continued to grow, he felt the distributed leadership it provided was becoming increasingly vital.

The five new members he named were hands-on managers who shared his focus on the all-important finer details. Joining Taro Alepian and Pierre Robitaille as executive vice-presidents would be Roger Nichol and Robert Tribe of the Transportation Division, Normand Morin, the head of the company's Industrial Division, Tony Rustin, who ran the defence division, now called Industrial Technologies, and Michael Novak, the Senior Vice-President of Law. With the exception of Novak, a lawyer by training, the new members had all been top project managers at one time in their careers.

With the doubling of the size of the Office of the President came a change in its role. Its members would no

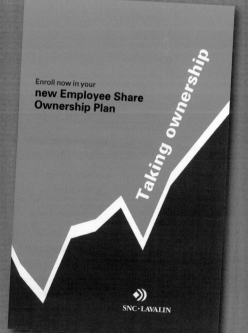

Jacques the Conqueror: Jacques Lamarre's remarkable reversal of fortunes earned him the cover of *Commerce* magazine in 1996.

A PROGRAM FOR EVERYONE

IN LATE 1995, GUY SAINT-PIERRE, PIERRE ROBITAILLE, AND GILLES LARAMÉE WERE DISCUSSING SHARE OWNERSHIP PROGRAMS AT SNC-LAVALIN. FOR SEVERAL YEARS, THERE HAD BEEN A REGIME FOR SENIOR MANAGEMENT, AND NOW THEY WERE LOOKING AT RENEWING IT. DURING THE MEETING, LARAMÉE SUGGESTED LAUNCHING A NEW PROGRAM THAT WOULD ALLOW MIDDLE AND JUNIOR LEVEL EMPLOYEES TO PARTICIPATE AS WELL. A MORE GENERAL PROGRAM, HE SAID, WOULD CREATE PERFORMANCE INCENTIVES ACROSS ALL LEVELS OF THE COMPANY.

SAINT-PIERRE AND ROBITAILLE LIKED THE IDEA, AND IN JULY 1996, THE EMPLOYEE SHARE OWNERSHIP PLAN WAS LAUNCHED. UNDER THE THEME "TAKING OWNERSHIP," EMPLOYEES WOULD NOW BE ABLE TO MAKE CONTRIBUTIONS TOWARDS THE PURCHASE OF COMPANY SHARES WHILE RECEIVING COMPANY CONTRIBUTIONS.

Enroll now in your
new Employee Share Ownership Plan

Taking ownership

SNC·LAVALIN

Friends and rivals. The gala dinner that preceded the International Symposium in 1996 provided a rare opportunity for SNC's and Lavalin's current and former top management to pose for a photograph. From left to right: Marcel Dufour, Jacques Lamarre, Guy Saint-Pierre, Camille Dagenais, and Bernard Lamarre.

longer be located up on the 21st floor with the CEO of the company. Lamarre now wanted them down among their teams. It was not just a matter of perception. He wanted them to be right in the thick of the action to field questions and help resolve issues as quickly as possible.

The change was even reflected in the way the Office of the President was remunerated. Previously, the management incentive program for its members had been tied exclusively to the overall performance of the SNC-Lavalin Group. Now, 50 percent of their compensation would be linked to the financial performance of the divisions under their control.

"You will continue to work closely with each other for the overall success of the group," Lamarre told them, "but I want all of you focused on the bottom lines of your units as well. Their success is your success."

INTERNATIONAL REDUX

Lavalin International had been the company's driver of global development during the 1970s and 1980s. After the merger, however, the division had lost some of its raison d'être. The difficulties seemed to stem from a lack of communication between the marketing reps and the group's business units. They didn't understand each other's needs.

As a result, too few of the prospects SNC-Lavalin International brought home were translating into contracts. It was a serious problem given how much the company had come to depend on international work. In 1995, for the first time in its history, SNC-Lavalin had generated more than 50 percent of its revenues from outside Canada.

When Lamarre took the reins, he assigned the new President of SNC-Lavalin International, Michael Novak, the task of making it relevant again. Novak saw that more could be accomplished for less if better channels of communication existed between International's regional representatives and the company's product experts.

He proposed that each product have its own manager. They would be expected to share information with the

existing regional representatives to ensure prospects were chosen wisely. The regional representatives, meanwhile, would hopefully be able to use that information to help divisions gain a foothold in countries where they were not yet present.

Novak planned to make use of the upcoming International Symposium in September to announce the changes. The internal meeting, held every 18 months, allowed business unit managers and regional reps from across the company to mingle and plot strategies. Novak knew very well that the get-together could accomplish a year's worth of networking in mere days.

between Kilborn and ByR, the company's new operating unit in Santiago, Chile. Kilborn had a small office in the country, and close ties to many of the big names in the business who were now launching projects there.

In March, SNC-Lavalin acquired the remaining 50 percent of ByR, merged it with Kilborn's Chilean operations, and enfolded both into its existing marketing office in the country, SNC-Lavalin Chile. Former procurement man Ivars Kletnieks became the new unit's President. His primary target would be the mining sector, but he would also be on the lookout for contracts in the region's booming energy, industrial, and infrastructure markets.

An expanded Office of the President: Taro Alepian, Pierre Robitaille, Roger Nichol, Robert Tribe, Normand Morin, Tony Rustin, and Michael Novak.

THE EXPANSION CONTINUES

In January 1996, SNC-Lavalin acquired a top Canadian mining firm called Kilborn. The company was widely recognized in the mining and metallurgy industry, and particularly for its gold and copper expertise.

The acquisition had grown out of a feasibility study for Inco's massive Goro Nickel project in New Caledonia, on which the two companies were currently collaborating. Working side by side with Kilborn had convinced Alepian that the company would make a valuable contribution to SNC-Lavalin's mining expertise. More specifically, he saw great synergies

MARKETING INTELLIGENCE AT OUR FINGERTIPS

IN NOVEMBER 1995, BENOÎT CÔTÉ (SEATED FACING COMPUTER), THE DIRECTOR OF MARKETING SERVICES, MADE A PRESENTATION TO THE BOARD ABOUT THE ONGOING IN-HOUSE DEVELOPMENT OF A NEW MARKETING INTELLIGENCE TOOL CALLED MARKIS. THE DATABASE WOULD GIVE MANAGERS AND THEIR STAFF ACCESS TO CURRENT INFORMATION ON PROSPECTS, ONGOING PROJECTS, AND COMPLETED PROJECTS, AS WELL AS OTHER VALUABLE MARKETING INFORMATION.

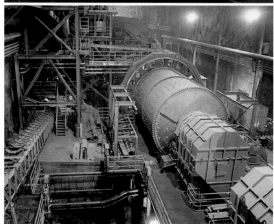

Two months later, Chile won its first significant contract, a gypsum wallboard production facility for Fletcher Challenge. Project Manager Melody Kratsios and Process Engineer Patrick Lamarre (Jacques Lamarre's son) were sent from Montreal to co-ordinate with a local team in Santiago.

In August, Alepian and Kletnieks had a breakthrough when the Andina division of Codelco awarded SNC-Lavalin Chile a contract to double the output of one of its copper concentrators from 35,000 to 64,000 tonnes per day. The project, led by John McCreight, was located 4,000 metres above sea level in the Andes. To protect the new facilities from the elements, including the occasional avalanche, they would be housed in an enormous cavern that SNC-Lavalin had to blast into the side of the mountain.

The project boosted SNC-Lavalin Chile's personnel to over 380, making it the largest Canadian-owned engineering firm in the country. Kletnieks was certainly feeling good about the business unit's prospects. "We have a good roster of projects now, with more to come," he reported in the company's internal magazine, *Spectrum*.

COURTING MONSIEUR PINGAT

Meanwhile, simultaneous inroads were being made in Europe. In early 1995, when Pierre Robitaille was given responsibility for the continent, he immediately fixed his attention on France. He saw that the standard of living was rising throughout the world. As a result, developing countries were becoming increasingly important consumers of high-end agrifood products, and France was a world leader in the industry.

The country was also an excellent platform from which to pursue a broad spectrum of contracts in the newly opened Eastern part of the continent. Since the fall of the Soviet Union in the early 1990s, former satellites like Poland had suddenly swung open their doors to Western companies. SNC-Lavalin felt that a stronger presence in France could provide a platform from which to bid on jobs in those countries.

After some research, Robitaille set his sights on a medium-sized family firm called Pingat Ingénierie, based in Reims. It went back nearly fifty years, and had built a solid reputation as the leading agrifood processes firm in the country. The question was: would an old French family-owned company want to be acquired by a Canadian multinational?

Robitaille established the first contact with its Managing Director, Jean Claude Pingat, in late August of that year and set up a meeting for the following week. Robitaille and Senior Vice-President and Controller Gilles Laramée flew to France to meet with Jean Claude and his father, André, the founder of the company.

They vaunted the capabilities and global reach of SNC-Lavalin and assured father and son that their company would have a special place within the organization. Jean Claude liked what he heard. He had a broad entrepreneurial streak and had long envisioned taking Pingat global. An association with a multinational company like SNC-Lavalin would finally give him the wherewithal to do that. His father saw things differently: Pingat Ingénierie bore the imprint of two generations of his family. Traditional and proud, André Pingat told his son that he preferred to hold on to the firm.

As the Pingats discussed the matter, Robitaille waited impatiently in Montreal. Two months later, with still no commitment from the owners, he decided to pull out all the stops. Robitaille invited Jean Claude to come to Canada in December to meet the company's management. It was a whirlwind tour designed to impress Pingat with the scope, talent, and expertise at SNC-Lavalin.

Within five days, he had met over 35 top managers at the head office in Montreal, including Jacques Lamarre, Taro Alepian, Pierre Dufour, Normand Morin, and Pierre Duhaime. It had the desired effect. By the end of the trip, Jean Claude was absolutely persuaded that the future of Pingat Ingénierie lay with SNC-Lavalin. Now he just had to convince his father.

"This is an amazing company, with incredible resources and expertise," he told his father when he returned to France.

André Pingat and his son, Jean Claude, in the 1970s.

From left to right: Jean Claude Pingat, André Pingat, and Jacques Lamarre, attend Pingat Ingénierie's 50th anniversary celebrations in 1997.

"We have built an excellent firm here, but associating with SNC-Lavalin will give us the resources to expand the way we've always wanted to."

It was not an easy conversation, but in the end André Pingat's trust in his son's judgment was enough to convince him to sell. "Alright, Jean Claude, if you really feel that the future of our company lies with SNC-Lavalin, then ... go ahead."

The acquisition was finalized in June of 1996. SNC-Lavalin fully expected Pingat to expand his organization, but the French business unit's growth would soon outstrip even the most optimistic projections. The entrepreneur in Pingat was about to be unleashed.

THE PETROTRIN PROBLEM

SNC-Lavalin had a serious problem in Trinidad. A fixed-price retrofit assignment at a Petrotrin petroleum refinery had become a runaway train.

The issue might have been resolved earlier had it not been for the lack of communication. The Calgary-based project team had stayed quiet about its troubles, hoping to fix them on its own. As a result, Taro Alepian had only learned of the scale of the problem in the summer of 1995, almost two years after the contract had begun. Now he needed an accurate assessment of the damage, and fast.

The job of putting a price tag on the remaining work went to Krish Krishnamoorthy, the Vice-President and General Manager of the Montreal Industrial Division. He travelled to Trinidad that summer with cost controls expert, John Romita, and the Vice-President of Construction, Gilbert Villeneuve.

What they found was chaos. The biggest problem was the enormous retrofit content of the job. Krishnamoorthy said such a project should never have been undertaken on a fixed-price basis, since it was impossible to know beforehand what they might run into. Calgary also urgently needed to put more of its own people on the ground in Trinidad to manage the work, he said. It would escalate costs even further, but at least it would give the company better control over project.

Alepian implemented the suggestions, and some progress was made. But projects that start off on the wrong foot are notoriously difficult to set right. In February 1996, with costs on the job continuing to spiral, Krishnamoorthy was transferred to the Calgary office as its new Senior Vice-President and General Manager to oversee the project full time.

That month, he and his new Vice-President of Operations, Ed Vogelgesang, took a trip to Trinidad to close up the project and settle all claims. SNC-Lavalin would eventually extricate itself from the fiasco, but it would take months and considerable legal resources.

Afterwards, Jacques Lamarre wanted to be sure that the lesson of Petrotrin resonated with the company's management. "What we've learned is the importance of communication," he told the Management Committee that fall. "I want this to be very clear. If you're in trouble on a project, tell us. We will be able to pool the company's resources to help you. If you stay silent, you are only further damaging your project and this company."

Krishnamoorthy had already lined up one possible contract in Saudi Arabia: the Qassim pipeline project for oil giant Saudi Aramco.

There was a problem, however. At the time, Aramco awarded contracts exclusively on a lump-sum turnkey basis, and Alepian had put an indefinite moratorium on fixed-price jobs out of Calgary. He had even taken the extraordinary step of moving the recently won Rhourde Nouss gas project in Algeria from Calgary to Montreal.

Krishnamoorthy had to convince his boss to let the office execute fixed-price jobs again.

"Taro, you've got to let us sign lump-sum jobs, because right now there are just not enough domestic clients," Krishnamoorthy pleaded. "We've made the necessary personnel changes in Calgary, and we have a team in place that is very capable of carrying out this project."

Alepian was not sure that the office was ready, but he had to give Krishnamoorthy the benefit of the doubt. He was right: the business unit would be in trouble unless it won a major job soon. He lifted the moratorium, and Calgary signed the contract later that year.

A man on a mission: Krish Krishnamoorthy was made Senior Vice-President and General Manager of the Calgary office in early 1996.

A NEW COURSE

Once Krishnamoorthy was assured Calgary's other projects were in order, he focused on the future. It looked bright, with oil prices finally on the rise once again, but he felt a major shift in strategy was needed to seize new opportunities.

For one thing, he anticipated that Alberta would become an ever more important market as investment in the oil sands increased. At the moment, SNC-Lavalin did not have bitumen (oil sand) processing expertise, so he began shopping around for a local firm that was recognized in the field.

He also felt the unit's international strategy was too opportunistic, and wanted to focus it on three or four key markets with the best potential, such as Saudi Arabia, Venezuela, and Oman.

CHAPTER 22 RISING TO THE CHALLENGE

The bar is raised for SNC-Lavalin in the late 1990s. The first challenge comes in the form of the Bre-X affair in 1997. The company must fight to prove its innocence, and the negative publicity takes a toll on its share price. Soon after, the company wins an EPCM contract for the Diavik Diamond Mines project in the Northwest Territories. Environmental restrictions force its team to devise cutting-edge techniques to satisfy the regulating agencies. The decade ends with SNC-Lavalin's consortium winning the Highway 407 concession in Toronto. The company itself is on the line since its investment in the deal is equal to the value of its shareholders' equity.

Highway 407 in Toronto.

On Wednesday, March 19, 1997, Michael de Guzman, the Head Geologist of Calgary-based mining company Bre-X, fell from a helicopter over the jungles of Borneo, Indonesia, plummeting 240 metres to his death.

The rumour mill kicked into high gear with de Guzman's apparent suicide. Since 1994, Bre-X had been making amazing claims about the gold at its site in Busang, Indonesia. The most recent projections had put deposits at anywhere between 70 and 200 million ounces. Now Bre-X's new partner in the venture, the mining company Freeport-McMoRan Copper and Gold, was carrying out a due diligence study at the site. De Guzman had apparently been on his way to an emergency meeting with representatives from Freeport.

On Thursday, March 20, the Jakarta business daily *Harian Ekonomi Neraca* confirmed the worst. The paper had gotten hold of an advance version of the Freeport study. It quoted the document as saying it was possible that the deposits were "not even economically exploitable." The journalist even went so far as to suggest that core samples had been "poisoned" (manipulated).

When the news hit Canada the next day, Robert Racine pulled Jacques Lamarre, Taro Alepian, Michael Novak, and Pierre Robitaille out of a Management Committee meeting on the 21st floor of Place Félix-Martin. There was bad news and worse news, he said: the bad news was that Bre-X was beginning to look like a scam,

and SNC-Lavalin's new subsidiary, Kilborn, had been hired to perform studies for the project before it was acquired. The worse news was that the Bre-X spokesperson quoted in the *Neraca* article had defended estimates by falsely suggesting that Kilborn had directly analysed its core samples.

Freeport and Bre-X were now preparing press releases to officially state their positions. Lamarre felt it would be important for SNC-Lavalin to issue a press release of its own explaining that Kilborn had been retained to calculate and estimate gold resources for the project based purely on data provided by Bre-X.

All three companies issued their press releases at around midnight on Wednesday, March 26. As expected, Freeport said it had found "insignificant amounts of gold." Bre-X conceded its gold resources were possibly "overstated," and said it had hired mining company Strathcona to conduct an independent due diligence study of the site. For its part, SNC-Lavalin stressed that Kilborn's studies had been based on "geological data, sample, and assay information provided by Bre-X."

When the Bre-X scandal broke in the spring of 1997, SNC-Lavalin's response was rapid and highly co-ordinated.

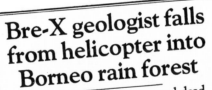

Bre-X geologist falls from helicopter into Borneo rain forest

Busang co-discoverer presumed dead

BY ALLAN ROBINSON
Mining Reporter

The No. 2 geologist for Bre-X Minerals Ltd. and co-discoverer of one of the world's richest gold de-

At that time, Bre-X was sticking, at least publicly, to its official estimate of 30 million ounces. The deposit is now estimated to contain at least 70 million ounces, and Mr. Felderhof mused about the possibility

CANADA'S BUSINESS NEWSPAPER
REPORT ON BUSINESS

©1997 The Globe and Mail

Thursday, March 27, 1997

Bre-X panic hits markets

Junior mining shares battered over fears that Busang gold find reserve estimates may have been overstated

Robitaille would head up investor relations, Robert Racine would handle the media, and Rick Dolan, the new Senior Vice-President of Law, would have the legal file. The only external member of the team was Vince O'Donnell of Lavery, de Billy, one of the country's top class action defence lawyers, although SNC-Lavalin still hoped it would not need to use his services.

Creso would be run with the seriousness and efficiency of a Richards Bay or an Ankara. The stakes were just as high: to the extent that those projects had helped build the company's reputation, the Bre-X affair now threatened to destroy it.

DIGGING FOR ANSWERS

Jacques Lamarre was working in his home office on Saturday, May 3, when he received an urgent call from Rick Dolan. "Jacques, the Strathcona interim report has been released. There's no gold at Busang."

Strathcona said it had found little, if any, gold. All signs pointed to massive fraud. ". . . the magnitude of the tampering with core samples that we believe has occurred and the resulting falsification of assay values at Busang, is of a scale and over a period of time and with a precision that, to our knowledge, is without precedent in the history of mining anywhere in the world," read the report.

SNC-Lavalin and Kilborn had already been named in one class action lawsuit, and the news that Bre-X was a total bust would likely bring others. That Monday morning, an emergency conference call was organized between the members of Creso in Montreal and about 50 employees at Kilborn's offices around the world who had been involved in the project. If SNC-Lavalin was going to have to mount a defence, no stone could be left unturned.

"We are in a very difficult situation," Lamarre said to the Kilborn employees. "If there is something you know, you have two days to tell Rick Dolan. It doesn't matter if it's bad news. The company will take responsibility for it if you tell us now. Otherwise, you will be held personally responsible for what you did not say."

As expected, the news caused panic selling of Bre-X shares the next day. Over $2.8 billion in value was obliterated in a single session when its shares fell from $15.80 to $2.50. SNC-Lavalin's stock took a hit as well, dropping from $18.45[1] to $16.00[2] since the announcement of de Guzman's death.

It was an unsettling development. Alepian feared that investors might start dumping SNC-Lavalin's stock if it looked like the company was going to be sued. And it was not just outside investors he was worried about. On May 6, following five years of preparation, all employee-owned class B shares, each now worth 14 votes, were going to be converted to common class A shares, which could be sold on the open market. If employees were spooked, they might be inclined to sell off their converted shares quickly, causing SNC-Lavalin's stock price to drop further.

It was not time to push the panic button, however. There was still a chance that it had all been an enormous misunderstanding. The Strathcona report, expected in four weeks, would put all questions to rest once and for all.

While the new investigation was under way, SNC-Lavalin formed Project Creso to monitor developments. Lamarre took the reins himself, and handed specific functions to several trusted executives. Taro Alepian would be in charge of tending to the company's professional reputation, Pierre

1. Adjusted for the stock split on March 10, 2006, the price would be $6.15.
2. Adjusted for the stock split on March 10, 2006, the price would be $5.33.

The Kilborn engineers, themselves in shock, were eager to help in whatever way they could. Over the next two days, they confirmed that the project team had acted professionally. Kilborn had done what it was asked to do by Bre-X, no more, no less. But while SNC-Lavalin was now sure Kilborn was blameless, the court of public opinion was still deliberating on the matter. News articles continued to appear almost daily, which only served to cloud the issue.

At a board meeting on August 8, 1997, Rick Dolan and Vince O'Donnell reviewed the class action suits that had been launched so far with Kilborn and SNC-Lavalin named among the defendants. There were now four, one for each month since the story had broken.

After their presentation, Lamarre said that he believed SNC-Lavalin could successfully defend itself, but that it would take years and many millions in legal fees before the company's name was in the clear. "You are going to have to be patient because we will be in this for at least 10 years," he told the worried directors. "But know that we are not going to back down. We are going right to the end of this thing."

Counsel Vince O'Donnell led SNC-Lavalin's defence during the Bre-X scandal.

Strathcona Mineral Services Limited
12th Floor, 20 Toronto Street, Toronto, Ontario, Canada M5C 2B8

Telephone: (416) 869-0772
Fax: (416) 367-3638

May 3, 1997

CONFIDENTIAL

BUSANG PROJECT - TECHNICAL AUDIT

FOR

BRE-X MINERALS LTD.

INTERIM REPORT

MAY 3, 1997

GF/ejh

An Independent Consulting & Project Management Service for the Mining Industry

AN ENVIRONMENTAL IMPOSSIBILITY?

If Kilborn, through no fault of its own, had embroiled SNC-Lavalin in the Bre-X affair, its team was proving an asset on every other front. It was through Kilborn that SNC-Lavalin won a preliminary engineering contract for Rio Tinto's Diavik diamond mine project in the Northwest Territories in March of 1998.

Mining diamonds is generally straightforward, but Diavik posed unprecedented environmental challenges. The diamonds were under a pristine arctic lake, so the only way to get at them was to build a horseshoe-shaped dike out from an island and pump out the water. The prospect of the lake becoming contaminated worried the inhabitants of villages along a nearby river.

The Mackenzie Valley Land and Water Board heard their concerns and drew a line in the sand: the project would not proceed unless Rio Tinto and its subsidiary, Diavik Diamond Mines, were able to prove the project could be carried out without a measureable impact on the local environment.

SNC-Lavalin's Project Manager in Calgary, Harry Sambells, knew the environmental criteria would be

Strathcona's Interim Report was the final nail in the Bre-X coffin.

Pineau could not believe his eyes. "There must be some typos in the email," Pineau wrote back. "There are too many zeros after the decimal point!"

There were no typos. Pineau and his lead water treatment engineer, Abdellatif Dellah, would, for all intents and purposes, have to design a potable water plant. The problem was that such plants were normally very large, and construction materials would be expensive to ship to Diavik. That meant that whatever facility they engineered would need to be both highly effective and very small.

Marcel Pineau (standing in the back) attended several of the community consultations for Diavik.

The cutting edge of technology: Diavik's environmentally friendly water treatment plant.

The Diavik project before the first dike was built.

strict, but even he was surprised when he saw the requirements for the project's water treatment plant. It looked like SNC-Lavalin would have to design a facility that could treat the turbid water from inside the dike to the standards of potable water.

Thinking that there had been some mistake, he sent an email to Marcel Pineau in Montreal, the Area Manager who would oversee its design. "The numbers seem low," Sambells wrote. "What do you think?"

Over the next three months, using the latest technology, the engineers developed a miniature test plant and had it built at Diavik. They needed turbid water, so six above-ground swimming pools were shipped to the site and filled with dirt and lake water. The results surpassed all expectations. There was no doubt that a scaled-up version of the plant—which would still be very small for a potable water treatment facility—would be able to meet the MacKenzie Valley Board's standards.

The news was greeted with scepticism by some, however, including a group representing the Aboriginal people of the region, who asked to see the treated water for themselves. "Yes, the numbers seem good," one of the visitors said to Pineau, "but I don't think you would drink the water!"

The engineer had no doubts about the quality of the water his plant was producing. Without hesitation, he dunked his coffee cup in the treated water and proceeded to chug its contents. Doubts vanished along with the last drop in Pineau's cup.

Once the team had demonstrated that it could process Diavik's waste water to the Mackenzie Valley Board's standards, the next challenge was to reduce the dike's footprint in the lakebed. Preliminary engineering had shown that the dike would need to be about 150 metres wide at the base to withstand the water pressure of the lake. The regulator felt that was too large and wanted a significant reduction in its

width. Anthony Rattue, SNC-Lavalin's dams and dikes specialist, had the job of figuring out how to do it.

By early 2000, the project had met all of the environmental criteria, and SNC-Lavalin had been awarded the EPCM contract for Diavik. But the Mackenzie Valley Board was still reluctant to give the project the go-ahead. Its members were unsure if the novel techniques used would be sufficient. Their main concern was the dike, which had an experimental design and would be built using an untested construction method. It looked fine in theory, they said, but how would it perform in a real-life situation? Rio Tinto was beginning to despair of ever getting approval.

It was at this point that Phil du Toit, the President of Diavik Diamond Mines, asked Rattue to make a presentation directly to the Mackenzie Valley Board to break the deadlock. Du Toit felt that Rattue would be able offer a technical rebuttal to the statements being made at the hearings.

The members had many questions, all of which Rattue was able to answer. It turned out that no one had taken the

AN ICE ROAD TO NOWHERE

THE DIAVIK DIAMOND MINE PROJECT WAS LOCATED IN THE CANADIAN SUBARCTIC ON A SMALL ISLAND IN THE MIDDLE OF A LAKE. THE ONLY MEANS OF ACCESS WAS AN ICE ROAD THAT LASTED BARELY THREE MONTHS OF THE YEAR. IT WAS ALL THE TIME HARRY SAMBELLS AND HIS TEAM HAD TO GET VAST QUANTITIES OF CONSTRUCTION MATERIALS, FUEL, AND EQUIPMENT TO THE SITE.

time to carefully explain the complex design, construction, and mitigation measures to them. The Q&A with Rattue had the desired effect: shortly after his presentation, the Mackenzie Valley Board issued a Class A environmental permit for Diavik.

Diavik's first dike, developed by Anthony Rattue, had an unprecedented but highly effective design.

Putting it all on the line: SNC-Lavalin would invest capital equivalent to the total value of its shareholders' equity for Highway 407.

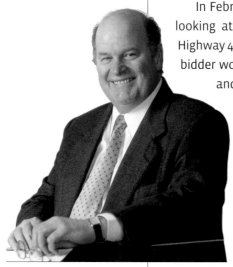

Roger Nichol

A LANDMARK DEAL

Mike Harris swept to power in Ontario in 1995 with a promise to cut the province's out-of-control deficit. He made good progress at first, slashing spending across the board, but by 1998 expenses were on the rise once again. With an election now expected in early 1999, Harris decided to employ some shock tactics to secure credibility as a cost-cutting premier.

In February 1998, the government announced it was looking at selling the existing 68-kilometre stretch of Highway 407 in Toronto to the private sector. The winning bidder would own the highway for an extended period, and generate revenue from tolls. They would also have to build much-needed eastern and western extensions as part of the deal.

SNC-Lavalin's Executive Vice-President in charge of Ontario, Roger Nichol, had been eagerly eyeing developments. In August, when he learned expressions of interest were going to be sought, he called Jacques Lamarre in Montreal and urged him to consider getting involved.

"Jacques, this is one of the biggest privatization projects in Canadian history," he said. "I think we should be there in some form."

Lamarre was interested, but with three consortiums already vying for the deal, he felt the playing field was overcrowded. "It's going to cost us between $5 and $7 million to mount a bid on our own," he said. "See if one of the three existing consortiums is willing to make room for us as designers and builders of the two extensions. If not, we'll look at forming our own team."

The answer from the other consortiums was a resounding no. Each had divvied up the investment between their own partners and had no intention of making room for another. That left only one option, but Lamarre would not even consider going in as an investor unless he was sure the traffic would be there to justify it.

Imad Nassereddine, SNC-Lavalin's Manager of Transportation Systems in Toronto, confirmed that it would. Since the 407 had become a toll highway in October 1997, volume had grown steadily. The increase was due to how badly the city needed the road. The 401, its main highway, was terribly congested, and, with Lake Ontario directly to the south, the 407 was practically the only east-west alternative for commuters.

The deal was beginning to look too good to pass up, but before making a final decision, Lamarre wanted to confirm that he had the full support of SNC-Lavalin's board, and particularly Chairman Guy Saint-Pierre. All felt that the deal warranted the large investment.

Lamarre then consulted an influential director from former years. He had remained friends with Stephen Jarislowsky since his retirement from SNC-Lavalin's board in 1996. At 75, Jarislowsky was still a feisty pillar of the Canadian business establishment, and a good spotter of new trends.

"This is absolutely enormous for us, Steve," Lamarre said over lunch at the former director's favourite Chinese restaurant in Montreal. "We've never sunk more than $25 million or so into an infrastructure concession before, but we'd be putting up hundreds of millions for this. Should we be venturing into this kind of thing?"

"This is the future," Jarislowsky said without hesitation. "It's a great investment for SNC-Lavalin."

"Then tell me what you think the key is to being successful with this deal."

"Bond ratings," Jarislowsky replied without hesitation. "When you refinance your bridge loans from the banks with a public offering of bonds, they *must* have an A rating from Standard and Poor's. No one has ever tried to sell bonds for a road concession in Canada before, so you'll need to make them as attractive as possible."

MISSION IMPOSSIBLE

The job of finding a partner with the toll road operation experience to complement SNC-Lavalin's design-build expertise went to Ken Walker, the Senior Vice-President of SNC-Lavalin's Ontario operations. With all the major contenders in North America already locked up in one of the three consortiums, he turned to an international trade magazine to scout for candidates. It was there that he found a write-up about Cintra, the subsidiary of the Spanish construction company Ferrovial. Cintra was number two in the world in toll road concessions, with a total of 13. Even better, it turned out they were looking for a Canadian partner to join them in a bid for 407.

As Walker and the Senior Vice-President of Law, Rick Dolan, were coming to an agreement with Cintra, Pierre Anctil, the new Senior Vice-President of SNC-Lavalin Equity, was leading the financial side of SNC-Lavalin's bid. He was getting close to securing a major investor. With dual engineering and business degrees, Anctil was able to merge the technical specifications and financial details into a strong sales pitch. The Caisse de dépôt et placement du Québec, the province's enormous pension fund, quickly came around.

Meanwhile, Project Manager Albert Sweetnam was leading the team that was preparing the designs for the road extensions. From the start, SNC-Lavalin saw that its greatest advantage lay in being able to deliver a quality road for a highly competitive price. The more cost-efficient it could be in the construction of the road extensions, the more capital it would have for the bid.

By January 1999, the three partners of the newly formed 407 Electronic Toll Road (ETR) International consortium had come to a preliminary agreement. But now that SNC-Lavalin had partners, it needed banks to provide bridge financing for the deal (i.e.: to lend the consortium the required capital until it refinanced its debt with a public offering of bonds). That would not be easy, since most of the major financial institutions in Canada were already committed to one of the other consortiums.

Hitching a ride
on the 407:
Pierre Anctil,
Christiane Bergevin,
Albert Sweetnam,
Ken Walker,
and Rick Dolan.

LAST-MINUTE SURPRISE

Pierre Anctil was speechless. With only days to go before the bid deadline of March 25, CITI Bank decided to pull its financing from the deal.

It had taken a great effort for Anctil and a team at SNC-Lavalin Capital, led by its new Senior Vice-President and General Manager, Christiane Bergevin, to line up financing from the Bank of Montreal, CITI Bank, and the Royal Bank of Canada. And now, out of the blue, CITI's Credit Committee had rejected the deal as too risky. A few recent U.S. toll roads were failing to live up to initial traffic forecasts, and they were concerned that the 407 would be more of the same.

Anctil immediately called his contact at the CITI Bank office in Toronto. "Listen, we can't accept this," he said. "I want to go and meet your Credit Committee in New York."

"We don't do that at CITI Bank, Pierre," the contact said. "The Credit Committee is purely internal. Investors never present their projects directly to the committee."

"I don't care," Anctil said. "I still want to do it."

While CITI Bank was not willing to let Anctil and Nassereddine meet the entire committee at once, it allowed them to speak to its half-dozen members one or two at a time. Over the next two days, the pair made the case for Highway 407 as a solid investment. It was an eye-opening experience for the committee members. Until now, they had only ever had the project explained to them by their banking colleagues. But here were engineers with a deep knowledge of the investment answering whatever questions they had.

Anctil reminded CITI Bank that the consortium had solid financial partners, and emphasized the careful way that the deal had been structured. Nassereddine, meanwhile, explained basic traffic and revenue forecasting to them. "That was like teaching an advanced transportation planning course to 50- and 60-year old university students with lots of money," Nassereddine quipped to Anctil after one meeting.

By the end of the two days, CITI was back on board.

THE BAY STREET SPRINT

It was March 25 and the clock was ticking. Walker sat by the phone staring nervously at the receiver.

SNC-Lavalin and Ferrovial/Cintra were currently in last-minute talks, attempting to finalize their offer. The cost for the construction of the two extensions, debt service, and working capital was already established at about $800 million. They had also come to an agreement on ownership percentages: 61 percent for Ferrovial/Cintra, 23 percent for SNC-Lavalin and 16 percent for the Caisse de dépôt. Ferrovial/Cintra would appoint the CEO of 407 International Inc., the company that would operate the road, while SNC-Lavalin would select its Chief Financial Officer (a decision had already been taken to put Ken Walker in the position, assisted by SNC-Lavalin's dynamic Controller and Treasurer, Gerry Grigoropoulos for the first years of the mandate). SNC-Lavalin and Ferrovial/Cintra would have equal voting rights, despite the difference in investments. SNC-Lavalin had earned that much by securing all of the financing for the deal.

The only thing now left to decide was how much the consortium would bid for the right to lease the highway for 99 years. It was what Walker was waiting impatiently to find out.

The call finally came in at 4:45 p.m., with only 15 minutes left before the submission deadline. "Okay, Ken, we have a final agreement with Ferrovial," Anctil said. "Do you have a pen and paper? Here it is: we'll bid $2.75 billion, that's 2-7-5-0-0-0-0-0-0-0-0… got it?"

Walker hastily wrote down the number, and slid the sheet into an envelope. The Merrill Lynch office where he had to deliver it was about 10 minutes away in normal traffic, but this was rush hour in Canada's most congested city. He had no choice but to hustle the envelope over on foot.

BEST AND FINAL OFFER

That evening, SNC-Lavalin learned that ETR International had one of the two top bids. The difference between them was within five percent, which meant they would now compete for the highway in a best and final offer round. ETR International had until April 7 to increase its offer and re-bid.

Rick Byers, the head of BMO Capital Markets, came to the rescue, offering to put up an additional $150 million in riskier junior bridge financing. The three partners then dug a little deeper and came up with additional equity to get the bid to $3.107 billion. It was a subliminal reference to 407 (3+1 = 4 and 07). SNC-Lavalin was now pushing it to the absolute limit: its share was $175 million in equity, and $175 million in subordinated debt, just short of the total value of its shareholders' equity.

ETR International submitted its second offer just in time once again. Two hours later, the team got the news that they had won. The importance of the deal to SNC-Lavalin could not be overstated. The company was now involved in one of Canada's largest privatizations ever, and one of the biggest road transactions of its kind.

Winning the deal was only half the challenge, however. The partners now had to refinance the bank debt. While the bonds were A rated, they were still unknown territory

for investors, so Walker and Nassereddine went on a cross-country tour with BMO that summer to secure buyers. The first issue exceeded all expectations, bringing in $1.1 billion by July. It was the biggest corporate public offering of bonds in Canadian history.

BUYING OUT BRACKNELL

By mid-1999, SNC-Lavalin and Bracknell Corporation had been enjoying a fruitful partnership for close to a decade. Their jointly owned facilities management company, ProFac, had done exceptionally well.

Things had accelerated considerably since August 1997, when ProFac was awarded a five-year contract by the Canadian Broadcasting Corporation to operate and manage all of its English-language network buildings. The next year

Clockwise:
Pierre Anctil (left) and Imad Nassereddine discuss progress on the construction of the extensions for the 407, paving in progress, and a completed interchange of the highway.

After two rounds of bidding, one of Canada's largest privatization projects was awarded to SNC-Lavalin's consortium.

In the 1990s, landmark ProFac contracts were signed with Canada Post, the Canadian Broadcasting Corporation, and the Ontario Realty Corporation.

had seen the partnership win a breakthrough international contract to rehabilitate and operate Lebanon's postal service. Most recently, in June 1999, the company had won a contract to operate and manage all the buildings belonging to the Ontario Realty Corporation in the Greater Toronto area and southwestern Ontario. That meant a total of 2,200 facilities, covering 28.8 million square metres.

But a chink had recently developed in relations between SNC-Lavalin and Bracknell. Bracknell's new President and CEO, Paul Melnuk, was indicating to his analysts that he wanted to either take full control of ProFac or sell off his share to SNC-Lavalin. It was not quite clear why he had taken that stance, but Jacques Lamarre found it undermined the credibility of the partnership.

SNC-Lavalin was certainly not ready to relinquish its share of ProFac. For one thing, the company saw potential synergies between its engineering and construction business and ProFac's operations and maintenance capability. At the moment, ProFac was only operating buildings, but there was no reason why the company could not do the same thing for SNC-Lavalin's engineering projects.

In the fall of 1999, Jacques Lamarre asked Melnuk to come to Montreal to discuss the matter. He had hoped to re-solve their differences and keep Bracknell as a partner, but it was soon clear that Melnuk had made up his mind.

"Okay," Lamarre said, "if you feel so strongly that you do not want to be our partner anymore, then we have a proposal for you."

"What's your offer," Melnuk asked dryly.

"I want you to make us an offer," Lamarre said. "Tell us what you would be willing to pay for our share of ProFac. We will then have the option to sell our share, or buy your share for that same amount. I also want to maintain the option to do neither and remain partners."

One week later, Melnuk was back with an offer. Bracknell was willing to acquire SNC-Lavalin's share of ProFac for $22.5 million. While Lamarre usually felt that he paid too much for acquisitions, he immediately recognized that it was a fair price.

When he brought the deal to the Office of the President the following day, there was overwhelming enthusiasm for accepting it. Many saw the synergies that could be developed between their divisions and a wholly owned ProFac. Lamarre also checked confidentially with ProFac's clients. He learned that many actually preferred having a single owner, since they felt it made for a more stable company.

With that, Lamarre informed Melnuk that SNC-Lavalin was going to buy Bracknell's stake. By May 2000, the deal was closed and SNC-Lavalin ProFac was born.

PART
7

BEYOND
FRONTIERS

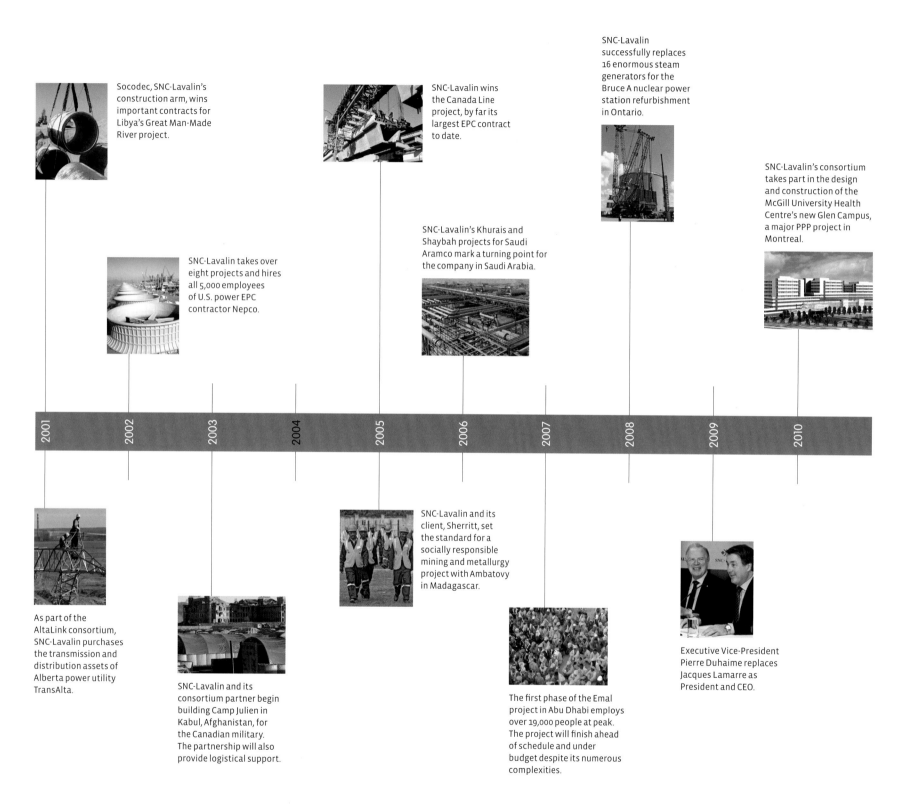

Socodec, SNC-Lavalin's construction arm, wins important contracts for Libya's Great Man-Made River project.

SNC-Lavalin wins the Canada Line project, by far its largest EPC contract to date.

SNC-Lavalin successfully replaces 16 enormous steam generators for the Bruce A nuclear power station refurbishment in Ontario.

SNC-Lavalin's consortium takes part in the design and construction of the McGill University Health Centre's new Glen Campus, a major PPP project in Montreal.

SNC-Lavalin takes over eight projects and hires all 5,000 employees of U.S. power EPC contractor Nepco.

SNC-Lavalin's Khurais and Shaybah projects for Saudi Aramco mark a turning point for the company in Saudi Arabia.

2001 2002 2003 2004 2005 2006 2007 2008 2009 2010

As part of the AltaLink consortium, SNC-Lavalin purchases the transmission and distribution assets of Alberta power utility TransAlta.

SNC-Lavalin and its consortium partner begin building Camp Julien in Kabul, Afghanistan, for the Canadian military. The partnership will also provide logistical support.

SNC-Lavalin and its client, Sherritt, set the standard for a socially responsible mining and metallurgy project with Ambatovy in Madagascar.

The first phase of the Emal project in Abu Dhabi employs over 19,000 people at peak. The project will finish ahead of schedule and under budget despite its numerous complexities.

Executive Vice-President Pierre Duhaime replaces Jacques Lamarre as President and CEO.

PREVIOUS PAGE

A partial view of the McGill University Health Centre's Glen Campus in Montreal.

CHAPTER 23 | A WORLD-CLASS COMPANY

SNC-Lavalin begins the new millennium with the healthiest balance sheet in its 90-year history. Record cash reserves allow it to target new acquisitions and investments. The company's Power Division gains transmission and distribution (T&D) expertise in Alberta, followed by thermal power know-how in Washington. As a majority partner in AltaLink, SNC-Lavalin moves into the power concessions market in Alberta. Meanwhile, two lagging divisions are rehabilitated: SNC-Lavalin's construction arm, Socodec, roars back to life after a year of losses, while its mining and metallurgy group is given a new raison d'être.

The Gila River thermal power plant in Arizona.

On May 4, 2000, Jacques Lamarre took the podium at the annual employees' meeting in Montreal and looked out into the audience. The glare from the projectors made it difficult to pick out individuals, but it was clearly a good-sized crowd.

"We have had significant success together this year," he began. "Supported by its world-class products, global reach, and entry into new high-growth sectors of activity, SNC-Lavalin has performed better than most of its peers."

Lamarre was referring to 1999, but he could just as easily have been talking about any of the previous eight years. During that time, there had been an impressive ascent in profitability: in 1992, following the merger, the company had netted a mere $9.3 million on revenues of $747 million. In 1999, after years of optimizing its operations, it had made a profit of $49.5 million on revenues of $1.3 billion. A similar story could be read in the company's fattening revenue backlog, which had gone from $1.5 billion to $2.7 billion. There

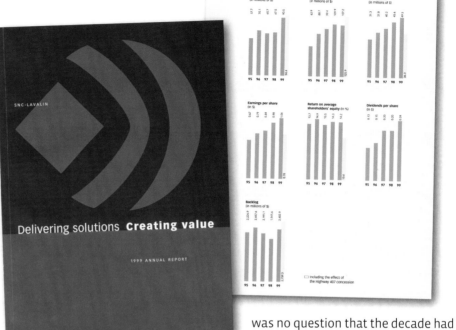

was no question that the decade had been good to SNC-Lavalin.

Sitting up front in the audience, Lamarre's Executive Vice-President of Finance, Gilles Laramée, saw opportunity in those numbers. For the past year, SNC-Lavalin had been searching for ways to fuel the next stage of its growth, and Laramée was convinced that its solid track record made issuing debentures an option. They did not offer security to investors in the form of assets, so only highly regarded companies could hope to sell them.

In the past, SNC-Lavalin had financed its development by issuing shares and tapping bank lines of credit. The drawback of a large share issue was the downward pressure it exerted on the company's stock price. Lines of credit, on the other hand, were subject to swings in interest rates, and could be shut off at a moment's notice.

Debentures had none of these downsides. They had no direct connection to the company's shares and would give SNC-Lavalin a measure of independence from banks— something that Lamarre and Laramée always liked. There would also be fringe benefits: SNC-Lavalin would receive a credit rating to help it secure favourable terms for the multi-million-dollar bank guarantees it needed for projects. Even the prospect of throwing open the company's books to rating

Jacques Lamarre

Gilles Laramée

agencies each year was greeted enthusiastically. If anything, it would help make SNC-Lavalin a more watertight ship.

Over the next three months, Laramée and Michael Ioffredi, the company's Vice-President and Controller, prepared the financial information required by the Canadian Bond Rating Service and the Dominion Bond Rating Service. In July, the two agencies assigned SNC-Lavalin's debentures a rating of BBB, or stable. Held against the company were its audacious move into large-scale concession investments like Highway 407 and its fixed-price contracts in developing countries. The upsides were its strong performance since 1992 and its healthy balance sheet. The agencies also awarded high marks for revenue diversification, world-class products, and long-standing client relationships. Importantly, both acknowledged that SNC-Lavalin had outperformed many companies in its sector over the past several years.

By September, the debentures had raised $105 million—$5 million more than hoped for. Not bad for its first foray into the debt capital market. Laramée was satisfied, but he knew that a rating of BBB+ was not beyond SNC-Lavalin's grasp. He would continue to aim for it. Over time, he was sure that the market would increasingly recognize the company for the solid investment it was.

THE RISE OF SOCODEC

By the mid-1990s, Sami Bébawi had made a name for himself in Quebec's project management world. After working on contracts like the James Bay LG-3 dam for Lavalin, he had founded his own project management firm called Géracon and gone head-to-head against some of the biggest players in the industry. To the amazement of all, his little company had snatched up a coveted owner's manager mandate for the Alouette aluminum smelter in Quebec.

Impressed by his audacity, and a little concerned by Géracon's success on SNC-Lavalin's playing field, Lamarre asked to meet him for dinner in mid-1998. He felt Bébawi was the right man to rehabilitate Socodec. SNC-Lavalin's fabled construction arm was heading for a loss of over $14 million for the year. The only thing holding the division together at the moment was a well-drilling mandate for the Great Man-Made River (GMMR) Authority in Libya, and that was wrapping up.

"Sami, we're getting big," Lamarre said. "We need major jobs, but Socodec is not living up to our expectations. If you're interested, I'll make you President of the Division and an Executive Vice-President." He was making a major exception:

Clockwise: Sami Bébawi, repair work on the Great Man-Made River, and an emergency water project in Algeria.

competition from other Western firms was thinner, like Algeria, Libya, Venezuela, and the Dominican Republic. Bébawi also wanted to go big: Socodec had previously been targeting contracts that were between $25 and $50 million. Now he upped the ante and took aim at projects in the $100 to $150 million range.

In this, Bébawi would have help from a newly hired management team, which included Réjean Carrier, his Senior Vice-President of Operations, and long-time Socodec veterans like Riadh Ben Aïssa, the division's Vice-President for Libya.

Ben Aïssa had been instrumental in securing the first mandate for the GMMR in 1995. It had been a maddening contract, fraught with challenges, including a crippling embargo, but SNC-Lavalin's team had not thrown in the towel. It was with this credibility that Ben Aïssa was able to secure a large-scale repair contract for two pipelines in the GMMR's Sarir-Sirt/Tazerbo-Benghazi conveyance system in August 2001.

Eight months later, in April 2002, Ben Aïssa and the Socodec team moved in on another job to repair and manage the factory that produced the GMMR's enormous pipes. While SNC-Lavalin had been a natural choice

never before had an outsider been hired directly to the Office of the President.

"I'm flattered, Jacques, but I have 25 employees at Géracon. I'm not prepared to just walk away and leave them high and dry."

"So we'll hire them too," Lamarre said. "We'll acquire Géracon and you'll all come to SNC-Lavalin."

When Bébawi became President of Socodec in December 1998, he had already decided to use the division's GMMR experience to make it a major player in the water sector. He would start by going after fixed-price jobs in regions where

to head up a large-scale pipe replacement mandate, refurbishing and running the facility that made them was another matter. When Socodec picked up the contract, it was clear that the division had not lost its ability to rise to new challenges.

By then, the division's prospects were brightening by the week. A team that included Socodec's new Vice-President of Infrastructure, Kebir Ratnani, and its Vice-President of Water Technology, Abdellatif Dellah, had been making inroads in neighbouring Algeria.

In September 2001, they won a contract for a water conveyance tunnel to supply drinking water to Algiers. It soon became clear, however, that the capital could not wait until 2004 for the additional supply. In May 2002, following months of drought, Socodec was asked to shorten the delivery date from two years to six months. It was an unheard of schedule for such a job, but Bébawi was not about to turn down a $140-million contract when Socodec had only just moved out of the red.

Socodec closed out the year with a second mandate for an urgent water project in Algeria. The first one had gone well enough to convince the government to award SNC-Lavalin a similar contract to supply drinking water to the city of Skikda, about 400 kilometres from Algiers. Together, the two Algerian jobs would add 264,000 cubic metres per day of badly needed production capacity to the country's aging system.

In the space of three years, Socodec was transformed from a money loser to the group's third most profitable operating unit. Its projects in 2002 generated an operating income of over $22 million on revenues of $413 million. The division was not resting on its laurels, however. Having succeeded in the water sector, Bébawi now wanted to try his hand at power, operations and maintenance, and infrastructure concessions.

Socodec was back in business.

BEHIND THE WIRE

By mid-2001, Ron Rhodenizer had been successfully managing the company's Maritime Coastal Defence Vessels in-service support contract with the Department of National Defence (DND) for over six years. It was a time-consuming mandate, but he had never stopped trying to get SNC-Lavalin involved in other DND projects.

A few months earlier, DND had officially decided to assign the operations and maintenance of its international military bases to the private sector. Rhodenizer saw that SNC-Lavalin was a perfect fit for the contract, officially called the Canadian Forces Contractor Augmentation Program, or CANCAP. Over the past 40 years, the company had operated project camps from deep in the heart of the Indian jungle to

A POWERFUL PROJECT MANAGEMENT ALLY

DURING THE 1980s, SNC's PROJECT MANAGEMENT SOFTWARE HAD BEEN NURTURED AND DEVELOPED BY KEITH CARRIER AND KRIKOR DER-GHAZARIAN INTO AN EXCELLENT MANAGEMENT TOOL, BUT CHANGES IN TECHNOLOGY EVENTUALLY REQUIRED A SHIFT TO A WINDOWS-BASED SYSTEM. IN 1999, ALONG WITH GÉRACON, SNC-LAVALIN ACQUIRED THE NUCLEUS OF A MORE MODERN, WINDOWS-COMPATIBLE SYSTEM DEVELOPED BY THE FIRM'S IT SPECIALIST, HUU NGUYEN. AS OF 2001, LOUIS DAGENAIS, SNC-LAVALIN'S VICE-PRESIDENT OF INFORMATION TECHNOLOGIES, BEGAN EXPANDING PM+'S CAPABILITIES WITH THE HELP OF DER-GHAZARIAN'S TEAM. A FULLY INTEGRATED TOOL SET WAS SOON INSTALLED ON A CENTRAL INFRASTRUCTURE TO ENSURE UNIFORMITY OF THE SOFTWARE AND GLOBAL ACCESSIBILITY. VERY QUICKLY, THE SOFTWARE WOULD BE RECOGNIZED AS ONE OF THE BEST OF ITS KIND BY SNC-LAVALIN'S CLIENTS.

altitudes of over 4,000 metres in the Andes. The only thing SNC-Lavalin lacked was operational experience in a combat zone. To get it, Rhodenizer formed a joint venture with Pacific Architects and Engineers (PAE), which had supported the U.S. military during the Vietnam War.

SNC-Lavalin and PAE's combined resumé resulted in a winning proposal. However, DND still wanted a concrete demonstration of the partnership's ability to rapidly mobilize for and support remote camps. Tony Wachmann, the new Project Manager on the Diavik Diamond Mines project in the Northwest Territories, urged Rhodenizer to bring them up there.

"Diavik is the ultimate example of remote site management. We're on a small island in the middle of a lake in the subarctic," he said. "Bring DND up here, and they'll see logistical support and remote site management taken to an extreme."

A group of representatives was flown up in November 2002 and given a tour of the site by Diavik Construction Manager Nick Mills. It was indeed an impressive display of resourcefulness. The project and its 800 personnel were humming along at maximum efficiency despite bitterly cold temperatures and an ultra-remote location. A tiny hamlet in the subarctic, Diavik was accessible by an ice road for only 12 weeks each year, but had to otherwise be reached by plane.

The final validation came a few months later, when the CANCAP team was asked to prove itself during an exercise

The Diavik diamond project in northern Canada helped SNC-Lavalin win the CANCAP project.

Camp Julien in Afghanistan was located next to a bombed-out palace.

Don Chynoweth

at a training base in Wainwright, Alberta. Over the course of three weeks, CANCAP personnel supplied food, accommodation, fuel, medical, transportation, and engineering services to more than 4,600 soldiers from across the country.

The joint venture's success in Wainwright convinced DND that the team was ready for the real thing.

In May 2003, SNC-Lavalin/PAE was asked to construct and support Camp Julien in Afghanistan, Canada's largest expeditionary base since World War II. By then, CANCAP was being led by SNC-Lavalin's new Senior Vice-President of Defence Programs, Don Chynoweth. His team, which included Program Manager Sam Feola, Site Project Manager Ian Malcolm, and Engineering Manager Bill Morton, quickly overcame what seemed like insurmountable obstacles, including a woefully deficient supply chain and a serious lack of resources.

Despite these challenges and more, the camp was soon ready for the 2,500 Canadian Forces soldiers.

IN SEARCH OF A LEADER

When Noranda's Chief Operating Officer, David Goldman, retired in 2001, Jacques Lamarre saw an opportunity to use his expertise to help the company find its footing in the mining and metallurgy (M&M) world. With the acquisition of Kilborn in 1996, SNC-Lavalin had emerged as one of the best-qualified Canadian engineering companies in the sector, but it was failing to live up to its full potential.

Between 2000 and 2001, revenues from mining and metallurgy activities had crashed by 42 percent. The drop in the sector's contribution to the company's net income was even more dramatic, plummeting by nearly 66 percent. The cause of the division's underperformance lay partly in unspectacular metal prices, but it also seemed to be tied to deeper, internal issues.

In typical Jacques Lamarre style, the instructions were brief and to the point. "David, I'd like you to go to Toronto and tell me what you think," he said. "Come back with recommendations on how we can make the most of the division."

In May 2001, Goldman set up shop at Kilborn. The former Noranda executive had decided not to conduct formal interviews. Instead, he would become a fly on the wall and simply observe the company's day-to-day operations. The only digging he would do would be on the accounting side. Working with the subsidiary's controller would give him a detailed picture of how the organization was structured, where it was making and where it was losing money.

One thing was immediately clear: the office had developed a morale problem. The look in the faces of some of its managers and engineers spoke volumes. Bre-X had been a traumatic blow from which they had never fully recovered. Kilborn also had several contracts tangled up in claims from clients, some of which reached into the hundreds of millions of dollars. The combined effect had sapped its personnel of motivation, and its backlog had dwindled.

Goldman's other observation had to do with the current structure of SNC-Lavalin's mining and metallurgy group. He felt that Kilborn was working in a deep silo, cut off from the central nervous system of the company. Goldman believed SNC-Lavalin was wasting an opportunity to market all of its mining know-how as one unified set of expertise.

By September, he was back in Montreal to deliver his recommendations to Lamarre. "Jacques, I think it's time that you bring things together in another way," he began. "You have a wealth of expertise in Toronto that you're not getting credit for because those people are off operating on their

THE MAGNOLA SAGA

BY THE LATE 1960s, DECADES OF ASBESTOS MINING IN QUEBEC HAD PRODUCED GREAT MOUNTAINS OF CRUSHED ROCK TAILINGS. IN THE MID-1980s, LAVALINTECH AND NORANDA HAD TAKEN AN INTEREST IN A NOVEL TECHNOLOGY THAT WOULD MAKE USE OF THOSE TAILINGS BY EXTRACTING THE MAGNESIUM THEY CONTAINED. THE PARTNERSHIP, CALLED MAGNOLA (A COMBINATION OF **MAG**NESIUM, **NO**RANDA, AND **LA**VALIN), PROCEEDED TO DEVELOP THE PROCESS. IN THE MID-1990s, NORANDA PURCHASED SNC-LAVALIN'S INTEREST AND PLANNED TO COMMERCIALIZE THE TECHNOLOGY IN PARTNERSHIP WITH THE SOCIÉTÉ GÉNÉRALE DE FINANCEMENT DU QUÉBEC.

IN 1997, NORANDA WAS AT LAST READY TO BUILD A FIRST COMMERCIAL PLANT. SNC-LAVALIN WAS AWARDED THE EPCM CONTRACT, AND GEORGES RODE'S PROJECT TEAM COMPLETED THE SMELTER ON TIME AND WITHIN BUDGET IN JUNE OF 2000. MAGNOLA'S FUTURE LOOKED BRIGHT, BUT AS THE FACILITY WAS RAMPING UP, THE MAGNESIUM MARKET WAS SUDDENLY OVERWHELMED BY AN UNFORESEEN SUPPLY OF LOW-COST METAL FROM CHINA. MAGNOLA COULD NOT COMPETE, AND THE SMELTER WAS MOTHBALLED IN APRIL 2003.

David Goldman

Pierre Duhaime

Marylynne Campbell

Goldstrike in Nevada.

only one candidate whom they both felt was up to the task—the current Senior Vice-President of the Industrial Division in Montreal, Pierre Duhaime.

"I've known this guy since his days at Noranda," Goldman said. "He's tenacious, and he has a solid reputation with clients. They respect him for his expertise and straightforward approach—what you see is what you get. On top of all that, he's got a great work ethic."

Lamarre had a favourable opinion of Duhaime, but before making a final decision, he sounded the waters to see if those who would report to him were in favour of the appointment. It was a tactic he used each time he promoted someone into a senior position, since no one could succeed without the support of their team. A dozen quick phone calls confirmed his choice.

On October 10, 2001, Lamarre announced the change. In addition to Kilborn, the company's mining and metallurgy offices in Montreal, Winnipeg, Vancouver, Denver, the U.K., Australia, South Africa, and Chile would now report to Duhaime. The rest of the Toronto units' activities, which included environment, transportation infrastructure, and industrial, would be separated off and given to the Senior Vice-President of Human Resources, Marylynne Campbell.

Lamarre did not hide what was at stake for the 47-year-old Duhaime. The challenges would be nothing short of enormous. If he succeeded, on the other hand, Lamarre told him he would be assured a place in the Office of the President. As for Goldman, Lamarre was impressed enough with his analysis to recommend that he be considered for election to SNC-Lavalin's board of directors.

DAMAGE CONTROL

Pierre Duhaime had no illusions about what awaited him in Toronto. Part of the problem stemmed from the depressed price of base metals, but, as Goldman had noted, there were also extensive internal issues to sort out. The most pressing was a series of completed contracts on which clients had made large claims.

own. I think you should consider naming someone to head up everything you have in the sector worldwide."

Goldman proceeded to review a few managers with Lamarre whom he felt could take on overall responsibility for mining and metallurgy. It was soon clear that there was

Duhaime knew he had to settle the claims if he was going to get the division off the ground. His years at Noranda had given him an innate empathy for the client's point of view, but his job now was to make them understand SNC-Lavalin's viewpoint.

"I think that if we step back, we can agree that we've both made some mistakes," he told clients. "Let's sit down and review the project from A to Z. We'll break it down and find out exactly what went wrong. I'm sure we can figure this out without going to court." Many responded positively to Duhaime's proposal, recognizing that he was looking for a genuinely equitable solution.

At the same time, Duhaime was pursuing new contracts. The only way to lure top talent was to bring in projects that would interest them and challenge their skills. To do that, however, he first needed to rebuild the division's reputation.

Duhaime spent the next year on a continual road trip, bringing his enthusiasm from client to client, and talking to them about SNC-Lavalin's unique mining and metallurgy expertise. He said he was making it his personal mission to ensure every project executed by the division delivered total client satisfaction.

While he worked on bringing in new contracts, an old client, Barrick Gold, remained an invaluable lifeline. Kilborn had designed every one of its processing plants, starting in the early 1980s with Goldstrike in Nevada. Now, in 2001, there were new Barrick contracts for the Veladero and Alto Chicama projects in Argentina and Peru. Seasoned project managers Dale Clarke, Terry Walbaum, and Bruce Randall were assigned to the jobs. They would keep the hearth lit while Kilborn rebuilt its client base.

GOLD AT THE TOP OF THE WORLD

THE VELADERO AND ALTO CHICAMA GOLD PROJECTS WERE LOCATED AT ELEVATIONS THAT WERE DEEMED TO BE AT THE LIMITS OF WHAT HUMANS COULD ENDURE FOR EXTENDED PERIODS. ALTITUDE SICKNESS COMES ON IMPERCEPTIBLY, AND THE LACK OF OXYGEN BEGINS TO MAKE PEOPLE IRRITABLE, ERODING CONCENTRATION AND THE ABILITY TO GET A GOOD NIGHT'S REST. IT WAS IMPORTANT, THEREFORE, TO ENSURE EVERYONE REGULARLY HAD A CHANCE TO GET BACK TO SEA LEVEL TO RECUPERATE. BOTH PROJECT TEAMS WERE PUT ON MANDATORY FIVE WEEKS ON, TWO WEEKS OFF SCHEDULES. IT WAS NOT WORTH RISKING THEIR HEALTH OR TAKING THE CHANCE THAT THEY MIGHT MAKE A CRITICAL MISTAKE ON THE PROJECT FROM A LAPSE IN CONCENTRATION.

AltaLink's T&D assets supplied power to over 80 percent of Alberta's population.

Pierre Anctil

POWER PLAY

Since starting up SNC-Lavalin's Equity Division in 1997, Pierre Anctil had been on the lookout for deals that would provide a steady stream of income while spinning off work to the company's engineering divisions. Highway 407 was a shining example, but he knew there were plenty of others out there.

In April 2001, he found one. A contact at Macquarie North America offered SNC-Lavalin a chance to go in on a deal to purchase a big chunk of Alberta's electricity transmission and distribution (T&D) assets. TransAlta, the public utility which owned them, was paring down its operations to focus exclusively on power generation. The contact told Anctil that a first bid was due in six weeks, and the lead partner in the deal, General Electric (GE) Investment, had just decided to reduce its stake. Was SNC-Lavalin interested in picking up the slack, equivalent to a 15-percent participation?

There were several things that Anctil liked about the deal. First, the 12,000 kilometres of lines and 250 substations on the block supplied power to over 80 percent of Alberta's population. Second, the province was a rock-solid market, and indications were that its growth would maintain a blistering pace as the oil sands continued to draw investment. Finally, of particular interest to SNC-Lavalin, the TransAlta Engineering Division, which did all the work on its lines and substations, was also being thrown in.

Jacques Lamarre liked what he heard and instructed Anctil to secure TransAlta's engineering arm as part of any deal. Anctil was in Toronto the next day for a meeting with the "AltaLink" consortium partners, which also included the Ontario Teachers' Pension Plan and Trans-Elect.

"We're interested," Anctil began, "and we feel we're well qualified to integrate and run TransAlta's engineering unit. Let us have it as part of the deal, and we're on board." No one could deny that SNC-Lavalin was best suited to further develop the unit's engineering capabilities. Anctil left the meeting two hours later with an agreement in principle to make SNC-Lavalin a 15-percent partner in AltaLink, and the sole owner of TransAlta's Engineering Division.

Everything seemed to be settled until a couple of weeks later, when GE Investment pulled out entirely. The company had taken a hard look at the pros and cons of investing in the regulated Canadian power market, and now considered it too risky. Lamarre, who was growing more enthusiastic about the deal by the day, told Anctil to up the company's stake to 50 percent.

AltaLink's offer of $850 million was accepted on July 4, 2001, although it would take another eight and a half months before the sale was granted regulatory approval. In the meantime, Anctil had to resolve the question of who would run the new company. He wanted Scott Thon, TransAlta's Vice-President of Transmission, for the job, but Thon was not currently part of the deal. He was not even in the country—TransAlta had sent him down to the U.S. for a new assignment following the sale.

After securing the permission of TransAlta's CEO, Anctil approached Thon directly in early August. One week later, the two men met face-to-face in Calgary. Thon knew little about SNC-Lavalin, but he could see that Anctil and the company he represented were serious about making AltaLink an example of operational excellence. It was a condition that he insisted on before agreeing to take the job.

"So we have a deal?" Anctil asked.

"We absolutely have a deal," Thon replied.

THE BIRTH OF A DIVISION

Klaus Triendl had come up through the ranks. Beginning as one of SNC's project managers on the Idukki arch dam in India in the 1970s, he had gone on to lead other hydropower mandates in the country like Chamera 1. Triendl's contribution was recognized in 1999 when he was named to the Office of the President and given the Power portfolio.

He came into the position with an ambitious plan to expand SNC-Lavalin's capabilities in the sector. Power had once been the backbone of the company's growth, but in the last decade it had slipped in importance. Triendl felt that SNC-Lavalin had come to depend too much on its hydropower and nuclear expertise, ignoring other rapidly growing sub-sectors. The company's acquisition of TransAlta's engineering unit, now called SNC-Lavalin Alberta Transmission Projects (ATP), was definitely a step in the right direction.

Turning the new division into a commercial company was not going to be automatic, however. Decades with TransAlta had given ATP invaluable insight into how utilities function, but understanding the internal mechanics of public power providers and winning contracts from them were not one and the same. ATP had never once had to engage in business development or launch a single marketing campaign.

The division's second life as a commercial engineering T&D company was kick-started under the leadership of former TransAlta managers Cindy Andrew and John Husch, who arrived soon after. The learning curve was steep, but SNC-Lavalin ATP passed an important test in late 2003 when it won a contract to design and build an underground transmission line for Three Sisters Mountain Village near Banff National Park. The subterranean line had to run under train tracks and

Klaus Triendl

The Three Sisters Mountain Village T&D project in Alberta was a proving ground for SNC-Lavalin ATP.

a geological obstacle course of mountains, mine shafts, and streams. The division's success on the project would leave no doubt that its transformation into a commercial engineering company was complete.

ENGINEERING A RESCUE

During a meeting at Hydro-Québec in mid-2001, a high-level contact told Klaus Triendl that the natural gas company TransCanada had just secured permission to build a gas-fired thermal power plant in Bécancour, Quebec. TransCanada was going to sell the majority of the power generated to Hydro-Québec under a long-term purchase agreement.

When Triendl naturally expressed interest in the project, the contact said the job required a level of expertise SNC-Lavalin did not really have. He recommended Triendl join forces with a major American firm if he wanted the contract.

The news was all the more frustrating because SNC-Lavalin had been searching for years to build up its thermal power expertise. The company had a small office of experts in Vancouver, led by Dave Parsons, and a partnership agreement with Washington Group International, but neither gave SNC-Lavalin the critical mass required for Bécancour. The new prospect made the need to find a major acquisition in the sector all the more pressing.

A few months after the meeting with Hydro-Québec, Parsons called Triendl to tell him that he had found a candidate. Enron, a high-flying energy broker headquartered in Houston, Texas, had recently filed for bankruptcy, leaving its many subsidiaries, like thermal power contractors National Energy Production Corporation (Nepco), dangling in the wind.

"Enron is finished," Parsons said, "but Nepco has a lot going for it. It's one of the most highly regarded and experienced companies in the business, with billions of dollars worth of ongoing contracts just waiting to be finished, including two of the largest gas-fired thermal plants in North America."

REPORT ON BUSINESS

CANADA'S BUSINESS NEWSPAPER ▪ FOUNDED 1962 ▪ GLOBEANDMAIL.COM ▪ THURSDAY, MAY 30, 2002

STOCK IN THE NEWS

Power-plant deals fuel SNC's ascent

Analysts expect signing of more contracts

SNC-Lavalin CEO Jacques Lamarre: 'It has always been part of our strategic plan to strengthen our presence in the thermal power sector, and these agreements provide us with the opportunity to meet that goal.'

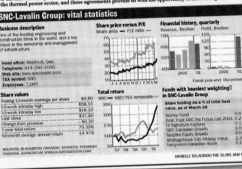

Triendl moved quickly. After obtaining permission from the board, he mounted a negotiation team, which included SNC-Lavalin's Executive Vice-President of Finance, Gilles Laramée, and counsels Réjean Goulet and Jean Hoffman-Zukowski. They were in Bothell, Washington, by the end of the week, talking to Nepco President John Gillis and his Vice-President of Project Management, Mike Ranz.

Months of intense negotiations followed, culminating, on May 15, 2002, in a deal that would see SNC-Lavalin hire Nepco's employees and complete eight of its projects, the outstanding portions of which were worth US$900 million. Over 5,000 jobs would be saved as its operations were absorbed into the newly created SNC-Lavalin Constructors.

On May 21, Lamarre, Triendl, and Marylynne Campbell were in Bothell to officially welcome employees at Nepco's offices. Other less formal meetings were held at the eight project sites SNC-Lavalin would be taking over. The Senior Vice-President of the Energy Division, Paul Dufresne, travelled to El Dorado, Arkansas, while Tony Rosato, the Vice-President of Marketing for Power, addressed questions from atop a cafeteria table at a project in Southaven, Mississippi. Their goal was to ensure the workers signed on with SNC-Lavalin to complete the projects. Few knew anything about their new employer, but they were relieved to learn they still had jobs.

A FLY IN THE OINTMENT

Not everyone viewed the transaction in a positive light. As SNC-Lavalin was celebrating the Nepco deal, Standard & Poor's (S&P), which had recently purchased the Canadian Bond Rating Service (one of the credit agencies that had given the company its first rating), was questioning its soundness. On the day when the acquisition was formally announced, S&P placed the company on CreditWatch, citing uncertainty surrounding the "size, scope, and potential cash outflows of the contracts." Following a review, it would decide whether to maintain or to downgrade SNC-Lavalin's hard-won BBB status.

It was a shock given how cautiously the company had sidestepped any liabilities and risks. Almost all of Nepco's fixed-price contracts had been renegotiated on a cost-plus basis. Convinced that S&P simply needed to have the deal properly explained to them, Lamarre, Triendl, Laramée, and Gillis flew to New York in early June to talk to its analysts.

Their message was that SNC-Lavalin had done nothing to merit being put on CreditWatch. If anything, they said, the deal had added to the company's lustre as an investment opportunity. As a result of the acquisition, its backlog had moved past $5 billion, and it now had thousands of skilled employees who could be put to work on thermal projects. True, the U.S. power market had cooled, but there was much potential work in Canada, Central and Eastern Europe, and North Africa.

With all the details laid out before them, S&P could not deny that the deal was essentially sound. On June 6, SNC-Lavalin was removed from CreditWatch without fanfare. By then, of course, Triendl and Gillis had begun mounting a proposal for Bécancour. SNC-Lavalin Constructors would go on to win the first phase of the project in mid-2003.

About 5,000 Nepco employees signed on to complete the company's thermal power projects with SNC-Lavalin.

The Bécancour thermal power project in Quebec.

CHAPTER 24 | WE CARE

Oil prices are on the rise, giving a further boost to SNC-Lavalin's Chemicals and Petroleum (C&P) Division. Major C&P contracts in Canada, South America, and the Middle East are won, and a game-changing decision is made to transform the Saudi Arabian project office into a full-blown operations unit. Meanwhile, the Transportation Division successfully pursues the Canada Line, an enormous mass transit project in Vancouver. By 2005, SNC-Lavalin has launched its WE CARE value statement—a commitment to health and safety, its employees, communities, the environment, and quality.

The Canada Line rapid transit project in Vancouver.

By early 2003, Jacques Lamarre was starting to get used to media interviews. SNC-Lavalin's profile was rising with each successful year, and he was being drawn into the spotlight along with the company. The latest was with a journalist from *Canadian Business* magazine, which had named him "Top CEO" for 2002. Lamarre was going to be the subject of a profile in the April 2003 issue.

Canadian Business credited him with delivering outstanding value to shareholders. Results for 2002 had been good by any standard of measurement. Revenue had jumped from $2.3 billion to over $3.4 billion. The real story, however, was net income. Bolstered by the sale of some of its shares of Highway 407, SNC-Lavalin's profits had skyrocketed to $202 million, a sixfold increase over the previous year. The company's share price had responded in kind, rising nearly 24 percent during May alone.

Lamarre was not taking all the credit, however. He spent much of the interview talking about the benefits of his "distributed leadership" approach. It was a managerial philosophy rooted in trust. Those he designated to lead the company's divisions and business units were the top in their fields, so he felt comfortable giving them the latitude to make decisions.

Lamarre could point to the two newest members of the Office of the President as evidence of the merits of his system. Pierre Duhaime had rehabilitated and unified the company's Mining and Metallurgy Division, while Marylynne Campbell had been instrumental in forging links between its different human resources departments. Lamarre had put his trust in them, and they had returned the favour by making SNC-Lavalin a more profitable and integrated company.

Distributed leadership did not mean that Lamarre had completely given up his hands-on style, however. It meant that he was focusing his attention on the problem areas now. Lamarre let his leaders lead, but when they faltered, he rolled up his sleeves, enlisted the entire group's resources, and climbed into the muddy trenches with them. SNC-Lavalin's

2002 was a very good year for SNC-Lavalin, and Canada's "Best CEO," Jacques Lamarre.

AIR CANADA: WHY IT FAILED, HOW IT CAN SUCCEED

CANADIAN BUSINESS

MINTZ: Why a US-EU rift could spell tax trouble
How MICHEL LEBLANC is defying Jetsgo's skeptics
INVESTOR ALERT: How safe are income trusts?

APRIL 28, 2003

ALL-STAR EXECS
MEET CANADA'S BEST CEO

SNC-Lavalin boss Jacques Lamarre leads off this year's lineup of the most investor-friendly managers in the country

+ The top-performing execs in Finance, Technology, Sales and Operations

canadianbusiness.com
$4.26

PUTTING OUR MONEY WHERE OUR MOUTHS ARE

BOTH SNC AND LAVALIN HAD BEEN INVOLVED WITH UNITED WAY / CENTRAIDE FOR MANY YEARS AT THE TIME OF THE MERGER IN 1991. SNC-LAVALIN'S EMPLOYEES REMAINED COMMITTED TO THE CANADIAN CHARITY FOR THE UNDERPRIVILEGED, REGULARLY DONATING HUNDREDS OF THOUSANDS OF DOLLARS EACH YEAR DURING ITS FUNDRAISING DRIVES.

board members sometimes joked that the company's CEO knew as much about what was happening on challenging projects thousands of kilometres away as some of the people who were actually on the jobs.

A TAILOR-MADE PROJECT

One of Krish Krishnamoorthy's goals when he had taken over the Calgary-based Chemicals and Petroleum (C&P) Division back in 1996 had been to secure more work in Alberta. By 2002, he had overachieved in that regard: the number of employees at the C&P offices in the province had shot up from 300 to over 1,400 on the strength of major projects for Syncrude, Petro-Canada, and Suncor.

Now a new project in the province had appeared for which Krishnamoorthy felt SNC-Lavalin was ideally suited. It was Husky's 30,000-barrel-per-day bitumen processing plant in Tucker Lake. The project would employ the steam-assisted

gravity drainage (SAGD) process to recover oil from bitumen, expertise that SNC-Lavalin had obtained through its 2001 acquisition of the Calgary engineering company Titan. Krishnamoorthy had also heard that Husky wanted to award the project on a lump-sum basis. If so, it would be the biggest fixed-price SAGD job ever carried out in Alberta's oil sands. While the prospect of signing such a contract in a superheated market made other engineering firms nervous, Krishnamoorthy knew SNC-Lavalin had the systems, experience, and talent to pull it off.

Sensing an opportunity, he went to speak directly to the President and CEO of Husky, John Lau. A shrewd and mercurial businessman, Lau was known for not liking to waste time, so Krishnamoorthy knew he would get only one chance.

"John, we'll do it on a fixed-price basis," Krishnamoorthy said. "Give us the specs for the front-end engineering that's been done so far, and I'll get you a fixed price within eight weeks."

Husky's Lloydminster refinery on the Alberta-Saskatchewan border.

"You realize we'd be taking a risk if we do that," Lau answered. "What if your guys come back to us with a price that we feel is too high? Then we'll have wasted two months, and our project will be no closer to getting started."

"Give us all your studies and specs, and I assure you that we'll get back to you with a very competitive price."

Lau looked at Krishnamoorthy for a moment. SNC-Lavalin had done a good job on a recent upgrader assignment for Husky's Lloydminster refinery, and he personally knew Krishnamoorthy as a man of his word. "Okay Krish," he said, slapping his hand down on the table. "You've got eight weeks."

Two months later, Krishnamoorthy was back with a price for Lau. It was a fair offer, backed up by real expertise thanks to Titan. Lau and his project team quickly came to the conclusion that their project would be in good hands with SNC-Lavalin.

A "NO CHANGE" MINDSET

The project kicked off in July of 2004. SNC-Lavalin had exactly 24 months to build Husky its facility. Given the steep penalties for a late delivery, the team, led by Project Sponsor Harry Sambells and Project Manager Dan Chan, took every precaution to ensure targets were met.

They secured vendor information and expedited long-lead equipment as soon as possible. They also made a decision to limit the number of changes to the design of the facility during construction. Some adjustments are inevitable (and beneficial) on large projects, but excessive alterations once work has begun inevitably lead to cost escalation. Shifting a single wall on an engineering plan translates into tens of thousands of dollars once tradesmen get around to making the change.

Luckily, SNC-Lavalin's project team had a watchdog who vigilantly pushed back against any changes he considered unnecessary. Tony Eddy, the Head of Engineering for Tucker Lake, liked to say that "changes breed excuses." Once you started allowing alterations on a project, valuable momentum was lost.

Why meet my deadline, some would ask, when the project is just going to change anyway?

If a component of the design was safe, of good quality, and met regulatory standards, Eddy flatly refused to accept any modifications to it. Of course, he would not have been able to keep the floodwaters at bay without the support of the rest of SNC-Lavalin's project team, Husky, and consortium partner PCL Industrial Management. When SNC-Lavalin pushed back, all of the project's stakeholders pushed back, too.

SNC-Lavalin's Husky Tucker Lake team. From left to right: Philip Lamb, Barry Docherty, George Propopappas, Roy Ledford, Venkat Machiraju, Tony Eddy, Eric Gloster, Dan Chan, and Murthty Nadella.

The completed Husky Tucker Lake project.

In the end, Tucker Lake was completed two weeks ahead of schedule, and the facility was turned over to Husky with less than $800,000 worth of changes on a $300-million job, a nearly unheard-of result for a project of that scale.

SETTLED IN SAUDI

Krishnamoorthy had not neglected international opportunities while he had been putting down roots in Alberta's hot C&P market. In the late 1990s, the division had staked its claim with successes in Venezuela, Oman, and, particularly, Saudi Arabia.

Since winning Saudi Aramco's Qassim pipeline project in 1996, SNC-Lavalin had picked up a steady stream of control system mandates for the oil and gas giant. By 2002, the company had executed so many of them that Aramco had officially classified it a "control systems expert." Krishnamoorthy was happy his division's expertise had been recognized by Aramco, but he was also eager to break out of the box and win larger, multidisciplinary jobs.

In mid-2002, it looked like SNC-Lavalin might have an opportunity to do that. Aramco had announced that it intended to carry out more engineering in the kingdom. The plan was to give a boost to the employment and training of Saudi nationals by increasing the local execution of oil and gas projects. If SNC-Lavalin could team with a Saudi firm, there would be a good chance of picking up some of the work.

Since 1992, the company's office in Al-Khobar, Saudi Arabia, had maintained a staff of two or three employees, but now Krishnamoorthy wanted to transform it into a full-blown operating unit. A volunteers' list was posted advertising the position of General Manager in Al-Khobar, but it was taken down when Krishnamoorthy learned that his Vice-President of Project Operations, Ed Vogelgesang, was interested in the job. He was familiar with Aramco, understood project execution, and could certainly run a medium-sized office.

Over the next six months, the Al-Khobar office's communications capabilities were improved to allow its engineers to directly access SNC-Lavalin's databases. To generate some badly needed income, Krishnamoorthy then agreed to pull

Clockwise:

Ed Vogelgesang

Working at the Al-Khobar office. From left to right: Mohammed Al-Sunni, Faiq Majid, Maher Al-Johani, Ken Cridland, and Hussain Al-Abbas.

Hadi Alajmi

back some Aramco control-systems work being done out of Calgary and relocate it to Saudi Arabia, along with six expatriate engineers.

With the help of Calgary-based project manager Alfy Hanna and International Marketing Manager Hadi Alajmi, Vogelgesang began making presentations to Aramco on SNC-Lavalin's full range of capabilities. It now looked likely that the oil giant was going to launch a major in-kingdom project management program, and Vogelgesang was trying to convince them that SNC-Lavalin should qualify.

The breakthrough came in December 2005, when the Al-Khobar office was awarded one of two five-year contracts for the In-Kingdom Project Management Services (IKPMS) program. It was no small feat, considering 14 local companies and their international partners had also bid hard for the contracts.

The program would be led by Chris Goodwin, a project manager recently hired to lend weight to SNC-Lavalin's proposal. His team would be assigned to smaller preliminary engineering and project management jobs, but being at the front end of the planning process would give SNC-Lavalin an invaluable window into Aramco's larger upcoming EPC opportunities. The oil and gas giant had just announced that it planned to invest US$50 billion over the next five years: it would be an expansion program unlike anything the industry had ever seen.

TO BID OR NOT TO BID

In early 2003, the British Columbian government sought expressions of interest for a major mass transit project it wanted to build in time for the 2010 Winter Olympics. The Richmond-Airport-Vancouver (RAV) line would slice through the downtown core of Vancouver, en route to Richmond and the Vancouver International Airport. It would also be one of the biggest public-private partnership (PPP) deals in Canadian history. British Columbia wanted the private sector to chip in hundreds of millions of dollars toward construction and then operate the line for 31 years.

THE HEART OF THE AMERICAN OIL INDUSTRY

THE JANUARY 2003 ACQUISITION OF GDS ENGINEERS BROUGHT TOGETHER THE EMPLOYEES OF SNC-LAVALIN AMERICA'S HOUSTON OFFICE WITH THOSE OF GDS IN HOUSTON, BAYTOWN, AND TEXAS CITY, TEXAS. SNC-LAVALIN GDS HAD 550 EMPLOYEES, INCLUDING MORE THAN 160 ENGINEERS SPECIALIZED IN EVERYTHING FROM SMALLER MAINTENANCE PROJECTS TO LARGE-SCALE EPCM WORK. THE ACQUISITION PROVIDED KEY EXPERTISE AT A TIME WHEN THE OIL AND GAS MARKET WAS HOTTER THAN EVER.

Jim Walters, Senior Vice-President and General Manager of SNC-Lavalin GDS.

Jim Burke, SNC-Lavalin's Senior Vice-President of Transportation in Vancouver, was on the fence about RAV. He was interested, of course, but he had just sunk more than $15 million into a proposal for a PPP mass transit system in England that had now been shelved. RAV was not certain to go ahead either, despite all the fanfare surrounding it. Serious budgetary concerns had split the Vancouver transit authority's board over whether or not to proceed.

Burke expressed his reservations to Jacques Lamarre during a Bid and Investment Approval Committee (BIAC) meeting in the fall of 2003. "I don't feel comfortable putting so much money on the line for a project that might never see the light of day," he said. "I'm considering not bidding."

Lamarre did not like what he was hearing. Ankara and Kuala Lumpur had been the twin peaks of his career. They had made his reputation and bolstered SNC-Lavalin's balance sheet, but the company had failed to win any mass transit contracts since then. Lamarre saw RAV as a chance to get back on the mass transit map with a high-profile and prestigious project.

Jim Burke

"Jim, you're going to bid," Lamarre said. "I know you're stretched to the limit, but you need to find a way to bid on this. You always tell me you have an excellent team. You can find a way."

Burke may have had reservations at the outset, but once he committed to bidding, he put everything into winning the project. He knew the key would be to deliver the system the province wanted for the price they were willing to pay.

Much of the RAV line had to run along historic Cambie Street, the most direct route to the airport. The current plan was to bore tunnels along Cambie between 2nd Avenue and 37th Avenue in the downtown core, run cut-and-cover tunnels between 37th and 49th, then finish up with an open-trench track up to 63rd. The biggest problem with this proposal was that it would cost the government far more than it was willing to spend. The other issue was aesthetic: the open trench portion of RAV would effectively obliterate Cambie Street's cherished tree-lined median called Heritage Boulevard.

The solution that Scott Anderson's civil works team came up with was to run a cut-and-cover tunnel the entire length of Cambie. It would shave many millions off the project price, accelerate construction by allowing work to proceed on several fronts at once, and leave Cambie Heritage Boulevard intact. Cut-and-cover tunnels also ran closer to the surface than bored tunnels. That would increase accessibility, a characteristic known to boost ridership.

SNC-Lavalin proved to have the right combination of affordability and functionality on January 13, 2005, when it was named "Preferred Proponent" for RAV. The deal still had to reach commercial and financial close, however. For that, Burke relied on his Senior Vice-President, Allan Cuthbert. Burke counted on him to negotiate a fair commercial deal with the government, concessionaire, and lenders. For 28 weeks, Cuthbert worked closely with SNC-Lavalin's technical operations team, SNC-Lavalin ProFac, and the company's investment group, led by Jean Daigneault.

On Friday, July 29, their hard work paid off. InTransit BC, a joint-venture company equally owned by SNC-Lavalin, the British Columbia Investment Management Corporation, and the Caisse de dépôt et placement du Québec, signed the contract for RAV, now called the Canada Line. As planned, SNC-Lavalin was sub-contracted the biggest EPC contract in its history by InTransit BC, while its subsidiary, ProFac, won a milestone 31-year operations and maintenance agreement.

Some members of the RAV design team. From left to right: Yuming Ding, Melissa Duckham, Chris McCarthy, and Mabel Kwok.

An aerial view of Vancouver.

MANAGING A MEGAPROJECT

RAV WOULD HAVE TENS OF THOUSANDS OF MOVING PARTS SPREAD OUT OVER A WINDING 19.5-KILOMETRE WORKSITE. IF SNC-LAVALIN TOOK ITS EYE OFF ANY OF THEM, PROBLEMS COULD EASILY ENSUE.

THE SOLUTION JIM BURKE CAME UP WITH WAS TO ENSURE HIS TEAM WOULD BE DIRECTLY INVOLVED IN ALL ASPECTS OF CONSTRUCTION. SNC-LAVALIN WOULD WORK WITH CONTRACTORS TO EXECUTE THE ELEVATED GUIDEWAYS, BORED TUNNELS, AND THE CUT-AND-COVER TUNNEL. THE ONLY PART OF THE PROJECT THAT WOULD BE FULLY CONTRACTED OUT WAS THE STATIONS, BUT EVEN THERE, SNC-LAVALIN STAFF WOULD DIRECTLY MANAGE THE CONTRACTORS.

WHEN BURKE WAS CONFIDENT THAT HE COULD MAINTAIN CONTROL OVER CONSTRUCTION, HE FOCUSED ON DEVISING A SYSTEM THAT WOULD KEEP AN IRON GRIP ON COSTS. HIS SOLUTION WAS TO PUT ONLY 12 PEOPLE IN CHARGE OF ALL THE MONEY HE HAD FOR THE JOB. HE WOULD SIT DOWN WITH EACH OF THEM ONCE A MONTH TO FIND OUT HOW THEIR BUDGETS WERE FARING. IF NEEDED, MONEY WOULD BE TRANSFERRED FROM ONE PART OF THE PROJECT TO ANOTHER, OR, IF NECESSARY, THE CONTINGENCY FUND WOULD BE TAPPED.

MAKING IT REAL

Back in early 2002, Jacques Lamarre was taken aback when a senior executive of BHP Billiton suggested SNC-Lavalin was putting out mixed signals when it came to social responsibility.

"You know, Jacques, you guys really should define your commitment to social responsibility," the executive had said during a meeting. "Look—we have a commitment to zero harm," he added, handing Lamarre a steel-encased calculator with the slogan next to BHP's logo.

Lamarre could not believe what he was hearing. SNC-Lavalin had maintained environmental and health and safety policies for over a decade. It had operated under a formal code of ethics for more than 40 years. On top of all that, SNC-Lavalin was about halfway through an expansion of the Mozal smelter in Mozambique for BHP, one of the best organized and most extensive social responsibility successes in aluminum history.

The first phase of the project, led by Pierre Dubuc, had achieved an almost unheard of safety record for projects in the region. Extensive education, prevention, and treatment programs had been set up at the project's work camp to manage AIDS and other sexually transmitted diseases, a serious problem in Africa, and a large-scale training program had been created to teach valuable skills to thousands of local tradesmen. Now, the expansion, under Brent Hegger, was going even further, training more locals and putting even more focus on AIDS prevention. Yet somehow the client still felt SNC-Lavalin lacked a clear message in matters of corporate social responsibility.

BHP's Zero Harm logo touched off discussions at SNC-Lavalin that led to the launch of WE CARE in 2005.

WE CARE

NOUS VEILLONS

A PPP DOUBLE HEADER

ON JULY 4, 2005, ONLY WEEKS BEFORE IT WON THE CANADA LINE PROJECT, SNC-LAVALIN'S VANCOUVER OFFICE SIGNED A CONTRACT WITH THE GOVERNMENT OF BRITISH COLUMBIA TO DESIGN, BUILD, OPERATE, AND MAINTAIN THE WILLIAM R. BENNETT BRIDGE IN KELOWNA. THE BRIDGE WOULD REPLACE THE CURRENT THREE-LANE OKANAGAN LAKE BRIDGE, WHICH WOULD NOT BE ABLE TO SUSTAIN THE MORE THAN 69,000 VEHICLES EXPECTED TO USE THE CROSSING DAILY BY 2017.

THE NEW BRIDGE WOULD HAVE FIVE LANES TO ACCOMMODATE THE PROJECTED INCREASE IN TRAFFIC. IT WOULD ALSO BE A FLOATING BRIDGE, SINCE THE LAKE'S DEEP WATER AND GEOTECHNICAL CONDITIONS MADE A CONVENTIONAL ELEVATED STRUCTURE FAR MORE EXPENSIVE. A FLOATING DESIGN WAS ALSO FAVOURED BECAUSE IT WOULD HAVE VERY LITTLE IMPACT ON KELOWNA PARK, LOCATED ON THE LAKE'S EAST SIDE.

Lamarre kept the calculator in a prominent place on his desk as a reminder of the work needed to demonstrate to clients that SNC-Lavalin was serious about corporate social responsibility. Later that week, he told the members of the Office of the President that the time had come to crystallize the company's commitment to its underlying values.

"This is a part of our culture," he said. "We all know that, but we're failing to communicate it effectively to our clients. I don't just want some new slogan, though. It has to be meaningful to us, and it has to be reflected by real action."

The ideas began to come in. Many were rejected because they did not capture the full scope of the company's commitment. Others like HSECQIRE (health, safety, environment, community, quality, industrial relations and empowerment) were initially accepted, but eventually discarded as too cumbersome and formulaic.

In early 2005, a name was found that effectively embodied all of SNC-Lavalin's values. During yet another round of discussions at the Office of the President, Klaus Triendl suggested "We Care."

"That's it, Klaus, you've got it," Lamarre said immediately. "It groups everything together in two simple words."

An hour later, Lamarre had called Gillian MacCormack, the Vice-President of Global Public Relations, into his office to ask her to draft a value statement under the heading of "We Care." First, however, he wanted her to understand how important it was to him.

AWARDING EXCELLENCE

THE 2005 INTERNATIONAL SYMPOSIUM GALA DINNER MARKED THE FIRST PRESENTATION OF THE SNC-LAVALIN AWARDS OF EXCELLENCE FOR OUTSTANDING ACHIEVEMENT. THERE WOULD NOW BE INTERNAL RECOGNITION OF PROJECT TEAMS THAT HAD DELIVERED TOP-TIER RESULTS IN THE CATEGORIES OF SUSTAINABLE DEVELOPMENT, ENGINEERING, PROJECT MANAGEMENT, AND HEALTH, SAFETY AND THE ENVIRONMENT.

Jacques Lamarre presents an Award of Excellence to some members of the Hillside 3 aluminum smelter project team. From left to right: Jacques Lamarre, Adrian Owens, John Romita, and Oraham Hedow.

"I'm not sure where you grew up," he said, "but I was raised in the Saguenay region of Quebec in the 1940s and 1950s. There was a lot of industrial investment there when I was young. Over time, those companies were able to align their own interests with those of the people of the region. The result is amazing to see now. We have to follow that example."

MacCormack spent the next few months collecting input from Lamarre, Executive Vice-President Marylynne Campbell, and the Vice-President of Environment, Mark Osterman, to come up with a set of values that reflected the company's commitment to health and safety, its own employees, communities, the environment, and quality. By the end of the year, the "We Care" message would be disseminated company-wide.

It was essential that the initiative resonate with employees since they were the platform on which the company's values rested. Head office could proclaim the importance of "We Care" all it liked, but in the end it was up to individual employees to apply its values.

Gillian MacCormack
Mark Osterman

A MODEL INDUSTRIAL TOWN

WHEN THE ALUMINUM COMPANY OF CANADA BUILT ITS FIRST SMELTER IN THE SAGUENAY REGION OF QUEBEC IN THE 1920s, A NEW TOWN WAS REQUIRED TO HOUSE THE FACILITY'S MANY WORKERS. BEFORE LONG, THE TOWN OF ARVIDA, NAMED AFTER PIONEERING INDUSTRIALIST *ARTHUR VINING DAVIS*, BEGAN RECEIVING ITS FIRST RESIDENTS. GREAT EFFORT WENT INTO ENSURING THE COMFORT OF ITS INHABITANTS. THE ORIGINAL HOMES WERE BUILT ON WINDING, TREE-LINED STREETS, AND EACH HAD A SIZABLE GARDEN AND ITS OWN DISTINCT ARCHITECTURAL STYLE. SCHOOLS, CHURCHES, AND RECREATIONAL CENTRES WERE ALSO ADDED TO PROVIDE RESIDENTS WITH ALL OF THE CONVENIENCES OF AN OLDER, MORE ESTABLISHED TOWN. NOW PART OF THE AMALGAMATED CITY OF SAGUENAY, ARVIDA HAS A POPULATION OF 12,000 AND IS CONSIDERED A SUCCESSFUL EXAMPLE OF THE MERGING OF COMMUNITY AND INDUSTRIAL NEEDS.

THE GLOBE AND MAIL · SATURDAY, NOVEMBER 13, 2010

NEWS · **A23**

DISPATCHES

Alcoa tycoon Arthur Vining Davis founded Arvida in the 1920s as 'a model town for working families.' It became known as the City Built in 135 Days on 'a North Canada steppe.'

URBAN AMBITION

Saguenay 'utopia' dreaming big again

Arvida, the town that aluminum built, forgotten by history, deserves a place on the UNESCO World Heritage list, its boosters say

INGRID PERITZ SAGUENAY, QUE.

To stand in the heart of Arvida, with its plume-spewing smoke-stacks looming nearby, it's tough to feel you're getting a glimpse into a modern-day Eden.

Yet this remote Quebec community was born as a model city and cutting-edge town, a Silicon

CHAPTER 25 | WALKING THE TALK

SNC-Lavalin demonstrates that its success and corporate values walk hand in hand. In Madagascar, the company carries out a social responsibility showcase project for Sherritt. In Vancouver, it limits disruptions to the lives and livelihoods of residents and merchants affected by the construction of the Canada Line. Meanwhile, other megaprojects move ahead. SNC-Lavalin acquires full ownership of Canatom and wins a pair of important contracts for Bruce Power's nuclear facility in Ontario. In the Middle East, the company makes dramatic inroads into the aluminum sector, picking up contracts for two of the largest smelters ever built.

Workers at the Ambatovy nickel project in Madagascar.

Pierre Duhaime, the Executive Vice-President of Mining and Metallurgy, and Feroz Ashraf, his Senior Vice-President of Commercial and Strategic Development, made a good team. Duhaime was a natural at forming and nurturing relationships with clients, while Ashraf had a talent for negotiating and winning the division's contracts.

By early 2006, they were on a three-year tear in the nickel sector. The winning streak had begun in June 2003 with Voisey's Bay in Newfoundland and Labrador, and continued with the gigantic Goro project in New Caledonia a year and a half later. More recently, in May 2006, they had pulled in Ambatovy, a 60,000-tonne-per-year behemoth of a nickel project in Madagascar for Dynatec, Sumitomo, and Kores.

Not only was Ambatovy easily one of the biggest EPCM contracts in SNC-Lavalin's history, the company would also be taking a five-percent investment stake in the project. Dynatec had asked SNC-Lavalin to demonstrate its confidence in the project's novel process to investors and lending institutions by putting some of its own equity on the table.

The complexities of Ambatovy went beyond the process, however. Building a megaproject in a developing country with a unique natural environment required extraordinary sensitivity. In April 2007, the natural resource company Sherritt acquired Dynatec and became the project's majority managing partner and operator, but its vision of the project was the same as Dynatec's had been: the company wanted respect for Madagascar's people and its fragile ecosystems to be front and centre.

It was up to Project Manager Albert Sweetnam (Dale Clarke would take over in 2008) and his team to handle training and development of the local workforce. One of the solutions SNC-Lavalin came up with was called the Local Resource Development Initiative (LRDI). Managed by Jean-François Gascon, it was similar to what had been done for Mozal and other major projects in Africa, only more ambitious. Over 10,000 locals would be taught bricklaying, formwork, rebar bending, painting, and welding, all while receiving instruction in health and safety. Hundreds of local businesses would be asked to register their interest in project opportunities, and

SNC-Lavalin would assist them with tendering, work scheduling, and health, safety, and environmental management. Mentorship programs would even be set up on the premises of some businesses when required.

The project's in-country environmental leader would be SNC-Lavalin's Jo Bayah. He would oversee the implementation of environmental management and protection plans, including an extensive re-vegetation initiative and training for contractors. On its side, Sherritt established a biodiversity program to protect vulnerable wildlife, including the country's large lemur population and its native species of amphibians and flora. SNC-Lavalin Environment advised Sherritt's on-site personnel every step of the way, offering various solutions to protect these species and their habitats.

Clockwise:

At the Ambatovy ground-breaking ceremony: Albert Sweetnam (left), Mitsuhiko Yamada of Sumitomo Corporation, and Marc Ravalomanana, the President of Madagascar.

One of the country's many lemurs.

Training under way for the Ambatovy project.

Cambie Street under construction, and concreting of the line's bored tunnel component.

Ambatovy would be different things to its different stakeholders. To Sherritt, it would be a chance to demonstrate its leadership as a sustainable producer of nickel. For SNC-Lavalin, it would be an opportunity to show that the company could put all the pieces together in a socially responsible manner and tackle the most challenging project being undertaken in the mining and metallurgy world.

A FEAT OF COMMUNITY RELATIONS

Steve Crombie

Steve Crombie had a pretty good idea of what he was getting himself into when he signed his contract with SNC-Lavalin in May 2005. As the head of Communications and Community Relations for the Canada Line rapid transit system (formerly known as RAV), he would have the challenging job of liaising with the many residents and merchants affected by its construction.

It was clear from the outset that much of his focus would have to be on Cambie Street in downtown Vancouver, which accounted for over a quarter of the 19.5-kilometre route. The province, the city, and the regional transit authority wanted to do everything possible to avoid unnecessary impact on the lives and livelihoods of those whose houses and businesses lined the street, but no one believed it would be anything less than a major challenge.

Working with the project's owner, the Canada Line Rapid Transit Company, Crombie's communications team mounted one of the most extensive community relations programs in the history of mass transit projects. Every avenue for getting information to the public was fully exploited. There were regular construction alerts on the radio and in community newspapers. There was an interactive website and a 24-hour hotline for those without access to a computer. There were construction monitors at key locations to quickly address the concerns of merchants and residents. There were regular public information sessions, where Project Manager Mike O'Connor was able to explain the project directly to those most affected by it. Most importantly, there were safety programs for local school children, which included tours of the construction sites so they would know what to watch out for.

Most acknowledged that a serious effort was being made, but it was not always easy to see the light at the end of the tunnel. A good part of Crombie's job, therefore, was to remind merchants on Cambie that they would be among the primary beneficiaries once the line was up and running. It would inevitably bring increased pedestrian traffic and there would be significant streetscape improvements. In short, the area would become more vibrant and appealing.

Even Jim Burke got into the act. Halfway through the construction of the Canada Line, he found himself sitting next to the owner of a hotel along the route while on a flight back to Vancouver from a fishing trip. When the hotelier realized who Burke worked for, he decided to give him a piece of his mind.

"You work for SNC-Lavalin? You know, you guys are building a station right outside my hotel and ruining my business," he said, visibly upset.

Burke, as mild-mannered and calm as always, had a question for him. "We're genuinely sorry for the inconvenience, and we're doing our best to minimize the effects on your business," he said. "But tell me, when the Canada Line is completed and you're the only hotel in Vancouver that has a station entrance directly outside your front door with a train that takes people to the airport in under 20 minutes, do you think that will be a good thing for your hotel?"

Upon reflection, the hotelier could not deny that the project would ultimately benefit his business. His demeanour soon changed, and the conversation turned to fishing.

Not all merchants were so easily persuaded, but all the project team could do was to limit the impact on them and keep focusing on the job at hand. The sooner the line was operating, the sooner the merchants would appreciate being located along what amounted to a mechanized river of daily customers.

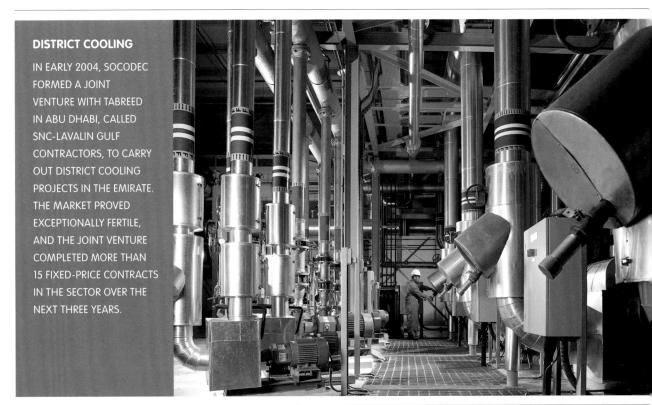

DISTRICT COOLING

IN EARLY 2004, SOCODEC FORMED A JOINT VENTURE WITH TABREED IN ABU DHABI, CALLED SNC-LAVALIN GULF CONTRACTORS, TO CARRY OUT DISTRICT COOLING PROJECTS IN THE EMIRATE. THE MARKET PROVED EXCEPTIONALLY FERTILE, AND THE JOINT VENTURE COMPLETED MORE THAN 15 FIXED-PRICE CONTRACTS IN THE SECTOR OVER THE NEXT THREE YEARS.

SUCCESS IN SAUDI

Following the win of the Saudi Aramco In-Kingdom Project Management Services contract in early 2005, the Al-Khobar office had picked up a few mandates. Among them were front-end engineering assignments for the massive Khurais water injection and Shaybah gas plant projects.

By the time SNC-Lavalin was wrapping up its design work in late 2005, however, Aramco found itself in a dilemma. Normally, the execution phases of Khurais and Shaybah would have been carried out using the lump-sum turnkey (LSTK) model Aramco favoured. But with major projects being kick-started worldwide on the back of record commodity prices, the oil giant decided market conditions were ripe for a "converted" lump-sum (CLSTK) approach. The

Jean Beaudoin

The Khurais and Shaybah projects in Saudi Arabia.

done the preliminary engineering for the projects, and it was one of few bidders with actual CLSTK experience. As hoped, the Al-Khobar office won important packages for Khurais and Shaybah in late 2005. For the Saudi team, the awards were the culmination of more than eight years of tireless campaigning.

With a major career goal accomplished, and his 63rd birthday rapidly approaching, Krish Krishnamoorthy decided the time was right to retire. In January 2006, Jean Beaudoin, the Senior Vice-President of the Industrial Division in Montreal, became a member of the Office of the President with the responsibility for Global C&P. He had good credentials, having successfully completed major EPC contracts for polytrimethylene terephthalate (PTT) and purified terephthalic acid (PTA) plants in Montreal's east end. It would be his job to finalize the contracts for Khurais and Shaybah with Aramco and ensure the megaprojects were executed efficiently.

FROM PECHINEY TO DUBAL

The aluminum industry was in the process of migrating. Aluminum smelters are power-intensive beasts and tend to go where energy is cheapest. Quebec, with its enormous quantities of inexpensive hydropower, had once been a primary beneficiary of this fact. Increasingly, however, the Middle East, the world's largest producer of natural gas, was becoming the new go-to region for aluminum production.

Seeing the writing on the wall, Bob Minto, the Aluminum Division's Vice-President of Technology, devised an expansion scenario for Dubai Aluminum's (Dubal) Jebel Ali smelter in 2003. It envisioned a five-stage program that would boost the smelter's production by 265,000 tonnes per year to a staggering 950,000. If Dubal went ahead with the plan, Jebel Ali would become the largest smelter in the world, hands down.

It was up to the division's self-starting Vice-President and General Manager, Pierre Ranger, to convince Dubal that it was feasible and that SNC-Lavalin could carry it out. In February of 2004, he got a rare opportunity to present the

risks to EPC contractors would be mitigated because the contract would lock in at a fixed price only once most of the engineering and equipment orders had been completed. As expected, the move got the attention of the EPC contracting world.

SNC-Lavalin now had to compete against a who's-who list of major players, but it had two distinct advantages: it had

IMPLANTED IN INDIA

IN JANUARY 2004, EXECUTIVE VICE-PRESIDENT KRISH KRISHNAMOORTHY AND CHIEF FINANCIAL OFFICER GILLES LARAMÉE TOUCHED DOWN IN MUMBAI, INDIA. IT WAS A 40-MINUTE CAR RIDE THROUGH A CRUSH OF HUMAN AND VEHICULAR TRAFFIC TO THEIR DESTINATION, A SMALL ENGINEERING OFFICE BY THE NAME OF RJ ASSOCIATES. THE PAIR HAD FINALLY PREVAILED ON JACQUES LAMARRE TO LOOK SERIOUSLY AT AN ACQUISITION IN THE COUNTRY. KRISHNAMOORTHY HAD ARGUED THAT HAVING ACCESS TO HIGH-QUALITY AND AFFORDABLE INDIAN ENGINEERING WOULD HELP SNC-LAVALIN COMPETE AGAINST COUNTRIES LIKE SOUTH KOREA, WHICH WERE BEGINNING TO UNDERCUT HIM ON JOBS. LARAMÉE HAD EMPHASIZED INDIA AS AN ENORMOUS POTENTIAL MARKET IN ITS OWN RIGHT. THERE WAS A HUGE AMOUNT OF INFRASTRUCTURE AND POWER WORK WAITING TO BE DONE.

IN THE END, LAMARRE HAD GIVEN THEM THE GO-AHEAD, AND RJ ASSOCIATES, A FULL-SERVICE ENGINEERING AND CONTRACTING FIRM BASED IN MUMBAI, WAS SELECTED. THE ACQUISITION WAS COMPLETED UNDER THE LEADERSHIP OF JEAN BEAUDOIN IN MARCH 2005. IT WAS A NEW MILESTONE IN THE COMPANY'S LONG RELATIONSHIP WITH THE SOUTH ASIAN COUNTRY.

R. Jaishankar, the CEO of SNC-Lavalin Engineering India.

expansion program directly to Dubal's board. In the engineering and construction world, it was the equivalent of jumping a queue that wound right around the block.

Ranger was given five minutes—just long enough. He focused on Potline 7a, the first step in Minto's plan, and assured them his team could upgrade it by 74,000 tonnes per year within only 18 months. Ranger spoke with confidence because he knew that he had top expertise backing him up.

Over the past 20 years, SNC-Lavalin had built many of the major smelters in the world, and had generally done so with excellent budgetary and schedule performance: Grande Baie, Laterrière, Lauralco, Reynolds, ABI, Tomago, Alouette, Richards Bay, Mozal and Alba ... the list went on.

Since Dubal would be an expansion, the company's most relevant recent experience was a 75,000-tonne-per-year capacity increase of Pechiney's smelter in the Netherlands. Now

Marc O'Connor

Philippe Parent

Pierre Ranger

man-hours. Ranger had a price for Dubal two hours later, and assurances from Nagib that he would receive a letter of intent by the end of the following week.

FROM DUBAL TO EMAL

The expansion of Potline 7a was completed in May 2005, five months ahead of schedule and significantly under budget. Seeing that they were working with a company that lived up to its promises, Dubal then awarded the project team expansions of the 7b and 9b potlines. Yet another solid performance led to further mandates in May of 2006, the expansions of potlines 5b and 6b.

The 40-pot expansion of 6b had been a special project for Dubal. It was intended to be a showcase for its latest aluminum reduction technology, called DX. Dubal hoped to sell the process to other aluminum producers around the world. Their pitch was that DX produced higher quality aluminum than its D20 predecessor while using less electricity.

The Mubadala Development Company, a state-owned enterprise of the Abu Dhabi government in the United Arab Emirates, was enthusiastic about DX. In early 2007, Dubal and Mubadala formed a joint venture called Emal to build the world's largest single-site smelter in Abu Dhabi using Dubal's new technology. SNC-Lavalin, which had helped Dubal develop DX, was awarded Emal 1, the first phase of the project, in May 2007.

The facility was to aluminum smelters what James Bay once was to hydroelectric developments. SNC-Lavalin would be building a 750,000-tonne-per-year mega-smelter requiring more than 19,000 workers at its peak, and using pre-assembled modules that were nearly as large as some of the first potlines SNC and Lavalin had built in the 1970s. Such an enormous smelter would naturally require a huge amount of power. In this case, it would

The Dubal aluminum smelter in Dubai.

Riadh Ben Aïssa

wrapping up, the project was ahead of schedule and under budget. Ranger sweetened his offer to Dubal by proposing to put the smelter's Project Manager, Philippe Parent, and Construction Manager, Marc O'Connor, on their project.

Ranger walked out of the boardroom feeling good about his presentation, but doubting that anything could come of such a brief appearance. As he was leaving to return to his hotel, however, the Managing Director of Dubal, Mohammed Nagib, came out and stopped him. "Okay, Pierre, can you give us a price for your services?" he asked. "We'll give you two weeks to get back to us."

Ranger did not need weeks to come up with a reliable ballpark figure. The job included only services, so he just needed to accurately calculate

be provided by a 2,000-megawatt thermal plant—the same capacity as the legendary Boulder Dam in the United States.

Before SNC-Lavalin won the contract, Jacques Lamarre and Pierre Duhaime had agreed to transfer the company's aluminum projects in Abu Dhabi and Dubai over to Socodec. They had come to the conclusion that the division's extensive list of contracts in the region made it the natural choice to oversee these projects.

Familiarity with the region and an extensive local network would prove crucial. In August of 2007, Socodec's new President, Riadh Ben Aïssa, was forced to reorganize the project team when he realized that Emal, the most challenging smelter the company had ever built, was being treated like any other project. Emal had not gotten off on the right foot.

His first decision was to transfer Jerzy Orzechowski to Emal as its Project Manager. Having led the Hadjret en Nouss thermal power project in Algeria, he was at ease running large-scale projects. He would also be able to lend his particular expertise to the construction of Emal's gigantic power plant. Marc O'Connor was then drafted onto the job as Construction Manager, along with other experienced aluminum hands like Pierre Ranger and Brian Murphy. Jacques Erasmus, a seasoned Health, Safety and Environment Manager, was also added to the mix.

With the right ingredients in place, things started turning around. Emal 1 would come on line a little more than three years later, four months ahead of schedule and comfortably under budget. Its health and safety performance would break records for large industrial projects in the region. Most importantly, SNC-Lavalin would have a satisfied customer.

The Emal aluminum smelter in Abu Dhabi was a feat of project and personnel management.

GOING NUCLEAR

The history of Canatom's ownership looked like a ping-pong match. The shares of the nuclear engineering company had bounced around between different parties for the past 25 years. The only constant during that time had been SNC-Lavalin.

By 2004, however, the company saw a chance to acquire total ownership of the nuclear services provider and bring it some much needed stability and growth. Aecon, SNC-Lavalin's partner in Canatom, was amenable to selling its 38.75-percent stake, and

Jerzy Orzechowski

Preparing to lift the first of Bruce Power's steam generators into the plant.

would rapidly improve. SNC-Lavalin purchased Aecon's stake in December of that year.

Canatom soon became SNC-Lavalin Nuclear, and Patrick Lamarre began building a team to give it what it lacked, a "project culture" with full EPC capability. It was what he needed to win two major contracts for Bruce Power's nuclear plant in southwestern Ontario: one to replace 16 steam generators and another to refurbish the main section of the plant. As hoped, the new and improved team had won SNC-Lavalin both jobs by December 23, 2005.

It was less expensive for Bruce Power to refurbish the plant and replace its existing steam generators than to build an entirely new facility. Cheaper did not mean easier, however. Replacing 16 submarine-sized steam generators in a 27-year-old plant had its risks, especially given the limited amount of time SNC-Lavalin Nuclear had to complete the work. Its team, led by Project Director Walter Tomkiewicz and Project Manager Brian Savage, would have to carry out the operation with the utmost efficiency to meet the project's deadline and technical specifications.

In April of 2007, a massive crane with a 1,600-tonne capacity was used to lower the first of the 16 steam generators though an opening in the roof of the plant. There was no room for error: it would have to connect within a millimetre with the existing machinery at 12 different points. Any misalignment once the generators were in place would greatly impact the budget and schedule.

Nerves were beginning to show, but there was an underlying feeling of confidence among the team. SNC-Lavalin Nuclear had used a state-of-the-art metrology imaging system to see where human eyes could not and plot each connection with absolute precision long before the drop. Congratulations spread through the site when it became clear that the connection points had been perfectly calculated.

The remaining steam generators followed in quick succession and the project finished ahead of schedule and within budget in 2009. It was a remarkable achievement that put SNC-Lavalin Nuclear at the top of what looked like a growing niche market. A first indication of this would come when the

Executive Vice-President Klaus Triendl and the SNC-Lavalin-appointed President of the subsidiary, Patrick Lamarre, seized the opportunity. It was true that Canatom was in trouble at the moment, but if its expertise were expanded, its prospects

division was awarded a contract by Xcel Energy in January 2010 to replace the steam generators at a nuclear generating plant in Welch, Minnesota. It would be the first time steam generators in the United States would be refurbished by a company other than one of the major American or French contractors.

GORED BY GOREWAY

Jacques Lamarre had good news and bad news to deliver at the shareholders' meeting in Vancouver on May 4, 2007.

The good news was that 2006 had been a spectacular year on all fronts. Net income had taken a big leap from $129.9 to $158.4 million, and major new projects had swollen the company's backlog to a record $10.4 billion, an increase of nearly $3 billion over the previous year. Among the biggest new assignments were the Qatalum aluminum smelter in Qatar, an electrical transmission line between Alberta and Montana, the Hadjret en Nouss 1,227-megawatt gas-fired thermal power plant in Algeria, the Canaport liquefied natural gas terminal in New Brunswick, and the Khurais and Shaybah Saudi Aramco projects.

The bad news was the first quarter results for 2007. For the first time in 13 years, SNC-Lavalin had failed to increase its quarterly net profit. The damage stemmed from difficulties on a $757-million fixed-price contract for the Goreway gas-fired power project in Brampton, Ontario.

Some of the problems were linked to the collapse of Deltak, the supplier of Goreway's steam generators. SNC-Lavalin not only lost the money it had provided as a down payment to Deltak but also had to assume the job of co-ordinating with its manufacturers in China to ensure the equipment would be delivered. SNC-Lavalin had brought in several of Deltak's employees and assigned some of its own people to manage them.

Despite the company's best efforts, however, it looked like there would be no way to avoid a major delay in the schedule. That meant "liquidated damages," a dreaded legal term that made even the most battle-tested project managers

quake in their construction boots. SNC-Lavalin would have to compensate the client for each lost day of production after the deadline, which could mean millions of dollars in penalties.

Shareholders were not hearing the news for the first time. When SNC-Lavalin's management learned of the projected loss on Friday, March 23, they had not wasted time in alerting the market. An Office of the President meeting had been called that Sunday, followed by an emergency board

Patrick Lamarre

From the Bruce Power project in 2007. From left to right: Brian Savage, Leslie Davis, and Walter Tomkiewicz.

A MAJOR PLAYER IN ITS SECTOR

IN AUGUST 2007, SNC-LAVALIN GATHERED ITS QUEBEC-BASED EXPERTISE IN MATERIALS ENGINEERING AND GEOTECHNICAL STUDIES UNDER ONE ROOF. THE NEWLY CREATED QUALITAS DIVISION—A MERGER OF GROUP QUALITAS, TERRATECH, AND THREE RECENT ACQUISITIONS, LABORATOIRE SOL ET BÉTON, TECHMAT, AND QUÉFORMAT—WAS A POWERHOUSE IN ITS SECTOR.

"THERE WILL BE NO SHORTAGE OF MATERIALS ENGINEERING AND GEOTECHNICAL WORK IN THE COMING YEARS IN QUEBEC," SAID CHARLES MALENFANT, THE DIVISION'S SENIOR VICE-PRESIDENT AND GENERAL MANAGER. "WITH NEARLY 800 EMPLOYEES AT MORE THAN 20 OFFICES AND TESTING LABORATORIES THROUGHOUT THE PROVINCE, THE QUALITAS DIVISION HAS A CRITICAL MASS THAT ALLOWS IT TO COVER THE MAXIMUM OF THESE PROJECTS."

Jacques Lamarre addressing shareholders in Vancouver.

The Goreway thermal power project in Ontario.

Even as Lamarre spoke, SNC-Lavalin's risk management experts were looking for ways to further shore up the company's procedures to avoid a repeat of Goreway. Patrick Lamarre, who would soon be named Executive Vice-President in charge of Power, ordered an in-depth analysis of the project to determine if other lessons could be drawn from it. For now, SNC-Lavalin would proceed cautiously, and a cost-plus approach would be encouraged on certain thermal power projects.

BUT THANKFULLY...

By sheer coincidence, SNC-Lavalin had sold its Munitions Manufacturing Division, SNC-TEC (formerly Canadian Arsenals), to General Dynamics in January 2007 for $335 million. The decision had been motivated by a strong desire to refocus on the company's core engineering and construction expertise.

Before SNC-Lavalin could go ahead with the sale, the federal government had asked the company to secure the buy-in of the subsidiary's two unions. SNC-Lavalin had held meetings with their leaders. In the end, it had not been difficult to convince them that they would have a brighter future with General Dynamics. While SNC-Lavalin had been able to generate respectable returns from the unit, General Dynamics, which was specialized in defence products, would be able to greatly expand the subsidiary's horizons.

Part of the credit for making SNC-TEC more attractive went to Executive Vice-President Michael Novak, who had taken over the subsidiary in September 2003. During his brief tenure, he had enhanced SNC-TEC's relationship with the Canadian government, improved its health and safety performance, and generally shaped the subsidiary into a leaner, more efficient organization.

The irony was not lost on anyone who had been around in the late 1980s, when problems with Canadian Arsenals had led to a major loss. Now the $83-million gain from the sale would help cushion the blow from Goreway considerably and allow SNC-Lavalin to make a reasonable profit in 2007.

meeting a few hours later. By Monday, a press release had been issued before markets opened warning of a "forecasted loss on a major power project" in the first quarter of 2007.

But now, as Jacques Lamarre addressed shareholders in Vancouver, the damage was no longer forecast—it was a reality. "We are aware that this major financial impact on our first quarter results in 2007 will disappoint you, our shareholders, as well as our other stakeholders," Lamarre said. "We will absorb it the SNC-Lavalin way, and regard it as a learning experience and an opportunity to become better. We will be humble and responsible about it, but we are also determined to improve our performance in the future."

CHAPTER
26 TOWARDS THE FUTURE

Now approaching 65, Jacques Lamarre decides the time has come to retire, and Pierre Duhaime is chosen to take up the mantle of President and CEO. His clear strategic vision and six years of solid results give the board confidence that he will be able to see the company through an impending recession. While 2009 does indeed prove challenging, the company bounces back in 2010, winning major projects like the MUHC hospital complex in Montreal, a public-private partnership deal for which it will carry out one of the largest EPC contracts in its history. SNC-Lavalin begins 2011 with some of its best results to date and a record backlog.

A computer-generated image of the MUHC's Glen Campus in Montreal.

Jean Claude Pingat anticipated that a tremendous consolidation movement would take place in the first decade of the new millennium. He believed that a few national players were going to emerge from a multiplicity of local firms.

Joining SNC-Lavalin in 1996 had given Pingat's firm the administrative structure and capital base it needed to establish an operational presence throughout France. Within a decade, he had created a national network through the acquisition of companies in key geographic markets: firms had been purchased in Paris, Lyon, Lille, Bordeaux, Strasbourg, Nantes, and Toulouse, among others. He had not confined himself to his agrifood roots, either. The acquisitions had ranged from the biotechnology and pharmaceutical sectors to infrastructure, transportation, environment, buildings, and industrial engineering.

He had also made use of an indirect marketing strategy. In 1998, the company had signed a management contract to operate and develop the Paris-Vatry cargo airport under a 20-year concession agreement. Pingat had realized that, while the project itself would generate modest revenues, the publicity his division would receive as the operator of a major airport was invaluable. After all, it was the first time in French history that a significant airport had been handed over to the private sector.

Pingat was rewarded for his efforts in August 2004 when he was named to the Office of the President and put in charge of most of SNC-Lavalin's European operations. SNC-Lavalin France became SNC-Lavalin in Europe. It would take a lot of work, but Pingat's ultimate intention was to one day become as prominent in the European market as he had in France.

In March 2007, he took a step in that direction with the acquisition of Intecsa-Inarsa, a 500-person firm with offices throughout Spain. The country had received more than $100 billion Euros from the European Union since 1986, much of which had gone towards developing ambitious programs for high-speed rails, highways, ports, bridges, and tunnels. In the process, local engineering companies such as Intecsa-Inarsa had acquired extensive infrastructure know-how. The firm had more than one skill set, however. It also had expertise in industrial facilities like gas compression plants. Equally important for Pingat, the acquisition brought the number of personnel at SNC-Lavalin in Europe to the symbolically important figure of 2,000.

A map showing SNC-Lavalin's expanded presence in Europe in 2005.

Jean Claude Pingat and the President of Intecsa-Inarsa, Diago Ibanez Lopez (both seated in the centre), share a word at the signing of the deal to acquire Intecsa-Ianrsa.

SOUTH AMERICAN EXPANSION, TAKE 2

Brazil held its first democratic presidential elections in 1989, following decades of military dictatorship. A privatization program ensued that transformed many of the country's most prominent government-owned enterprises, such as Companhia Vale do Rio Doce (CVRD), into publicly traded corporations.

Brimming with new economic strength and large reserves of key natural resources, Brazil opened up to foreign investment, while its flagship, CVRD, targeted international opportunities of its own. One of the first was Canada's Inco, the world's second largest producer of nickel. On October 23, 2006, Inco shareholders accepted an offer from CVRD to buy the company for $17 billion. If Inco found itself with a new owner, SNC-Lavalin now had a new client. It was at work on Inco's massive Goro nickel project in New Caledonia when the mining company was acquired.

Executive Vice-President Pierre Duhaime had wanted to open an operating office in Brazil for some time, but the failures of several international companies in the country had dissuaded him from taking the risk. With Brazil's corporations now going abroad, however, he reasoned that conditions had become favourable to foreign investment. The door of international investment always swung both ways.

Marco Pires, the head of Nickel projects at CVRD, confirmed Duhaime's hunch. "There are opportunities for you now in Brazil with CVRD, Pierre, but we have to see you," said Pires. "You have to have an engineering presence in the country."

Duhaime had two options: he could either set up a new office in Brazil or buy a local firm. Past experience had taught him that purchasing a company in a foreign country was really the only way to secure instant credibility. He gave the job of finding one to his Senior Vice-President of Commercial and Strategic Development, Feroz Ashraf.

Ashraf took multiple trips to Brazil throughout the spring and summer of 2007. He met with several firms, but none impressed him as much as SNC-Lavalin's current joint venture partner in the country, MinerConsult. Some years earlier, Ashraf had identified the firm as a partner for the Kinross

Feroz Ashraf

Outside the Barro Alto project site. From left to right: Walter De Simoni of Anglo American, Vladimir Carvalho, Dale Clarke, and Luis Carlos Guimares of SNC-Lavalin.

An aerial view of the project.

Gold Paracatu and Anglo American Barro Alto nickel projects in Brazil. The execution phase of Paracatu had gone well. The study for Barro Alto was also progressing smoothly and, with any luck, SNC-Lavalin and MinerConsult would win the EPCM mandate for the project in a few months time. Importantly, MinerConsult also had an ongoing relationship with CVRD (now known as Vale), a company Duhaime was eager to continue working with after Goro was finished. Ashraf strongly recommended that Duhaime move to acquire MinerConsult.

As SNC-Lavalin and MinerConsult were in acquisition talks in August 2007, their joint venture won the contract for the next phase of the Barro Alto contract. It was a good omen: the award added energy and enthusiasm to the negotiations, and the acquisition was finalized in December.

THE HARDEST DECISION

The morning of July 30, 2008 was balmy, and Jacques Lamarre had a big day ahead of him. It would begin at exactly 8:00 a.m., when he would walk into the 21st-floor conference room and formally announce his retirement to the board.

He had wrestled with the decision for weeks, until he realized that what he had been struggling with was the urge to hold on to the job for his own sake, because he loved it. In the end, he could not deny that the timing was right to exit the stage. Lamarre was now 64, and there were strong candidates waiting in the wings who were themselves not getting any younger. They had put in their time, made major contributions, and deserved a shot at what he had often called the "best job in the world."

The company was also in good shape: net income had bounced back following the troubled Goreway project, hitting $146.2 million for the first two quarters of 2008 compared to $21.3 million for the same period in 2007. True, the unfolding global financial crisis was sure to do some damage to the world economy, but he was confident that SNC-Lavalin's backlog of $9.4 billion would allow it to ride out the worst of the impending storm.

Lamarre knew the company's greatest strength, however, lay in the broad diversity of its expertise and its geographical coverage. Over the last two decades, it had gained market share in several new countries and had nearly doubled the spectrum of expertise it was able to offer its clients. This brought added stability, since recessions rarely impacted on all sectors and all regions at the same time.

That did not mean there would not be challenges for his successor, however. The global market was roiling and the stock market was deep in bear mode. For all these reasons, the process to select a new leader would have to be approached with the utmost care. There would be multiple interviews with the board's Human Resources Committee during which new CEO would need to distinguish himself on multiple fronts. He would have to be a true leader,

with a broad vision capable of overseeing all of the group's diverse activities. He had to have contributed to the company's profitability, and he had to know how to talk to employees, clients, investors, and the media. In short, he would need to be at once an entrepreneur, a communicator, and a visionary.

SNC-Lavalin's Human Resources Committee in 2008: David Goldman, Pierre Lessard, Lorna Marsden, Larry Stevenson, and Hugh Segal.

O&M MEETS E&C

IN AUGUST 2007, CHARLIE RATE, THE SENIOR VICE-PRESIDENT OF OPERATIONS AT PROFAC, WAS MADE PRESIDENT OF THE SUBSIDIARY. THE GROWING IMPORTANCE OF OPERATIONS AND MAINTENANCE (O&M) WITHIN THE GROUP WAS CLEAR WHEN RATE WAS IMMEDIATELY NAMED TO THE OFFICE OF THE PRESIDENT.

WHEN SNC-LAVALIN HAD ACQUIRED FULL OWNERSHIP OF PROFAC IN 2000, THE ASPIRATION HAD BEEN TO CAPITALIZE ON WHAT WERE SEEN AS LATENT SYNERGIES BETWEEN ITS O&M EXPERTISE AND THE COMPANY'S ENGINEERING-CONSTRUCTION (E&C) CONTRACTS. BY THE TIME RATE HAD BEEN NAMED TO THE OFFICE OF THE PRESIDENT, THERE WAS NO QUESTION THAT THE DREAM HAD BECOME A REALITY. PROFAC WAS BOTH CANADA'S LEADING OPERATIONS AND MAINTENANCE SOLUTIONS EXPERT AND HAD IMPORTANT SUBCONTRACTS FOR SEVERAL RELATED ENGINEERING-CONSTRUCTION PROJECTS, INCLUDING A POWER PLANT IN ONTARIO, AN EXTENSION OF THE TRANS-CANADA HIGHWAY INTO NEW BRUNSWICK, THE WILLIAM R. BENNETT BRIDGE, AND THE CANADA LINE IN BRITISH COLUMBIA.

PASSING THE BATON

It was March 6, 2009, and the press had been informed that SNC-Lavalin was about to make a big announcement regarding "succession." At exactly noon, journalists were led into the conference room on the third floor of Place Félix-Martin. About 15 minutes later, Chairman Gwyn Morgan, Jacques Lamarre, his wife, Céline, and Pierre Duhaime entered and took their places at the long table at the front of the room.

"The decision by a board of directors to select a new chief executive is, without a doubt, its most important responsibility," said Morgan. "We have followed a robust process, from annual succession planning to considering the requirements needed to lead SNC-Lavalin to continued success. This morning our board resolved to appoint Pierre Duhaime as the next President and CEO, effective immediately following the May 7, 2009 Annual Meeting of Shareholders."

"It is with great pride and confidence in the future of SNC-Lavalin that I am passing the baton to Pierre," said Lamarre, following Morgan's introduction. "Pierre has demonstrated extraordinary leadership in heading the Mining and Metallurgy Division of SNC-Lavalin, and I am fully confident, Pierre, that you will guide this company to new zeniths."

In a market where consolidation had drastically reduced the number of clients, Duhaime's client-friendly approach had earned big dividends. SNC-Lavalin had become a service provider of choice for many of the largest movers in mining and metallurgy, including Anglo American, Rio Tinto Alcan, Vale, and Barrick Gold. In the process he had taken his division from one of the company's weakest profit-earning segments in 2001 to its strongest in 2008.

"I would like to thank Jacques for his leadership, vision, entrepreneurship, and success in building a winning team," said Duhaime. "These exceptional characteristics have turned

The announcement that Pierre Duhaime had been selected to replace Jacques Lamarre as President and CEO of SNC-Lavalin was followed by media interviews and a farewell cake.

SNC-Lavalin into the great company it is to work for today, and a company that is ready to move forward."

Beneath all the formality and procedure, there was real emotion. Lamarre was in great spirits, but it was clear that it was a bittersweet moment for him—a man who had devoted all his time to SNC-Lavalin, who had never drawn a line between his professional and personal life. Sitting next to him, Duhaime maintained a composure that belied not only the great humility he felt in having been selected, but also his sense of the challenges to come, now squarely on his shoulders. The task of piloting the company through a recession would be his.

Duhaime's place as the head of Global M&M would now be assumed by his right-hand man of several years, Feroz Ashraf. A global thinker and sound strategist, he seemed like the best candidate to continue the expansion in a challenging commodity market. For now, however, all attention was on the company's future CEO.

GOING FOR GROWTH

On May 15, 2009, Pierre Duhaime took the stage at the Management Committee meeting at the Palais des congrès in Montreal. He had officially been named CEO only eight days earlier, so this was his first opportunity to lay out his strategic vision to SNC-Lavalin's management as a whole. He was not concerned about securing their buy-in, however. One-on-one conversations with many of them over the last months had confirmed to him that he had their support.

His first message was that there would be no drastic changes. "SNC-Lavalin has processes and strategies that have proven valuable and effective," he

Outlining a new vision:
Pierre Duhaime addresses
Management Committee
members at the meeting
on May 15, 2009.

2010 MANAGEMENT'S DISCUSSION AND ANALYSIS

The following seven strategic priorities will ensure that SNC-Lavalin continues to grow and be successful by serving the needs of its clients, employees, shareholders and the communities where it is active.

STRATEGIC PRIORITIES		KEY IMPLICATIONS
Operational excellence	>	Successful project delivery is at the heart of achieving operational excellence which is required for SNC-Lavalin to retain the trust of its clients, existing and new. Successful project delivery includes exceeding targets for health and safety performance, budget, schedule and client satisfaction.
Improve competitiveness	>	A focus on cost-efficiency, supported by strong capabilities and experience, will be key to ensuring that the Company is consistently selected by clients as their partner of choice on major projects.
Stronger relationships with clients	>	Creating strong relationships with clients will ensure that SNC-Lavalin remains top-of-mind and becomes a true partner to its clients.
Geographic diversification and growth of markets and offerings	>	Expansion of geographic, product and sector coverage will be an important component to access growing markets where the Company can continue its successful growth trajectory. The ability to deliver local projects using local resources will be a key component in delivering the geographic growth strategy.
Recruit, identify and develop the best talent in the industry	>	SNC-Lavalin will continue to attract the best talent and offer compelling career opportunities to retain that talent, supported by a strong talent management approach. The Company will use a global approach to finding talent which will enable it to have highly skilled resources across the globe.
Financial strength	>	Maintaining a strong balance sheet and financial performance is important not only for the Company's shareholders and credit providers but also to provide its clients with the knowledge that it is able to maintain stability while delivering projects it undertakes on their behalf.
Corporate social responsibility	>	The Company has deep respect for its social obligations and will act, and be known, as a socially responsible company. This includes engaging itself with the broader community wherever the work is performed.

A RECIPE FOR THE FUTURE

IN THE YEAR THAT FOLLOWED HIS APPOINTMENT AS PRESIDENT AND CEO, PIERRE DUHAIME ELABORATED A SEVEN-POINT STRATEGY FOR THE NEW CHALLENGES THE INDUSTRY WAS FACING.

began. "We are strong and well positioned, with an excellent balance sheet. We have a diverse array of activities in key regions throughout the world. We're not going to overhaul something that is clearly in good working order."

One thing he certainly did not want to alter was the company's steady growth over the past 13 years. Since 1996, when Jacques Lamarre had become CEO, SNC-Lavalin's revenues had increased by a multiple of seven, and its net income by a multiple of 10 while its shares had done even better. Duhaime boldly declared that he fully expected the winning streak to continue.

The company would do this by expanding in key growth markets like India, Saudi Arabia, Russia, and Brazil. Duhaime wanted to put more operating units in these countries, and give them the systems and procedures to become increasingly self-sufficient. He hoped the day would soon come when far more of SNC-Lavalin's international offices were exporting expertise to one another.

"Yes, a global recession seems to be taking hold, but with enough flexibility, the company will continue to thrive during tough economic times," he said. "After all, recessions have made SNC-Lavalin the successful company it is by forcing us to stay lean and enhance our expertise."

THE AGE OF UNCERTAINTY

There were three key areas where Duhaime proposed to enhance the company's existing practices. SNC-Lavalin's Risk Management group, managed by Vice-President Adam Malkhassian, would be given additional resources to help it better identify, follow, and mitigate risk throughout the life of a project. Every business unit would soon have its own risk manager.

Duhaime's second priority was human resources. For well over a decade, the talk in the business world had been of the impending collapse of the North American workforce following the retirement of the Baby Boom generation. Duhaime planned to tackle the problem simultaneously on several fronts. The Human Resources Department would be given greater means to locate and reel in top candidates, and there would be a formal cross-company program designed to foster leadership across all levels. He would also hire a new Executive Vice-President and member of the Office of the President for Human Resources. Given what was at stake, he felt HR should have a representative on the company's main decision-making body. (Darleen Caron, who had 20 years of experience in Human Resources with multinational companies, would be named to the position in November 2010.)

Finally, Duhaime took aim at the company's global image. As he had done with Global M&M, he would get more SNC-Lavalin business units speaking the same language and using the same procedures and systems. He wanted an engineer who was transferred from Toronto to an office in India to feel equally at home in that work environment. With a common way of doing things, it was easier to get more divisions collaborating on projects, which was Duhaime's ultimate goal.

The harmonization of SNC-Lavalin also needed to happen on a marketing level. Duhaime wanted even more consistency in the way that the company sold itself to clients from office to office and region to region. One way to ensure that the company was front and centre in all marketing efforts was simply to include SNC-Lavalin in the names of its more prominent subsidiaries. To begin with, Socodec would become SNC-Lavalin Construction. ProFac would become SNC-Lavalin Operations and Maintenance, and more of SNC-Lavalin's offices in France would bear the SNC-Lavalin brand.

SECURING A SUPERHOSPITAL

In October of 2008, a mega public-private partnership (PPP) project in the province of Quebec was formally given the green light. A request for proposals was sent out for the McGill University Health Centre's (MUHC) new Glen Campus. The project had been talked about for decades, and now it was a reality. Needless to say, in tough economic times, with projects being cancelled around the world, competition was going to be fierce.

BREAKFASTS WITH THE PRESIDENT 2.0

WHEN HE BECAME CEO, PIERRE DUHAIME DECIDED TO REVIVE AND REBOOT AN OLD SNC-LAVALIN TRADITION. LIKE GUY SAINT-PIERRE HAD DONE IN THE EARLY 1990s, HE WOULD HOLD BREAKFASTS WITH THE PRESIDENT MEETINGS TO COMMUNICATE DIRECTLY WITH EMPLOYEES. UNLIKE SAINT-PIERRE, HOWEVER, TECHNOLOGICAL ADVANCES WOULD ALLOW HIM TO SPEAK TO EVERYONE SIMULTANEOUSLY VIA THE COMPANY'S INTRANET. EMPLOYEES WOULD HAVE THE OPPORTUNITY TO SEND IN QUESTIONS AHEAD OF TIME, WHICH DUHAIME WOULD ANSWER DURING THE BROADCAST.

Bob Bieler

Charles Chebl

André Dufour

The winner would finance, design, and build the largest healthcare complex in Canada, then maintain it for a period of 30 years. Glen Campus would comprise 220,000 square metres of floor space in all, almost as much as the Empire State Building in New York City. It would have a centralized ambulatory service for all of its 25 departments, dedicated teaching areas, and a research facility that housed Innovative Medicine and Translational Biology centres. In total, there would be 20 operating rooms, along with 154 pediatric and 346 adult single-patient rooms, each with private bathrooms and space for visiting family members.

The bidders had to submit the technical proposal in August 2009, with the financial proposal following three months later. With no room for error, overall responsibility for the design and construction component of the bid went to Executive Vice-President Riadh Ben Aïssa, while the financing proposal was entrusted to Chief Financial Officer Gilles Laramée.

A design, planning, and estimating team of over 150, led by Charles Chebl, the Senior Vice-President of SNC-Lavalin Construction, and including Josée Éthier and Yves Gauthier, was formed and relocated to its own project office. Bob Bieler,

the Vice-President of Business Development at SNC-Lavalin Operations and Maintenance, headed up a team that included Camil Briand and Brigitte Dupuis. Meanwhile, the Senior Vice-President of SNC-Lavalin Capital, André Dufour, and his vice-presidents Dominic Forest and Claude Bourque went to work obtaining the capital needed to finance the project. With stock markets fluctuating wildly and the collapse of Lehman Brothers only a few months in the rearview mirror, they knew raising the required capital would be a challenge.

Over the next 10 months, no effort was spared to put a proposal together that would meet the government's budgetary objectives. Over 150 workshops were held with hospital and government representatives, including physicians, nurses, planners, and medical equipment specialists. After each meeting, the proposal team then went back to review the concept and implement the recommendations.

By November 19, 2009, SNC-Lavalin had submitted both the technical and financial proposal for the project. Two months later, however, the government asked the bidders to prepare new proposals that were more in line with a revised budget. An unforeseen best and final offer round would now take place between the leading two bidders, one of which was SNC-Lavalin. They had until March 15, 2010, or 60 days, to significantly reduce the cost of their proposals without touching any aspect of the hospital that had to do with functionality and patient care.

The proposal team went back to the drawing board. On March 15, SNC-Lavalin submitted a new proposal that met the requirements of the technical program and fell within the revised budget. All team members had pushed hard to reduce the costs associated with their contributions—the designs were optimized, engineering was refined, construction was streamlined, operations and maintenance was rationalized, and the borrowing costs of the financing package were reduced.

All their effort paid off on April 1 when SNC-Lavalin was informed that it had won the project. It was one of the largest EPC contracts in the company's history, and a major boost to its growing PPP portfolio.

RESURGENCE

After a minor lull due to the global recession, the company began reaping dividends from its all-out effort to win new jobs.

One of the first had come in May of 2009, when SNC-Lavalin and its partners were awarded a prestigious PPP project to design, build, operate, and maintain the new concert hall for the Montreal Symphony Orchestra, a mere stone's throw from SNC-Lavalin's headquarters. The resurgence started in earnest by the second quarter of 2010 with a series of megaprojects, including an iron ore processing facility in Brazil and a contract to design and build the Waneta Expansion, a 335-megawatt hydroelectric power facility in British Columbia, Canada. The biggest numbers, however, were put up by the EPC component of the MUHC Glen Campus Hospital contract, which added $1.6 billion to the backlog in the third quarter.

These were trend-defying results. Many of the world's engineering and construction firms had taken a hit from the slowdown in contracts that had come on the heels of the economic crisis, and SNC-Lavalin's ability to bounce back so quickly confirmed what Pierre Duhaime had been saying all along—the contracts were there, and the results in 2010 were going to surprise analysts.

On March 4, 2011, Duhaime, Chief Financial Officer Gilles Laramée, and Investment Relations Vice-President Denis Jasmin were able to announce an exceptional performance in 2010.

"As you saw in our press release this morning, we achieved good results for the year and ended 2010 on a very strong note," Duhaime said during the quarterly conference call to analysts. "Net income increased by 21.6 percent to $437 million, compared to $359.4 million for the same period in 2009." Duhaime acknowledged that the popular uprising in North Africa had stalled some of the company's projects, but assured analysts that the outlook for the coming year remained excellent.

"We expect 2011 to be another good year for SNC-Lavalin," he said. "We see good potential in all sectors and are confident that the situation in North Africa will resolve itself soon. You know, over the last century, SNC-Lavalin has risen to countless challenges. Each time it has learned new lessons that have made the company stronger. Our engineers and constructors know how to adapt, innovate, and keep moving forward."

Site of the future Waneta Expansion in British Columbia.

A computer-generated rendition of the Montreal Symphony Orchestra's new concert hall in Montreal.

EPILOGUE

It is April of 2011, and Pierre Duhaime is gazing out onto the Montreal skyline from his 21st-floor office in Place Félix-Martin. He sees a cityscape transformed by the company he leads. So many of its bridges, highways, schools, hospitals, exhibition halls, arenas, stadiums, petrochemical plants, and water treatment stations have been built by SNC-Lavalin. And he knows that if he could see further, many thousands of miles beyond, he would glimpse a whole country, an entire world that now bears the indelible imprint of his company.

Duhaime takes great pride in knowing that he stands at the crest of a 100-year tradition of exacting work, quality, and entrepreneurship. He feels humbled by the tens of thousands of employees who have come before him, who have dedicated their lives to building the company he now heads.

There have been great leaders. There have been world-class project managers and brilliant engineers. The company has seen strategic visionaries, great gentlemen statesmen, mathematical geniuses, outstanding construction managers, fine lawyers, marketing masterminds, and financial maestros . . . the list of contributors is unending. They have come from around the world, speaking different languages, representing many cultures. Each one has poured the full measure of his or her talent into the company to fashion it into the organization it is today, and Duhaime is grateful for their legacy.

And what of SNC-Lavalin's current and future employees, the foundation on which its fortunes will rise? Duhaime has complete confidence they will meet the challenges of an increasingly global and competitive world. Throughout its history, the company has always benefited from adversity, using the opportunity such moments present to strengthen its practices and refocus its vision. It has grown and improved as a result of such challenges, and that will not change.

In the end, Duhaime knows that the great changes the industry must undergo to become more ecologically and socially sustainable will be made possible by engineers and constructors. Without them, the world's major environmental and resource challenges can never be met and its call for new infrastructure will go unheeded. Without engineers and constructors, the broad spectrum of progressive ideas that are emerging to shape the world of tomorrow will never be translated into reality.

There is no question that SNC-Lavalin's employees will be at the centre of the coming century. The next 100 years are only just beginning.

Looking back with pride and forward with confidence, President and CEO Pierre Duhaime.

ACKNOWLEDGEMENTS

The publishing of a history book requires a veritable battalion of dedicated professionals to see it through to completion, and that is certainly true in this case. I have had help and encouragement from a great number of people throughout this process.

First, I want to thank my research assistant, Lorraine Gagnon. As the months passed, I came to think of her as more of a partner than an assistant, seeking out her opinion on a variety of issues. Her hard work, enthusiasm, and perfectionism have greatly benefited this project.

The formal approval committee was also gratifying to work with. Each member took the time to carefully read the various chapters submitted to them, and provided useful comments. If not for them, this book would be both less accurate and less interesting. They are Pierre Duhaime, Jacques Lamarre, Gilles Laramée, Yves Laverdière, Leslie Quinton, Dominique Morval, Mary Brett, and, in the first months of the project before her retirement, Gillian MacCormack.

The book was simultaneously translated into four other languages as I was writing it. You can imagine the logistics and complexity of such an undertaking. That we succeeded is due to the dedication and skill of our Linguistics Department in Montreal, headed by Christine Christophory. And while Lorraine and I did most of the research for this book, we had enthusiastic support from Fiona McNaughton's Library Services team, as well as the Archives Department, headed by Simeon Ivanov.

The graphic design and editing team at IQ Press took their work very seriously. Pierre-André Derome did a fine job of laying out the book, Keren Penney was a vigilant language editor, and Isabelle Quentin put much work into reviewing the French proofs and co-ordinating with the printer.

The bulk of the information in this book comes from close to 300 interviews I conducted between January 2009 and December 2010. Speaking to so many enthusiastic and interesting employees, past and present, has been perhaps the most rewarding aspect of this project for me. These people were and are the top in their field, with tremendous experience and an infectious love of their work. I cannot name them all here, but there are quite a few whom I feel I must mention.

First, I thank our past presidents (in chronological order): Camille Dagenais, Bernard Lamarre, Jean-Paul Gourdeau, Guy Saint-Pierre, and Jacques Lamarre. It was nice to see that their deep interest in this company has not faded since their retirement. SNC-Lavalin's Office of the President was also useful in providing comments and oversight (in alphabetical order): Feroz Ashraf, Jean Beaudoin, Riadh Ben Aïssa, Jim Burke, Patrick Lamarre, Gilles Laramée, Michael Novak, Jean Claude Pingat, and Charlie Rate. In addition, I would like to thank: the Surveyer, Chênevert, Nenniger, Lalonde, and Valois families; Taro Alepian, Pierre Anctil, Bernard Arsenault, Christiane Bergevin, Georges Boutary, Marcel Côté, Armand Couture, Denis Crevier, José de Carvalho, Maxime Dehoux, Rick Dolan, Pierre Dubuc, Marcel Dufour, Pierre Dufour, George Filacouridis, Pierre Fortier, René Godin, David Goldman, Jack Hahn, Fred Heeley, Stephen Jarislowsky, Ivars Kletnieks, Krish Krishnamoorthy, Pierre Lamarre, René Landry, Peter Langlais, Jacques Larouche, Henno Lattik, Gaétan Lavallée, Nick Lee, Alain Lemay, Marie Lessard, Jean Lord, Henri Madjar, Yves Maheu, André Marsan, Bob Minto, Normand Morin, Jean-Pierre Mourez, Claude Naud, Ted Papucciyan, Marcel Pineau, Rock Poulin, Robert Racine, Pierre Ranger, Anthony Rattue, Tony Rustin, Pierre Robitaille, Tom Ross, Harry Sambells, Marcel Sicard, Walter Stensch, Larry Stevenson, Alex Taylor, Tony Thatcher, Anwar Thomas, Robert Tribe, Ed Vogelgesang, and Ken Walker.

While the people mentioned above provided much of the information in this book, I am also deeply indebted to those who have taken on this task before me. In particular, I would like to thank Suzanne Lalande, who wrote a lively history of SNC called *Engineering Beyond Frontiers* in the early 1990s. Many of the people she interviewed are no longer alive today, so her book served as an invaluable source of information for the first chapters on SNC, and several of its anecdotes also appear in this book. Her account of the merger of SNC and Lavalin, written while it was actually underway, is also drawn upon for the corresponding chapter here. Other books that were helpful to me include *Les Ficelles du Pouvoir,* by Carol-Marie Allard, and *Bernard Lamarre: Le génie d'une vie,* by Guy Samson.

Last, but certainly not least, I would like to thank my wonderful wife, Kim, and my son, Ethan, for putting up with the long hours and the many weekend work sessions.

Noel Rieder

INDEX

This book was printed on May 4, 2011
by Friesens, Altona, Canada
for IQ Press
on FSC Sterling paper.